D0900028

Developing Recreation Skills in Persons with Learning Disabilities

Lorraine C. Peniston

SAGAMORE PUBLISHING
Champaign, IL 61820

Production coordinators: James and Kathryn J. Meyer
Production manager: Susan M. McKinney
Cover design: Deborah M. Bellaire
Proofreader: Kathryn J. Meyer

ISBN: 1-57167-134-x

Printed in the United States

ACKNOWLEDGMENTS

■───────────────────────────────────■

I would like to thank God for keeping me alive throughout this writing process. He probably figures no one else would bother to finish the book.

Special thanks go to my mother, Carol, and brother, Carl, for their patience and support. To my dog, Monet, who did not devour any portion of this manuscript out of revenge for my lack of attention toward her. Appreciation goes to good friend, Melissa, for use of her literary collection on learning disabilities. And, last but not least, to Michael Bender, my developmental editor, who taught me the essentials about writing and the publishing business. Your support was greatly appreciated.

This book is dedicated to all those in the world who realize that "having fun is not easy."

CONTENTS

FOREWORD

Regina Cicci, Ph.D.

Perhaps nothing reveals so much about individuals as how they choose to play—how they invest their time and energy for leisure time. Leisure is that time free from demands of school, work, or required activities of daily living. Everyone needs regular recreation that develops skills, promotes good health, relieves stress, facilitates social interactions, and provides a general joy for living.

For recreation, we choose activities at which we can be successful. Good readers read. Athletes seek sports' activities. Musicians lose themselves in music. Visual artists paint or draw. Craftspeople create. Social individuals engage in group activities. Observers appreciate the efforts of others—whether a basketball game, painting, fine meal, or concert.

Children, adolescents, and adults with learning disabilities may find themselves with limited opportunities to fully enjoy leisure time. A lack of perceptual, motor, memory, linguistic, or organizational skills may cause them as much difficulty for leisure as they have at school or work. Fear of failure may limit their reaching out to access recreational activities. Just as we teach children with dyslexia to read, those with math disabilities to understand math, those with linguistic problems to better comprehend and use language, we must teach skills and provide practice so individuals with learning disabilities can achieve some recreational proficiencies. When skills are not as well developed as necessary and compensations are not made, agencies, institutions, instructors, and coaches can be helped to make necessary accommodations. Satisfying leisure time for persons with learning and other disabilities is as important as accomplishments at home, school, and work.

PREFACE

Dale S. Brown

It is an honor to write a preface for *Developing Recreation Skills in Persons with Learning Disabilities.* As a leader in the self-help movement for people with learning disabilities, dyslexia, and attention deficit disorder, I have seen the results of the lack of leisure. The saying "All work and no play makes Jack a dull boy" is proven by the lives of many people with learning disabilities who work so hard coping with a world without accommodation that they have little time for play. Their forays into the world of recreation have led to rejection, partially because the staff involved did not know how to make it possible for them to participate. They have an added problem—isolation.

It is critical that people with learning disabilities, like all human beings, create balance in their lives. Parents, special educators, therapeutic recreation specialists, and leisure professionals can be allies in all aspects of a high-quality life—school, work, and leisure.

This historic book, currently the only volume addressing the issue, can help many readers. People with learning disabilities themselves can go right to Chapter 6 and use the many accommodations and modifications to enhance their own leisure. Professionals in the fields of leisure and recreation can use this book to assure that they are in compliance with the Americans with Disabilities Act and to not lose revenue from people with learning disabilities who may be excluded. And finally, parents will find many ideas to advocate for their children.

When I was growing up, most organized recreation was extremely challenging to me. Learning disabilities were virtually unknown. My long hours doing homework did not leave much time for a social life. And my disabilities affected my ability to accurately perceive what other people were saying and doing. A few accommodations made then would have enabled me to have a happier childhood with periods of rest and renewal. This book will help the youth of today relax in situations where the youth of yesterday had to struggle.

I challenge the readers of this book to read it and take notes for the purpose of action. Write down what you will do differently. And do something about at least one of the points tomorrow. If at least one of you does that, somebody with learning disabilities will be better off. If most of you read and then act, we will change the system of recreation and leisure to be more open to people who have learning disabilities. And people with learning disabilities will be able to play and belong to many teams.

Dale S. Brown founded the National Network of Learning Disabled Adults and has helped over 200 local and statewide self-help groups develop and grow. She was a key player in the passage of the Americans with Disabilities Act and has written three books and hundreds of articles. She has won numerous national awards, including being selected as one of ten outstanding young Americans by the U.S. Junior Chamber of Commerce.

Chapter One

AN INTRODUCTION

Much positive publicity about disabilities during this past decade has been displayed through television, books, newspapers, and magazines. The passing of federal legislation (the Rehabilitation Act of 1973, Education for All Handicapped Children Act of 1975, Civil Rights Restoration Act of 1989, and Americans with Disabilities Act of 1990) confirms the government's role in promoting rights and equal protections to people with disabilities. Through the media and government entities, the public is beginning to understand the educational, economical, social/emotional, career, and access needs of people with disabilities.

Statistics are sketchy regarding how many people in the United States have learning disabilities. Harwell (1989) makes a broad estimate of from 2% to more than 20% of the population. The U.S. Department of Education (1994), in its *Sixteenth Annual Report to Congress on the Implementation of the Individuals with Disabilities Education Act*, reported the public schools having identified approximately 2.3 million students 6 to 21 years of age as learning disabled, which represents 4.09% of those in this age range (this excluded children in private schools). Learning disabilities as a whole has become the largest group of disabilities diagnosed in elementary, secondary, and postsecondary settings.

Learning disabilities are known among those who have them as the "invisible disability." One looks quite normal, may articulate and express oneself quite well, but in a given situation for some unknown reason experiences difficulties in reading, performing simple math problems, remembering, or misinterpreting what he or she hears in a particular conversation. The presence of these characteristics is often not consistent. A person may not exhibit problems spelling the word "government" on one day, but later in that week while working on the same writing assignment, he will misspell it "guvernmint," unaware to him. This inconsistency causes frustration. One cannot determine when it will occur nor stop it before the problem begins. The individual is not sure where he fits on the scale of having a disability, because sometimes the characteristics will not appear. A person with a hearing impairment who needs to use a hearing aid will use the aid every day, but the person having an auditory processing problem might only experience difficulty with interpretation of verbal information in a small group, short-timed, freely participated setting and not in a one-on-one situation. Teachers, coaches, parents, siblings, and friends misunderstand the person as being lazy, not trying hard enough, or not serious; they show disbelief of exhibited behaviors. A verbal comment of "Johnny must be faking" is often exchanged between the child's friends or between the staff working with this child. Because of the ever-changing covert and overt appearance that learning disabilities have, family members and professionals need to understand the complexities and display empathy to those who have it.

Learning disabilities are not concentrated in any specific gender, age group, geographic location, ethnic group, or socioeconomic income level. People with learning disabilities have high school, Bachelor, Masters, and Doctorate degrees. These individuals work in many disciplines and can achieve success in a particular career if they so desire. They take part in solitaire, group, active, or passive recreation activities. Some are leaders, attacking a problem straight on. Others are more diplomatic, analyzing players and obtaining consensuses from the group. These individuals are often resourceful and creative. Their approach to problem solving is unique, not like the "regular" population. These individuals can provide us "regulars" with innovative thoughts to attack problems for the future. As children or adults, they are not homogenous in level of difficulty, level of functioning, learning style desired, or accommodations preferred. It is important for professionals working with persons having learning disabilities, as well as the public, to understand each person as an individual. These individuals can make decisions, argue points of view, instruct others, plan activities, reach long-term goals, and excel in areas of interest. One should remember, it is called a *learning disability,* **not** *a learning inability.*

Early federal laws addressed the need for people with disabilities to receive equal opportunities within the community. Public Law 94-142, the *Education for All Handicapped Children Act,* and Public Law 101-476, the *Individuals with Disabilities Education Act,* required that a free appropriate public education, which includes special education and related services (recreation and recreation therapy), be available to children and youth with disabilities in mandated age ranges (3 to 21). These laws started the *least restrictive environment* concept that suggests that children with disabilities are to be educated, to the maximum extent possible, and are to participate in community leisure services, to the maximum extent possible, alongside nondisabled peers.

The Americans with Disabilities Act of 1990 was created to eliminate discrimination against people with disabilities in all aspects of American life. This law encourages inclusive programming instead of segregated programs, meaning an environment for the delivery of service in which interaction between people with and without disabilities is provided to the maximum extent feasible. Why? First, to provide opportunities for the nondisabled person to participate with someone having a disability. Schleien & Ray (1988) report studies in integrated environments where attitude change was measured, resulting in better acceptance and understanding of the individual having the disability by the nondisabled peer. Second, to allow persons with disabilities the freedom of choice of activities without limitations of time, place, or employee availability. Disabled and nondisabled peers can now register for the same activity session at the same time. All sessions of a recreation program are open to people with disabilities. Any program offered in a particular building is open to people with disabilities. A recreation leader who is working with the able-bodied population in his session also works with participants who have disabilities. Inclusion promotes equal access and participation in recreation programs for people having learning disabilities. The success of an inclusive recreation program requires that general program staff and a therapeutic recreation specialist, a special education teacher, or adaptive physical education teacher to work cooperatively. Private and public leisure service providers network to exchange ideas, offer solutions to problems, and share resources, making their environments as accessible as possible. The main goal is for the individual with a disability to have enjoyable and successful leisure experiences with nondisabled persons in community settings.

Numerous materials have been published on educational intervention, cognitive instruction, transition planning, and vocational training for individuals with learning disabilities. However, very little is written on how language, cognitive functioning, visual and auditory processing, and perceptual-motor difficulties can affect recreation and leisure pursuits. Recreation/Leisure ability and planning are part of a student's individual education plan and individual transition plan; credence must be given to this area to promote its importance and success in developing one to be a well-rounded individual. One's life is comprised of many interests and pursuits, not just the area of academics. In reading this book, teachers, educational specialists, counselors, practitioners, program directors, recreation therapists, and family members will gain additional knowledge to express to others the importance of recreation in the lives of those with learning disabilities. Acquiring the understanding of learning disabilities and the knowledge about diagnostic information, recognizing the benefits of leisure involvement, becoming concerned about proper delivery of recreation services, promoting the use of accommodations or modifications to programs, and gaining awareness of resources all provide readers with the foundation to assure equal access and participation in leisure activities of choice for the individual having learning disabilities.

Primary Focus of Book

The primary focus will be learning disabilities and leisure. The methods and examples explained in this book may have implications for programming leisure activities with other special populations, especially in the area of cognitive impairments. Professionals working with individuals having acquired head injury, attention deficit disorder, cerebral vascular accident (stroke), and communicative disorders might find the information and resources supplied in this book beneficial to planning and implementing leisure activities for these groups.

Chapter Two commences with the generally accepted definition of learning disabilities and an explanation of its different types. Understanding what constitutes learning disabilities is important for anyone working with this population. More than 18 different types of learning disabilities exist, one of which is perceptual-motor deficits. It is within this perceptual-motor area where difficulties with mirroring exercises and dance routines, balance, movement through space, eye-hand coordination, and directionality are displayed. In Chapter Two, the many stated learning disability types describe examples after the definition. This way readers can utilize the chapter as a quick-reference guide in assessing characteristics to determine if an individual should be referred for diagnostic screening or testing. A brief description of major evaluation tests commonly used in determining learning disabilities for children and adults will be explained. This section intends to familiarize the reader with the type of tests used and the testing process. Chapter Two continues to examine how learning disabilities are present in children and adults and presents its similarities and differences. The developmental life stages and life factors (i.e., adjustment and competency during elementary, secondary, and postsecondary education and employment; social interaction, peer acceptance, and teamwork; initiative and goal achievement) will be explored between the age groups. The chapter will conclude reviewing the misconceptions people in society have about those who have learning disabilities, multicultural perspectives of learning disabilities, and people with learning disabilities' perceptions of themselves and how the public views them.

Chapter Three takes on the topic of awareness. It discusses what self-awareness is, how the person having learning disabilities recognizes his or her own strengths and weaknesses, and why self-awareness is important. Once self-awareness is present, the individual can explore possibilities to solving continuous problems (i.e., where to go for help and who to ask) and can develop strategies to both improve areas of weakness and enhance leisure skills. In this book, the Five Levels of Competency and Cognitive Behavior Management strategies teach the reader how to instruct the participant in improving competency skills toward effective problem-solving. These skills will enable the person to reach a higher level of decision making, whereby becoming advantageous to self and situation. Awareness of strengths and weaknesses, as well as frustrations and exhilaration, in the person with learning disabilities should also become cognizant to the parents, sibling(s), and spouse of this individual. These behaviors become apparent when the parents, siblings, or spouse of the person with learning disabilities observe that person's behavior and ability during life skills activities (i.e., hygiene, academics, social skills, and recreation). Personal accounts and reports portray the frustration, anxiety, sadness, and happiness family members encounter in observing their love one's triumphs and tribulations in tackling daily tasks. In order to better understand the individual with learning disabilities, this book provides exercises to aid family members in discovering their perceptions about learning disabilities and how these perceptions, whether positive or negative are exchanged and understood amongst themselves. Professionals can teach these family members, through the use of additional chapter exercises, how it feels to process information at a slower rate, to constantly misinterpret oral and visual information, and to display poor coordination.

When one is given the diagnosis of learning disabilities and is aware of one's own strengths and weaknesses, the next step is to advocate for one's needs. Self-advocacy is addressed in this book through learning the proper procedures to seek information or services on accommodations and modifications for recreation activities. Advocacy and assertive skills are synonymous for achieving success in acquiring services. Information in this section supplies the reader with materials in teaching individuals what type of behaviors are exhibited when being assertive and the benefits of said assertive behavior. When a person decides that she is going to advocate for services, then disclosure of disability results. Various components of disclosure will be discussed: what disclosure is (i.e., the procedure that enables one to receive the accommodations or modifications needed); why a person should disclose her disability; the proper way to "disclose" to another individual; the pros and cons of disclosing one's disability to recreation program leaders, friends, and others; and concern about the confidentiality of the disclosure (i.e., who should know and not know about the disability).

This chapter will end by highlighting the impact advocacy has on the lives of those having learning disabilities, involvement in change that influenced policy and delivery of services, and ways to become an effective advocate for oneself and others.

The main focus in Chapter Four is what comprises leisure, the benefits of engaging in recreation activities, and reports from people with learning disabilities regarding how important leisure is to them. Selected generic recreation survey forms will be presented to help those with learning disabilities to discover and explore their recreational interests. The book continues with a look into the realization of how the characteristics of learning disabilities can affect one's recreation participation. The introduction of the Cognitive Leisure Indicator Instrument serves in determining to what extent learning disabilities might affect one's participation in recreation activities. This self-report type survey form contains seven sections that cover cognitive processes and leisure behavior. It is the scores within and between these sections that signify inability or preference not to participate in certain types of leisure activities. Specifics regarding the survey form's operation, validity, and reliability index are provided in the appendix section of this book. After exploring recreation participation ability, information on building and maintaining a successful leisure relationship with the person having learning disabilities will be examined, focusing on the following topics: communication, especially in relation to auditory processing difficulties; development of appropriate social skills; time management—scheduling time to participate in the leisure activity of choice; recreational interest—preference for types of activities (i.e., solitary, group, active, passive, leadership, or participant); organization of materials and ideas before and within leisure settings; encouragement to express need for accommodations; self-esteem within the recreation situation; and participation in the leisure activity. This chapter finishes with simple steps for guiding the person with learning disabilities to actual involvement in recreation activities.

Chapter Five, "Delivery of Recreation Programs to Persons with Learning Disabilities," explores the subject of creating an inclusive community recreation environment. Readers encounter the reasons behind inclusive community recreation and its benefits to people with disabilities. The discussion extends to specifics of the Americans with Disabilities Act and what effect this Public Law has made on recreation agencies. This chapter illustrates a number of scenarios regarding ways of creating accommodations and modifications of recreation programs that are in agreement with both the agency and the person with learning disabilities to demonstrate "good faith effort" and to avoid "undue hardship."

Next is introducing people with disabilities to the leisure service system and the purposes and philosophies of agencies within its subdivisions. This knowledge enables these potential participants to investigate the best options for selecting recreation activities at particular agencies or departments that will satisfy their leisure need. Extending to important aspects within a leisure service system, readers are exposed to how the participant's registration information guides the recreation leader's design of an activity session; the importance of the staff member's skills and their understanding to work with individuals having different levels of abilities; and the involvement of persons with disabilities in evaluating the agency's programs. The essential components of staff training and education about disabilities cover several topics: processes involved in learning, effective communication skills, knowledge about disabilities, accommodations and modifications, locations of resources, and leadership and group function.

This chapter's last section addresses the participant's role in program evaluation. In recognizing the participant as a "customer," and validating his or her contribution to improving existing services, the agency can succeed in achieving optimal quality satisfaction in service delivery. It is in the best interest of an agency promoting inclusive recreation programming to obtain input from people in the community that have disabilities—to network with area agencies to expand and satisfy participants' needs and create recreation opportunities. When the previous guidelines are met, the agency is on its way to achieving an effective and successful inclusive community recreation program.

Chapter Six furnishes specific suggestions for accommodations and modifications of recreation activities. An explanation will be provided about the differences and similarities between an accommodation and program modification. The multisensory teaching approach with learning styles theory will be explained relating to instruction of recreation and sport activities. This is an approach utilized in the academic setting that can contribute a unique and sensory-balanced approach to teaching recreation activities in the community setting. Teachers, coaches, recreation leaders, and recreation therapists need to know that everyone does not learn by "watch and do." This chapter explains compensation strategies utilized during both basketball and football instruction and in adapting game plays for athletes with visual acuity problems, auditory processing problems, and short-term memory difficulties. This book contains clear illustrations of simple directions, measurements (if required), and names of materials to be used as accommodations or for modifying recreation activities. Examples of modifications shown in this book cover the following areas: 1) sports and physical activities (badminton, racquetball, golf, aerobics), 2) passive activities (card games, e.g., Crazy 8, and table games, e.g., Word Yahtzee®, dominoes), 3) outdoor activities (fishing, hiking, gardening), 4) hobbies (photography, cooking, crafts), and 5) social/community activities (concerts, travel, volunteering). The modifications to be demonstrated focus on slight changes in game directions, allowances for extra time, use of color to assist in tracking the object, one-on-one game instruction, repetition of steps in the task, and uses of alternative teaching methods such as role playing and visualization.

The last chapter supplies a represented list of names and addresses of major organizations and agencies, commercial businesses, well-known publications, and actively-used visual media sources. The list of major organizations and agencies serves readers in networking with professionals in the field; acquiring information about an organization or agency (i.e., purpose and function); obtaining materials and publications about learning disabilities; and keeping abreast of the trends, discoveries, and issues of concerns in the field of learning disabilities. In this book, the organizations and associations contain national and international agencies that

- promote assistive technology and disabilities;
- provide information sharing, education, training, and support for family members or persons with learning disabilities;
- disseminate materials and information about various disabilities, including learning disabilities;
- encourage enhancing the leisure experiences (whether passive or active recreational pursuits) of people with disabilities.

Chapter Seven continues with providing company names and addresses on assistive technology equipment, materials, and supplies; printed materials depicting strategies, techniques, and personal experiences for enhancing the life of persons with learning disabilities; and electronic sources via the internet to foster quick communication between parties to aid in solving problems and implementing change.

In summary, implications that learning disabilities affected nonacademic portions of people's lives have been noted in books and articles throughout the years, yet attempts to explore its nature and derive solutions were not major areas of research. The emphasis of teaching these individuals formalized learning overshadowed social adeptness and leisure competence. Learning occurs in recreation; individuals would like to receive success in their leisure pursuits just as in their academic endeavors. Learning proceeds through one's life span just as recreation does. On the road of life, play never stops and learning never ceases to end. One hopes that play becomes more satisfying and learning more profound in future years. It is imperative that each individual with learning disabilities discovers both compensation strategies and game modifications and uses adaptive equipment to improve his quality of leisure throughout his lifetime.

References

Harwell, J.M. (1989). *Complete learning disabilities handbook.* West Nyack, NY: The Center for Applied Research in Education, Inc.

Schleien, S.J., & Ray, T.M. (1988). *Community recreation and persons with disabilities: Strategies for integration.* Baltimore: Paul H. Brookes.

U.S. Department of Education. (1994). *Sixteenth annual report to Congress on the implementation of the Individuals with Disabilities Act.* Washington, D.C.: Author.

Chapter Two

LEARNING DISABILITIES

Definition

There have been many definitions formulated over the decades about what constitutes learning disabilities. These definitions were created within federal legislation (e.g., Public Law 94-142, the *Education for All Handicapped Children Act*), associations serving individuals with learning disabilities, and individual state department of education and professional researchers in the field of special education and learning disabilities. This book will use the definition from the National Joint Committee on Learning Disabilities (NJCLD). The NJCLD is composed of organizations having a personal stake in learning disabilities. These organizations are the Association on Higher Education and Disability (AHEAD), American Speech-Language-Hearing Association, Council for Learning Disabilities, National Association of School Psychologists, Division for Children with Communication Disorders, International Reading Association, Learning Disabilities Association of America (which, however, did *not* adopt this definition), and the International Dyslexia Association. The 1988 NJCLD definition on learning disabilities reads as follows:

> *Learning disabilities* is a generic term that refers to a heterogeneous group of disorders manifested by significant difficulties in the acquisition and use of listening, speaking, reading, writing, reasoning, or mathematical abilities. These disorders are intrinsic to the individual and presumed to be due to central nervous system dysfunction, and they may occur across the life span. Problems in self-regulatory behaviors, social perception, and social interaction may exist with learning disabilities but do not by themselves constitute a learning disability. Although learning disabili-

ties may occur concomitantly with other handicapping conditions (e.g., sensory impairment, mental retardation, serious emotional disturbance), or with extrinsic influences (e.g., cultural differences, insufficient/inappropriate instruction), they are not the result of those conditions or influences. (National Joint Committee on Learning Disabilities, 1988, p. 1)

In using this definition, those working with people having learning disabilities will begin to understand the diversity of characteristics represented in this disability.

In regards to learning disabilities occurring with sensory impairment (e.g., hearing and visual impairments), it is very difficult for one to detect what affects a decrease in hearing and how inefficient auditory processing abilities play a part in learning orally presented information. Where this presumed dual difficulty exists, the person should seek evaluation services from more than one area (e.g., educational diagnostician and speech/language pathologist or school psychologist and ophthalmologist). The American Psychiatric Association (1994) classifies mental retardation in a person having below average intelligence (i.e., IQ level 70 and below). In this book, learning disabilities refers to a person having average or above average intelligence. This is one of the main criteria for determining if this disability is present. A person who has mental retardation can exhibit some of the same characteristics listed under "Different Types of Learning Disabilities" (see the next section), but this person is not given the diagnosis of specific learning disabilities. Mental retardation and learning disabilities are two distinct classifications and the two should never be confused. Another area of concern is with attention deficit hyperactivity disorder (ADHD). Silver (1990) refers to a number of reports stating that somewhere between 15% and 20% of children and adolescents with learning disabilities will have ADHD disorders. This is a syndrome characterized by serious and persistent difficulties in areas of attention span, impulse control, and sometimes hyperactivity. It can begin in childhood and extend through adulthood while having negative effects on the individual's life at home, school, and work. Silver (1990) comments that "ADHD is an associated disorder but is not a learning disability. ADHD does not impact on the brain's ability to learn. It can interfere with the individual's availability for learning" (p. 396).

The considered theories of cause for one developing learning disabilities are numerous. Hallahan, Kauffman, and Lloyd (1996) report:

that increasingly sophisticated technology in medicine and related biological sciences in the 1990s confirm the suspicion that learning disabilities are caused by differences in brain structure or functioning. Yet, there is no confirmed evidence of neurological dysfunction in the vast majority of cases. (p. 8)

Harwell (1989) lists possible causes as a familial factor—previous diagnosis in a close relative; difficult pregnancy; post-birth traumas (e.g., oxygen deprivation, intracranial infection, head trauma); and chronic ear infections and allergies. There are often accounts where the person or family member cannot find any incident occurring in the person's life that would indicate a cause for having learning disabilities. Basically, research has not found any single cause for learning disabilities that is consistent in all cases. As this area continues to be explored, parents, siblings, friends, spouses, and professionals need to become familiar with the disorders associated with learning disabilities and understand how these disorders affect the everyday life functions of people with learning disabilities.

Different Types of Learning Disabilities

Different types of learning disabilities pertain to the "heterogeneous group of disorders" statement within the definition. This statement refers to the types of disorders that can occur under the umbrella category of learning disabilities. Dale S. Brown (1980), in *Steps to Independence for People with Learning Disabilities,* listed numerous difficulties that can occur under the umbrella of learning disabilities. Some examples in the definitions were adapted by the author. The disorder includes the following:

Dyscalculia is the inability to do math.
Dysgraphia is the inability to write.
Dyslexia is the inability to read.
Associative Reaction is when one part of the body moves involuntarily because of the movement of another part of the body (e.g., the left arm may move when the right arm moves, or one arm may move when the head turns).
Auditory Perceptual Problems are when an individual has trouble absorbing information through the sense of hearing and/

or processing that information. (Processing pertains to how the information is interpreted by the sense; the length of time it takes to think about and to understand the incoming information in order to respond to the instruction, question, statement, etc.) People with this problem frequently hear inaccurately. The individual hears "formed" instead of "performed," "six" instead of "sixty," or "treats" instead of "streets." The person may experience difficulty in discriminating sounds from background noise. A common example is determining what someone is saying to you while in a restaurant. The background noise in this setting—the dishes clanging, music playing, and people talking or laughing—causes the interference. Auditory sequencing may be a problem, such as if one hears sounds in the incorrect order, such as "four-five" instead of "five-four," especially when listening to someone recite one's telephone number or scores in a card game.

Catastrophic Response is an involuntary reaction to too many sights, sounds, extreme emotions, or other strong stimuli. It is as if you overloaded your senses. The result may be losing one's temper, becoming dazed (unaware of one's present environment), or "freezing" for a short period of time.

Cognitive Disorganization is when an individual suffers complications with thinking in an orderly, logical way. People with this problem often jump to conclusions and have difficulty planning tasks and organizing time. Individuals also experience challenges in distinguishing between two similar concepts, such as love and like.

Crossing the Midline is when one has trouble in moving his limbs across the center of his body. This includes difficulty writing across a page, mimicking exercise movements, and catching a ball on either side of the body with the opposite hand.

Directional Problems are complications in automatically determining left from right; learning north, south, east, west; and learning the layout of a large symmetrical building. This disorder becomes quite apparent when a person experiences constant difficulty in placing herself during a rotation serve in volleyball.

Disinhibition is difficulty behaving appropriately in an automatic way. A person may laugh in inappropriate situations, exhibit poor social graces, abruptly interrupt a conversation, or barge into a person's office without knocking.

Intersensory Problem is having trouble using two senses at once or associating two senses (e.g., not realizing that the sighted letter "d" is the same as the sound "d" when it is spoken or not being able to listen to conversation and drive at the same time).

Short-term Memory Problem is when an individual has trouble remembering names, numbers, specific facts, and game plays that occurred only a few minutes ago.

Perceptual Motor Problems are difficulties in performing a task requiring coordination because inaccurate information is received through the senses. This is often exhibited in clumsiness or in a display of awkward movements.

Visual Motor Problem is difficulty with imitation of a task; for example, copying something off a blackboard or learning a dance step while watching the instructor.

Auditory Motor Problem is a complication in hearing something and then performing the task (e.g., following verbal directions or dancing to a rhythmic beat).

Proprioceptive Perceptual Problem is difficulty knowing where one is in space. This person might not be able to tell the position of his limbs with his eyes closed or may experience distress when maneuvering around close objects in a space (e.g., walking into the ends of tables or tripping over legs of chairs).

Tactile Perceptual Problems involve a couple of areas. One area is defensiveness—avoidance to being touched. It can also be a discrimination problem—determining the difference between similar objects, such as watercolor and newsprint paper, acrylic and wool yarn. This may cause the person to be extra careful or to ask for advice when selecting supplies for art projects. Tactile pressure problems cause one to misjudge the correct amount of pressure needed to do fine motor acts such as holding small or fragile items without breaking them (e.g., painting or adhering items on porcelain or ceramics pieces), rubbing too hard on paper and being heavy handed (e.g., tapping someone, throwing the basketball too hard).

Visual Figure-Ground Problem is suffering complications in finding a ball in the playing field, finding keys on a crowded desk, or picking out one line of print from the other lines in a book.

Visual Sequencing Problem is trouble seeing things in the correct order (e.g., seeing letters, words, or numbers in reverse order). The individual may copy game scores or team titles down incorrectly.

Visual Discrimination Problem is facing obstacles in identifying the difference between two similar objects, such as the letters "v" and "u" or "n" and "m" or the difference between two shades of one color.

Depth Perception Problem is when an individual has difficulty perceiving how far away or close an object is (e.g., how far to reach to put a glass of water on the table) (pp. 10-13).

Common characteristics noted during academic learning may have an impact on leisure activities, especially in reading game instructions, writing a journal , completing registration forms, expressing thoughts, explaining instructions to teammates, understanding verbal instructions from teammates or a recreation leader, and understanding abstract concepts (e.g., time).

In the area of *reading*, individuals with learning disabilities experience the following:

- confusion of similar sounding and looking words,
- poor word-attack skills,
- problems reading multiple-syllable words,
- difficulty using phonics,
- frequent misinterpretation of words,
- inability to locate the main idea of a reading passage,
- problems understanding and retaining material that is read,
- problems synthesizing information,
- habitual addition or omission of text that makes the sentence meaning incoherent,
- poor awareness of punctuation and verb tense in a sentence.

In the area of *writing*, individuals with learning disabilities experience the following:

- difficulty with sentence structure—they have an immature and limited vocabulary,
- constant use of incorrect grammar,
- omission of words,
- incorrect tense usage,
- frequent undetected spelling errors—phonetic spelling of words, inconsistent spelling,
- letter reversal,
- inconsistent use of capitals and punctuation,
- difficulty arranging thoughts in a sequential order,

- use of unrelated information—interruption of tangential thoughts,
- poor arrangement of ideas within the body of the essay.

Handwriting of individuals having learning disabilities often displays the following:

- a slower rate of writing from persons not having learning disabilities,
- awkwardly formed letters,
- preference to only print handwriting,
- inconsistent spacing,
- difficulty maintaining writing within margins or lines on paper,
- writing that is too large or too small.

In the area of *expressive language*, individuals having learning disabilities exhibit the following:

- difficulty expressing ideas orally (e.g., with ideas that a student has knowledge in and understands, he has a lack of connection with thoughts),
- difficulty retrieving the appropriate word for a situation (e.g., word-finding problems),
- problems describing events or stories in correct sequence,
- using incorrect words during a conversation (e.g., exceed for succeeding).

In the area of *receptive language*, individuals having learning disabilities would have difficulty with the following:

- understanding what others say (especially in an interactive group setting),
- quickly responding to a joke, answering a question, or demonstrating a task on the spot,
- determining what a statement meant the first time presented without asking for the question or statement to be repeated,
- not repeating the statement or question to assure understanding of the information that was just stated.

In the area of *cognitive abilities*, individuals having learning disabilities would show the following:

- difficulty organizing ideas and information,
- problems comprehending abstract concepts,
- limited awareness of cause-and-effect relationships,

- difficulty retrieving information from one's memory,
- difficulty remembering what one hears or sees,
- trouble remaining on task,
- difficulty distinguishing important from unimportant information during lectures,
- problems applying skills from one task or situation to another.

In the area of *study skills*, individuals having learning disabilities exhibit the following:

- problems working on task until completion,
- procrastination with assignments and projects,
- poor time-management skills,
- difficulty establishing short- and long-term goals,
- poor ability to break down a task and begin with primary requirements of the task,
- problems integrating information from various sources (e.g., textbook, classroom notes, and video to construct a report),
- lacking competent note-taking skills,
- difficulty outlining important information in a text,
- limited test-taking strategies,
- extreme test anxiety.

All these disorders and problems with academics do not occur in every individual having learning disabilities. One individual may experience mild difficulties in a variety of areas and another person may experience extreme distress in only one or two areas. Whatever the combination of disorders or characteristics, they are consistent and long-term. Individuals with learning disabilities need to be aware of their strengths and weaknesses, utilize present strategies that are successful, and build areas of weaknesses through compensation strategies.

In becoming familiar with the previously stated disorders and characteristics inherent to learning disabilities, professionals and family members, through observation and interaction with the person, can ascertain if a referral is needed for the evaluation of learning disabilities.

Diagnosing Learning Disabilities

The purpose for diagnosing learning disabilities is to determine exactly what types of disorders and characteristics the individual possesses and what degree of severity is present in order to better understand strengths, limitations, and learning styles of the individual and to determine what strategies and accommodations would be beneficial to the person. If a teacher, counselor, recreation leader, or therapist suspects someone may have learning disabilities, the first step is to refer the individual for diagnostic testing. The teacher, counselor, recreation leader, or therapist would approach the parent of the child or the adult participant with information about learning disabilities and suggest referral for testing.

With a child, the most delicate way to approach this topic is to call the child's parents and ask for a meeting to discuss this child's progress. The professional should arrange this meeting for discussion to take place in a private area and should assure the parents about confidentiality of the meeting. During the meeting, inform the parents that either you, as the professional, or other staff members have observed that the parent's child seems to be experiencing difficulties in school, recreation activity, interaction with peers, etc. The "experiencing difficulty" terms should allude to the characteristics of learning disabilities, and it is during this discussion that one should have some literature available on the topic to give to parents.

In approaching the topic of learning disabilities, try not to use the phrase: "I think your child has a learning disability." First of all, it is not certain the child has a learning disability and this cannot be determined without proper evaluation. One can only imply through the statement, "A few of us (or I) noticed your child exhibits these characteristics (e.g., misreading words, always asking for directions to be repeated, forgetting next play in game, etc.) during a soccer session and these are similar to characteristics of learning disabilities."

Addressing the matter in this way does not guarantee belief from the parents, a pleasant conversation about learning disabilities, or the follow through of the child being tested. It is merely addressing a concern that the professional (e.g., teacher, counselor, recreation leader, therapist, etc.) has about a child's abilities within particular noted tasks. Learning disabilities are mainly discussed in the realm of school performance. The public is more aware of these disabilities being present in the academic setting, so it might not come as a surprise for parents to deny a professional's observations of their child exhibiting learning disability behaviors during a leisure activity. It is possible that during this interaction the professional may discover that the child has been diagnosed with learning disabilities and that the parents chose not to disclose the information. The parents' feelings may be that the child has enough separation in school by attending special education classes and they do not wish for the child to be singled out as "different" in leisure activities. Perhaps the parents knew something was different about their child's performance but did not know how to treat the situation.

With an adult participant displaying learning disability behaviors, a similar approach can be taken to recommend the person for testing. Here, the professional can describe the characteristics she has noticed during the activity to the adult. Talk about this in a private area and before discussion ends, inform the adult about the confidentiality of the conversation, especially regarding a spouse or partner. In a midst of the conversation with the adult, one may find that the adult noticed these problems throughout his life, but he did not know who to discuss them with or where to seek help. A common phrase is, "I thought everyone did that." Because the behavior was exhibited for such a long time and did not receive corrective feedback from someone, the person thought his behavior was the norm.

When informing the parent of a child or the adult participant himself about noted characteristics of learning disabilities, be prepared to discuss this matter for a period of time; setting aside 30 minutes to one hour would be sufficient. Many of these individuals were not able to discuss this matter previously with anyone. The professional may hear years' worth of frustration, heartache, and concern from the parent of a child or the individual possibly having learning disabilities. Throughout this meeting, the professional is required to show patience and empathy, be an active listener, encourage parents or the participant to talk about concerns, and inform those concerned about resources available in the community (e.g., diagnostic testing, support groups, other service agencies).

Guidelines in Assessing Learning Disabilities

The diagnostic procedure of determining if someone has learning disabilities requires the use of numerous tests. The assessment instruments can take the form of screening checklists. In these self-evaluative checklists, the individual relays ideas on how she perceives areas of difficulties. The Student Referral Information form (see Figure 2.1) is used with an adult population (i.e., ages 17 and above) in postsecondary schools. The Self-evaluation Checklist (see Figure 2.2) is written on a sixth grade reading level, and used in grade six and above. The Evidence Checklist: Referral for Learning Disabilities (see Appendix A) is for professionals to use when observing behaviors in children or adults. These checklists serve as a screening device in justifying the continuation of diagnostic testing with standardized instruments. A combination of intelligence, cognitive and memory, academic, and information processing tests constitute a full-diagnostic battery for identification of learning disabilities.

Figure 2.1
Student Referral Information

Name of student: _____

Social security number: _____

Phone number: (day) _____   (evening) _____

How did you find out about our services? _____

_____

Instructions: As you read through the following characteristics, check only those that are clearly evident to you (that you notice occurring repeatedly in your life). When you check a characteristic, you should be able to say, "This really fits me." Be careful not to check the ones that you notice only occasionally. *Everyone* experiences most of these at some time. **Only check the ones that you feel interfere with your overall ability to learn.**

Cognitive
_____ difficulty putting events and ideas in order
_____ difficulty understanding abstract concepts
_____ difficulty in distinguishing important from unimportant information
_____ little awareness of cause-and-effect relationships
_____ memory (inability to remember what you've heard)
_____ poor visual memory (inability to remember what you've seen or read)
_____ difficulty staying on task
_____ difficulty in organizing ideas and information
_____ difficulty in applying skills from one task or situation to another

Figure 2.1 Cont.

Language

    Spoken

_____ difficulty understanding what others say

_____ use of poor grammar

_____ limited range of vocabulary

_____ difficulty retrieving the appropriate word for a situation

_____ inappropriate use of words or using a word where it doesn't belong

    Written

_____ imprecise and unclear expression (trouble getting your ideas across on paper)

_____ grammar errors (trouble with tense agreement, etc.)

_____ poor organization of thoughts

_____ incorrect use of punctuation

_____ seldom use phrases or sentences with long or difficult words

_____ compositions usually too short for purpose

Perceptual-Motor

_____ reversal of letters and numerals

_____ difficulty perceiving spatial attributes (e.g., trouble reading a map)

_____ difficulty dealing with three dimensional figures and/or shapes

_____ difficulty hearing differences in similar sounding words

Reading

_____ difficulty sounding words out

_____ poor ability to understand what was read

_____ poor ability to determine main ideas

_____ slow rate of reading

_____ difficulty remembering what was read

Spelling

_____ transpose letters when spelling words (such as writing "saw" for "was" or "fo" for "of")

_____ omit letters when spelling words

_____ phonetically spell most words (such as writing "guvernmint" for "government")

_____ general avoidance of writing words that are difficult to spell

Handwriting

_____ awkward and uncomfortable style of handwriting

_____ slow rate of writing

_____ poorly formed or not easily read letters

_____ writing that is overly large or small

_____ difficulty keeping writing within the margins or on the line

Figure 2.1 Cont.

Mathematics
_____ poor computational skills (adding, subtracting, etc.)
_____ incomplete memorization of multiplication tables
_____ poor mathematical reasoning (i.e., word problems)
_____ difficulty recalling the sequence of an operational process or formula
_____ failure to understand and retain terms related to math concepts

Social
_____ difficulty establishing good relationships with others
_____ difficulty working effectively with others
_____ poor family relationships
_____ problems saying what is thought or felt
_____ misunderstanding humor and sarcasm
_____ difficulty engaging in "small talk"
_____ few hobbies and interests
_____ difficulty relating to authority figures such as professors and advisors

Work and Study Habits
_____ poor organization and budgeting of time
_____ difficulty completing work when due
_____ difficulty getting work started
_____ difficulty staying with a task
_____ difficulty establishing short- and long-term goals
_____ inability to identify the basic requirements of a task
_____ difficulty bringing together information from various sources
_____ difficulty using the dictionary or other reference tools
_____ notes that are typically incomplete, inaccurate, or lacking
          important facts
_____ difficulty outlining important information in a text
_____ excessive test anxiety

Self-awareness
_____ low sense of self-worth
_____ lack of self-confidence
_____ over-dependence on others
_____ overly sensitive to criticism by others
_____ frustrates easily
_____ tendency to think negatively about outcomes of your own efforts
_____ unclear values about life
_____ tendency to respond immediately without thought about the outcome
_____ low degree of motivation
_____ excessive anxiety about things
_____ defensiveness in interacting with others

Figure 2.1 Cont.

Additional Comments: List any questions or concerns that you might have that you feel have not been covered.

_____

_____

_____

_____

Figure 2.2
Self-evaluation Checklist

	Hardly ever	Sometimes	Most always
Auditory Comprehension			
1. Do you have problems following spoken directions?	____	_____	____
2. Do you have problems remembering what you heard?	____	_____	____
Spoken Language			
3. Do you have problems telling a story so people understand?	____	_____	____
4. Do you have problems recalling the exact word you want to use?	____	_____	____
5. Do you have problems remembering names of people or things?	____	_____	____
Visual Comprehension			
6. Do you have problems remembering what you saw?	____	_____	____
7. Do you have problems using directions to put something together?	____	_____	____

Figure 2.2 Cont.

	Hardly ever	Sometimes	Most always
8. Do you have problems when someone shows you how to do something?	___	___	___
9. Do you have problems reading a newspaper?	___	___	___

Motor Coordination
10. Do you have trouble writing so that people can read it?	___	___	___
11. Do you have trouble drawing pictures?	___	___	___
12. Do you have trouble keeping your balance?	___	___	___

Orientation
13. Do you lose track of time?	___	___	___
14. Do you have problems concentrating on your homework?	___	___	___
15. Do you keep track of homework assignments in a book or log?	___	___	___
16. Do you complete assignments on time?	___	___	___

Study Skills
17. Do you understand the information you are reading?	___	___	___
18. Do you take notes from the reading?	___	___	___
19. When you find a word in your reading that you do not know, do you look it up?	___	___	___
20. Can you understand notes you have taken a day later?	___	___	___
21. In preparing for a test, do you group information to be memorized?	___	___	___
22. Do you proofread test answers before turning in a test?	___	___	___

Figure 2.2 Cont.

	Hardly ever	Sometimes	Most always
23. Do you organize your paper before writing it?	_____	_____	_____
24. Do you proofread for spelling and punctuation?	_____	_____	_____
Behavior 25. Do you understand rules and requirements?	_____	_____	_____
26. Do you have problems getting along with other people?	_____	_____	_____
27. Do other people have problems getting along with you?	_____	_____	_____
28. Do you get upset easily?	_____	_____	_____

As was mentioned earlier, the person being tested must have an average or above average intelligence in evaluating for learning disabilities. The psychologist, neuropsychologist, school psychologist, or educational diagnostician can choose from a variety of instruments. The instruments chosen must be appropriate to the age of the individual being tested and limited of cultural bias. The following is a list of commonly used intelligence tests with children.

Intelligence and General Ability Tests for Children

Test	Features
Wechsler Preschool and Primary Scale of Intelligence	age 4 to 6 1/2
Wechsler Intelligence Scale for Children-Revised	age 6 to 16 +
Test of Memory and Learning	age 5 to 19
Bender-Gestalt Test for Young Children	age 5 to 10
Stanford-Benet Intelligence Scale Form L-M	age 2 to 18
Woodcock-Johnson Psychoeducational Battery-Revised: Tests of Cognitive Ability	age 4 to geriatric

In addition to the intelligence test, academic and processing tests assist in discovering which area of the child's academic and processing abilities are affected by learning disabilities. The Wide Range Achievement Test (WRAT) Level I or II measures arithmetic computation skills, spelling, and ability to read words. The Peabody Individual Achievement Test (PIAT) determines the ability to comprehend reading material; the identification and selection of correctly spelled words; the comprehension of math; and knowledge about general information. The Key Math Test measures the ability to reason math problems with and without pencil and paper. The Woodcock Reading Test measures the ability to comprehend meanings of topics and to manipulate words in a variety of ways. The Test of Written Language-2 evaluates a child's ability for contrived and spontaneous writing. The Swanson Cognitive Processing Test (S-CPT) contains 11 subtests that measure different aspects of mental processing ability and potential. The following is a list of commonly used intelligence tests with adults.

Intelligence and General Ability Tests for Adults

Test	Features
Wechsler Adult Intelligence Scale-(III)	16 years to adult; determines cognitive strengths and weaknesses
Detroit Tests of Learning Aptitude - Adult	16 years to adult; measures mental processing strengths and weaknesses
Scholastic Abilities Tests for Adults	16 years to adult; measures cognitive and academic strengths and weaknesses
Luria-Nebraska Neuro-psychological Battery	15 years to adult; measures cognitive processing
Raven Standard Progressive Matrices	18+ years; assesses mental ability by requiring one to solve problems presented in abstract figures and designs
Test of Non-verbal Intelligence-2 (TONI)	5 years to adult; a language-free measure of intelligence and reasoning
Woodcock-Johnson Psychoeducational Battery-Revised	15 years to adult; measures cognitive and academic strengths and weaknesses

Adults also receive academic and processing tests adjunct to an intelligence evaluation. These tests consist of the following: the Nelson-Denny Reading Test evaluates vocabulary, comprehension, and reading rate; the Diagnostic Spelling Potential Test (DSPT) determines general spelling ability; the Bender Visual-Motor Gestalt Test is frequently used to measure visual processing; and the Woodcock-Johnson Psychoeducational Battery-Revised: Cognitive Processing section defines one's information processing ability. Some diagnosticians may add a learning style inventory within the testing repertoire (Learning Styles Sensory Modality Inventory; see Appendix B). These inventories measure sensory modality preference (e.g., visual, auditory, kinesthetic, or tactile), social preference (e.g., self-oriented, peer-oriented, adult-oriented, or combination) and learning theory (diverger, accommodator, converger, and assimilator), as in the Kolb Learning Style Inventory. The inventory results furnish information to the professional, family member, and the person with a learning disability regarding preference to learning style beneficial to grasping information efficiently. It also assists the professional in teaching information to individuals in a manner that complements all learning styles (see Chapter Six for teaching adaptations).

Eligibility criteria for learning disabilities in children and adults will vary from state to state. Some states may employ a discrepancy formula that compares standard scores across the areas of intelligence, academic achievement, and cognitive processing. The data from the combination of tests will generally indicate average to superior intelligence with a significant deficit in at least one academic area as well as in a specific area of processing ability. Discrepancies may also transpire between verbal and performance scores on an intelligence measure; however, this does not always occur. A significant discrepancy is defined as a negative difference of 20 standard score points (Hoy & Gregg, 1986) between the standard score on an intelligence test, the standard score obtained in an academic area, as well as in one area of cognitive processing ability (e.g., visual processing, auditory processing, verbal processing, and fluid-reasoning ability). This information will be supplied in a diagnostic report at the cessation of testing. In addition to significant discrepancy measures and a written explanation of findings, a thorough diagnostic report contains the demographics of the student (name, age, sex, school, social security number, educational level); date of concluded evaluation; name and qualifications of the diagnostician; referral source; tests administered; behavioral observations noted during testing from the diagnostician; test scores; and recommendations (see Appendix C for a Sample Educational Diagnostic Evaluation Report for an adult currently attending college). This is the information professionals should be aware of if given a report to view or if supplying recommendations for accommodations to the parents of a child or activity participant based on testing results.

Regardless of what age the diagnosis is discovered, learning disabilities present themselves differently throughout developmental life stages. The impact learning disabilities has on children will differ from adults, even though both age groups may exhibit the same disorders and characteristics. It is vital for family members, professionals working with persons having learning disabilities, and the individual having learning disabilities to become knowledgeable about the influences this disability has on one's developmental life stages (e.g., infancy and early childhood, the school years, the productive years, and the senior years).

Learning Disabilities in Children

The developmental life stages of early childhood and the school years will be examined in the child having learning disabilities. Early childhood is a period of time where rapid learning takes place and at-risk children require special attention. Weisgerber (1991) states, "The infancy and early childhood period is often the first time we become aware of emerging hearing and vision deficiencies or any delayed development in speech, physical growth, or learning, as well as motor and chronic health problems" (p. 11). Children who present any of the following characteristics should be referred to a pediatrician and/or other diagnostic programs for further assessment:

- limited visual response to objects and people in their environment;
- deviations in their responses to sound (e.g., no response, inconsistent response, hypersensitive to sound);
- lack of interest or no interest in people;
- display of no real words at age 2 and not combining words by age 3; limited vocabulary;

- difficulty following directions in comparison to peers;
- repeat or echo everything they hear with little understanding of content;
- difficulty formulating sentences after about 4 years of age;
- confusion with function of object (e.g., pounding thing or hammer);
- mixing up sounds (e.g., rabby bunnit for bunny rabbit);
- dislike of stories being read to them;
- not responding to questions; limited or unrelated response to topic of conversation;
- rejection of puzzles, small blocks, and games with numerous pieces.

(Adapted from Regina Cicci, *What's Wrong with Me? Learning Disabilities at Home and School*, 1995)

It is also important that during this life stage children are involved in a nurturing environment to stimulate development, such as a home-based structured program, Well-Baby program, Head Start, Montessori school, or a high-caliber day care facility. Teachers in the previous stated programs use structured and imaginative play, and selective materials they use are highly motivating, thereby encouraging children to use them during play. These teachers also monitor children's involvement in play as the context for educational activities. Schleien, Meyer, Heyne, and Brandt (1995) elucidate in their research that

> Play participation and increased leisure skills are related to increases in skill level in a variety of other curriculum areas. As a function of participation and instruction in play, collateral skill development has been documented for children and other areas such as language; problem solving; cognition; person-social behavior; gross and fine motor skills; and in older and higher function children, academics such as reading comprehension and mathematics. (pp. 4-5)

The following are some suggestive instructions to encourage and foster play in a child with learning disabilities:

- Introduce tools and materials that can be used in multiple ways; this encourages fantasy and imagination. Let children pretend with the objects first (e.g., a block takes on the characteristics of a car, person, animal, or food).

- Promote exploration of environment; have the child notice things: observe the shape, color, texture, smell, and sound of objects.
- Present large hard surface (e.g., wooden, plastic, sturdy foam) jigsaw puzzles, gradually introducing ones with more pieces. Extend the session to asking questions to child, such as, "Why did you put that puzzle piece in that place?" "What gave you the idea that this puzzle piece goes in this place?" "How do you know this puzzle piece will fit in this space?" This develops the process of recognition through cognitive analysis.
- Practice motor activities singularly and with apparatuses. Emphasize understanding and feeling the difference between taking large steps, skipping, jogging, running, and jumping; throwing a ball high verses throwing a ball low; throwing and bouncing different sizes of balls; moving one's body through various spaces.
- Provide a large enough space for conducting art projects (essential for a child exhibiting poor awareness of boundaries and it limits classroom skirmishes) where it is acceptable to create a mess. Have a giant variety of materials present for use (e.g., paper, markers, paints, glue, pencils, etc.) and encourage use of any or all materials available.
- Supply games and opportunities for matching pictures and objects. A good start is with computer interactive programs asking to match geometric forms (e.g., circles, squares, triangles, etc.), then advance to geometric forms having the same color, then to objects (e.g., animals, people, things in the community). Also, use a created game to match pre-letter forms (with various horizontal, vertical, and diagonal lines as well as circular forms that will later form letters). Finally, use letters and numerals that can be used for matching.
- Extend the matching game to discrimination of pictures or objects, within and between categories. For example, if a child associates a circle with a ball, that is between the categories of geometric shapes and equipment used in particular recreation activities, let's say baseball. Have the child state or select the difference between objects within a group. Select the one that does not belong with a group or set.
- Develop activities to improve auditory recognition and memory; children can be presented with a sound or word.

For example, a sound a dogs makes, "ruff," is introduced at the beginning of a story. The story talks about a dog named Simon and his adventures during a weekend. Every time the story states that Simon encounters a stranger, Simon says, "ruff." The child is instructed that every time Simon makes that "ruff" sound she is to raise her hand. This activity will determine if the child recognizes the "ruff" sound within the words of the story, can remember the "ruff" sound, and then recall what to do when the "ruff" sound is mentioned.

- Promote recognition of speech sounds. Carry out rhythmic games with made-up rhymes; say rhyming words during a drive to an outing; encourage a child to tell words that rhyme.

- Advance visual memory ability; supply games that fade out a visual object. The key is for the child to remember how the object looked, where it was located (if applicable), and when this object is used.

- Create an awareness of organization and scheduling to play. Before and within the activity, inform the child about the ending of a play session. Be specific to time; refer to the clock (e.g., at 2:30, or if the child does not understand time, say, "when the long hand gets on the 4, it is time to put away your toys"). Show the child the appropriate containers and shelves that hold objects and how objects should be placed in the containers and on shelves. The importance of ending this session is to begin another session to learn more and different things. The child can create a plan to schedule time in the week to complete the project or resume recreation activity (Cicci, 1995, pp. 20, 23-25, & 27).

The school years life stage encompasses the child being exposed to activities centered around structured learning in social settings (e.g., school environment, organized recreation activities). It is in these informative environments where learning and practice are experienced and personal characteristics are molded. Equal importance is held for displaying determination and tenacity, as well as acquisition of knowledge and skills. During this life stage, the child with learning disabilities has great difficulty adjusting to the formal education environment. This is partly due to the poor ability to organize, thus interfering in normal learning. They can't get started, have an awful time focusing, and then when they do finally focus, will not stop when instructed to do so (i.e., perseverance). This may present itself when a child is working on an art project; the teacher must physically remove the materials from the child at the end of a session, and with a poor ability to understand time and limits, the child creates a tantrum. Smith (1995) states,

> The learning disabled youngster of seven or eight is frequently similar in social behavior to the two- or three-year-old. The child can handle only one thing at a time, so very often he can manage best with just one person. He or she seems to need constant recognition of his existence long after the preschool years are over . . . . the discovery that helplessness brings swift attention, positive or negative, thus making the child center of attention. (p. 18)

Unable to impress peers, teachers, therapists, program leaders, and family members with their academic prowess, some children with learning disabilities utilize manipulation to receive the positive feedback they desire and need. These are called the "internal locus of control people," capable of handling major and minor life issues through the expertise and experience of others, by illustration of keen perception, charm, and persuasion. These children make friends with the smartest, easygoing, friendliest children in the classroom, and suddenly those children are helping them with their homework, assisting with class projects, and providing input to solving problems on a regular basis. When this behavior extends to adulthood, some guilt is expressed regarding the exploitation of others and not relying on oneself to problem solve.

At the opposite end are the children who exhibit the "external locus of control." These children display little control over their own lives. One possible reason for this is that everything has been done for the person by someone else, for example, a family member. When a professional or friend demonstrates to the child how to take care of a specific problem (i.e., asking the recreation leader to further explain or to repeat the explanation of steps in an activity) but will not do it for them, the child then becomes very angry. Implying to this type of child that he needs to do his own work or to solve his own problems is a frightening alternative because the child has little faith in his abilities.

New dilemmas appear in adolescence for the individual with learning disabilities. Hyperactivity persists into adolescence; finger tapping, foot tapping, and grimacing all are observed during classroom sessions. Fine motor coordination difficulties may linger, confirmed by uneven and laborious cursive handwriting. During this age, the individual might ask permission from her teacher to use print instead of cursive writing for all in-class and outside class assignments, thereby establishing acceptance for print writing.

These adolescents display more social skill deficiencies and poor self-concept due to repeated academic failure than younger students. They overrate deficiencies and underrate strengths and achievements; they assume that their failure in school is due to their own inadequacies and, therefore, doubt their own success in all domains. This defeatist attitude leads to avoidance of new challenges and promotes temptation to engage in maladaptive behavior rather than to risk failure with new pursuits.

It is important that the parent, teacher, recreation leader, or therapist expose the teenager to various leisure activities and promote interest in something socially acceptable and constructive. These activities can range from the debate club; creating one's own video; solitaire recreation activities (e.g., jogging, collecting, computer games, surfing the net, etc.); volunteer work; or trying out for a varsity sports team. Also, encourage the student both to talk with community business leaders and professionals with interests similar to the student and to visit area colleges and take group trips with family or friends to obtain ideas about possible interests.

At frequent times these teenagers do not overtly recognize their responsibility for outcome in social situations. They demonstrate the ability to verbalize attitudes pertaining to the use of appropriate social behavior, but they do not know when to use them. A role play exercise of presenting appropriate and inappropriate responses to a social situation would assist the teen having learning disabilities to recognize what behaviors cause what results to appear in a given situation (e.g., the display of good sportsmanship). Videotaping this exercise and having the teen view it when the conflict occurs again would reinforce the need to choose some other type of response that might bring upon a more favorable solution. Another strategy for improving interpersonal problem solving is called the FAST strategy. This mnemonic-based strategy focuses on 1) developing, questioning, and monitoring skills; 2) generating a range of solutions to problems; 3) evaluating the consequences of the alternatives and selecting the best plan; and 4) implementing the plan, monitoring the outcome, and providing self-feedback (see Figure 2.3).

Figure 2.3
FAST Strategy

1. Interpersonal Problem Solving (FAST)

F	**FREEZE.**	Don't act too quickly. What is the problem?
A	**ALTERNATIVES.**	What are all my possible solutions?
S	**SELECT ONE.**	What is the best solution in the long run?
T	**TRY IT.**	What do I need to implement the solution? And if it doesn't work, what else can I try?

2. Accepting Negative Feedback (SLAM)

S	**STOP**	what you are doing and look at the person with an appropriate expression.
L	**LISTEN**	to what the person is saying until they are finished.
A	**ASK**	a question about what you don't understand.
M	**MAKE**	a response or answer their concerns.

3. Making Friendship Overtures (PALS)

P	**PLAN**	to look for someone in the room or a group who seems friendly or approachable.
A	**APPROACH**	the person or group by walking over and saying hello.
L	**LISTEN**	to what the person or group is talking about before you respond or speak or ask a question.
S	**SAY**	something related to what the person or group is discussing.

(Reprinted with permission from Vogel, 1992, *Educational Alternatives for Students with Learning Disabilities, Social Intervention for Students with Learning Disabilities: Towards a Broader Perspective*)

Other characteristics noted occurring during the secondary school years: difficulty meeting responsibilities and timely deadlines; poor ability in clarifying life values; exhibiting high frustration levels with little patience for self-learning; inability in controlling impulsive behavior; lacking the ability to question results of actions; and viewing life prospects in a pessimistic manner. At a time in this person's life where peer acceptance, popularity, keeping up with the group, and achievement are of significant value, this can be a difficult stage regarding adjustment and self-actuality for the adolescent having learning disabilities. Exposing these teens to others with learning disabilities who are successful can help curb the cynicism. The International Dyslexia Association publishes a bi-yearly calendar highlighting outstanding dyslexics and promotes the readings of several autobiographies and biographies. These books are *Susan's Story: An Autobiographical Account of My Struggle with Dyslexia* by Susan Hampshire; *Something's Not Right: One Family's Struggle with Learning Disabilities, An Autobiography* by Nancy Lelewer; *The Runaway Learning Machine: Growing Up Dyslexic* by James J. Bauer; *The Language of My Soul: The Anatomy of a Dyslexic Mind* by Glenn Sheffield Leavitt; *The Gift of Dyslexia: Why Some of the Smartest People Can't Read and How They Can Learn* by Ronald D. Davis with Eldon M. Braun; *A Little Edge of Darkness: A Boy's Triumph Over Dyslexia* by Tanya and Alexander Faludy; and *The Scars of Dyslexia: Eight Case Studies in Emotional Reactions* by Janice Edwards (see reference section of this chapter for full book references). The society's newsletter, *Perspectives*, honors young dyslexic students who are recipients of the Remy Johnston Certificates of Merit; their struggle to achieve college success is chronicled in its summer issue. The Learning Disabilities Association of America (LDA) recommends these personal perspective readings: *YES YOU CAN! A Booklet to Help Young People with Learning Disability to Understand and Help Themselves* (Revised 1993), *Why Are You Calling Me LD?* (1995), and *The Dyslexia Scholar—Helping Your Child Succeed in the School System* (1995); these books and many others are available at cost through the LDA library (see Chapter Seven for addresses of organizations). This organization also has a list of famous individuals who have learning disabilities; specific information regarding that person's life can be researched through one's local library. Parents of a young person can inquire about these and other books in an audio format if available. Also, reading or listening to motivational or inspirational materials, especially being exposed to daily positive and humorous proverbs, always help the psyche prepare for the challenges that await it, and for the adolescent, these challenges are coping with adulthood.

Learning Disabilities in Adults

Many of the disorders and characteristics that the child with learning disabilities possesses carry on into the adult life stages, and to a certain extent, interfere with independence and daily functioning. The type of educational, social, and emotional intervention the adult received during the early years of her life will reflect in how she is able to cope with the challenges of adulthood. This is especially true if the adolescent has not obtained optional transition training to assume emergent adult roles in the community. These roles include employment, participating in postsecondary education, maintaining a home, becoming appropriately involved in the community, and experiencing satisfactory personal and social relationships (position statement on transition from The Division on Career Development and Transition, Council for Exceptional Children).

Research findings by Gerber and Ginsberg (1990) suggest that many individuals who are identified as learning disabled in their youth adjust quite well to the demands and complexities of adulthood. Due to the range of severity that can occur with learning disabilities, persons experiencing more severe problems might incur difficulties in adjustment to the later half of the school years life stage (e.g., college, university, or trade school) or in the productive years life stage (e.g., starting a family; obtaining, maintaining, and advancing in employment; utilizing leisure time).

A number of research finding in the late 1980s regarding self-assessment of capabilities (e.g., academic achievement skills, educational and occupational attainments, social and emotional functioning) by adults having learning disabilities produced the following results. College students with learning disabilities reported their self-concept, interpersonal skills, and processing and study skill abilities to be lower than the college student not having learning disabilities. Adults with learning disabilities identified reading and memory problems as interfering with employment. Poor readers often felt left out of their friends' conversations about the latest books or newspaper articles because they could not remember what they read. In self-reported behavioral studies, these adults described themselves as shy, insecure, self-conscious, overly passive, withdrawn, moody, and easily discouraged. Some dated for a long time before telling their mate they could not read and some simply nodded and laughed with others even when they did not "get the point" of a conversation. Occasionally, they asked friends or dates to explain things; but, in general, their problems made them feel very unsure of themselves socially. Many reported they desired support to elevate their level of self-esteem and self-confidence.

Vogel and Forness (1992) reported from early 1980 studies that "one of the observable manifestation of difficulty in making and keeping friends is level of participation in recreational activities .... non-learning disabled adults participated in many more social-recreational activities than learning disabled adults" (p. 380). These authors noted that participation in leisure activities was limited, and the adults in these studies were dependent upon family support for social activities. These authors also predicted the ability of some adults with learning disabilities to take part in recreational activities because they might be hampered by language deficits (saying the wrong word) and memory difficulties (interrupting conversation, forgetting the facts, or performing incorrect sequences of game plays). These adults' abilities to participate in word games, card games, dances, or sports was limited because of problems with language and motor coordination.

Some adults with reading problems would find out in advance if games were scheduled at a party or social event before accepting the invitation, while others often avoided parties where word games were to be played. A situation occurred where a woman found she could dance if she closed her eyes, concentrated on the rhythm, then verbalized the steps, but that did not assure a perfect dance. Others reported they could not dance and talk at the same time and realized they were poor dance partners.

In reviewing the situation of adults with sequencing and reversal tendencies, these individuals often have trouble remembering and writing telephone numbers correctly. They misinterpret street addresses and frequently misread numbers on buses or trains and on transportation schedules. It is not uncommon to hear these comments: "I took the wrong bus," "I was right on Main Street, but could not find your house" (having missed hearing or reading the S in South Main Street), and "I thought the sign said Exit 240, but I exited the highway at Exit 204." This type of situation becomes more embarrassing for the adult than the child. The child and teenager may always have someone reminding him where the person needs to be, but the adult is expected to be independent. Thus, it is the individual's responsibility to write down information correctly and attend an event on time. It is most likely that this type of adult would arrive late to a travel tour, thus holding the group up or missing the tour completely. Suggestions a teacher, therapist, or recreation leader can present to an individual having such a problem are as follows:

1. The person can write the frequently reversed or switched letter or numbers in a particular color; for example, if six (6) causes the person to see nine (9), use a multicolored pen to write all sixes (6) in red and all nines (9) in green.

2. Have a small tape recorder present during the session when the program leader explains directions on how to get to the event; or privately ask the program leader if the directions can be repeated for audio recording.

3. If the adult is going to the recreation event with a friend, have the adult ask the friend if it is okay to meet at her house and the friend can drive to the meeting place; emphasize politeness in offering the friend gas money or arranging some other kind of favor.

4. An adult can meet at a friend's house and follow the friend in her car to the meeting place.

5. Take a trial run to the meeting place, getting an idea of how long it will take. This prevents misdirection during the final drive and helps gain an awareness of reading signs incorrectly. The adult can add more information to the directions previously given to create easier navigation.

6. Read through train, bus, or airplane schedules with someone before going on an adventure; also, circle arrival and departure times of transportation on the schedule form.

7. Enlarge train, bus, or ferry schedules via a Xeroxing machine. Dividing the schedule into morning, afternoon, evening, and weekend sections on separate sheets of paper might make it easier to read.

8. Highlight routes in different colors (i.e., airline departing times in orange and arriving times in green; south train lines in yellow and north train lines in blue).

9. Utilize computer daily planners, inputting your travel itinerary.

10. Allow extra travel time (e.g., for unexpected road construction detours, slow traffic, getting lost, pulling off the road to read road signs, and necessary stops, such as a gas station).

11. Aside from setting the alarm clock in one's room, utilize the hotel wake up call system.

12. Become familiar with different time changes (e.g., Eastern, Central, Mountain, & Pacific); make a note of the time difference. For example, in New Mexico it is 2:00 p.m., but in San Francisco it is 1:00 p.m. One could also wear two watches (e.g., the brown watch has New Mexico time and the blue watch has San Francisco time).

There are numerous adults with learning disabilities that have learned efficient and effective strategies to accomplish a successful lifestyle. Not all studies provided negative findings in adults with learning disabilities adjusting to the adult lifestyle. The Gerber, Ginsberg, and Reiff (1992) study interviewed 71 successful adults with learning disabilities. High success meant having high levels in education, job satisfaction, eminence in one's field, income level, and job classification. The researchers found a number of major points relating to these adults' successes.

The first major point is control—making conscious decisions to take charge of one's life and adapting and shaping oneself in order to move ahead. This was an overriding and meaningful characteristic for both the high-success and moderate-success adults with learning disabilities.

The second major point involved internal decision making—having the desire to excel in order to excel; consciously setting goals that are closely related to the decision concerning desire; and re-framing— making a set of decisions related to reinterpreting the learning disability experience in a more positive or productive manner.

The third major point centered on adaptability, transferring those internal decision-making characteristics into actual behaviors. These behaviors are persistence, goodness of fit, learned creativity, and social ecologies. Regarding persistence, the comments from adults were, "I overcame my problem with sheer grit and accomplishments by working harder than others and gutting it out, and I never stopped trying" (p. 482).

In goodness of fit, the successful individuals demonstrated a strong passion for their work, and they selected work contexts wherein they could be their own boss or had the flexibility to control their destiny and to make significant decisions about their work. The success of the person's adaptability was a product of learned creativity; each used strategies, techniques, and other mechanisms devised to enhance one's ability to perform well. Learning from experience, these successful people became "quick studies." They shaped their reactions to various events or situations so that they would not be embarrassed, but, rather, could perform and excel.

The importance of social ecologies is surrounding oneself with supportive and helpful people (e.g., family, spouse, friends) and mentors. One woman executive in the study describes it in the following way: "it's basically that issue of knowing exactly the types of support you need ... so it's knowing what it is you can't do and when you need to call on help to perform" (p. 484). The major points listed are important to instill throughout a person's life stages and within the many facets of one's life.

In another study, Scuccimarra and Speece (1990) supplied an account that the majority of their subjects (60) were active and engaged in a variety of leisure activities with peers. A low percentage (24-29%) reported participating in only two or fewer activities, had no close friendships, and were generally dissatisfied with their social lives. The respondents who expressed the most satisfaction with their social lives were employed and were active socially.

These adults learned that leisure involvement is not influenced by parental interest, the school system, classrooms, or neighborhood peers, but by individual free choice of leisure activities, comfort with others, employment and family obligations, the financial situation, physical and mental ability, and motivation to meet goals and to succeed. Some adults with learning disabilities will incur no quandaries regarding selection, planning, and participation in leisure activity of choice, but others will not be so lucky. Participation in satisfying, constructive, entertaining, and fun leisure activities nearing the end of the productive years life stage helps provide a smooth transition to the senior years stage.

Society's Perceptions of Learning Disabilities

It can be said that individuals with disabilities are vulnerable to the negative thinking of others. Especially when the teacher, employer, or service provider is not fully informed about the capabilities people with disabilities display when rising to a challenge and the natural variability that exists within any subgroup of disabilities. We know the latter is true with learning disabilities. Therefore, it is not uncommon that assumptions are insinuated by people without disabilities to cluster people with disabilities together in adverse, stereotypic ways. Winbush (1995) describes the results of the March 1995 Roper poll:

> This poll showed that 85% of those surveyed responded affirmatively when specifically asked if mental retardation is associated with learning disabilities. When asked the same question, 79% of teachers responded in the same manner. Among Americans with learning disabilities, 44% perceive that they received less than equal treatment during the school year because of their disabilities. (p. 22)

Most of the literature available measuring perceptions of or attitudes toward individuals with learning disabilities targets college faculty, special education teachers, regular classroom teachers, student teachers, mothers of children with learning disabilities, regular college students, and non-learning disabled children who will be exposed to children in their classroom with learning disabilities (e.g., mainstreamed).

Again, with the emphasis of research in the area of education, it would be important to determine how perceptions of educators will affect individuals with learning disabilities. The results of these studies varied depending upon contact with a person having learning disabilities, previous knowledge about learning disabilities, rating one's competency level to teach or assist someone with learning disabilities, and difficulty in understanding a disability that is not readily seen consistently. Misperceptions from the groups about learning disabilities, especially the level of one's abilities and successes, were revealed. When these groups of people were presented with training and exposure to an individual with learning disabilities, the perception became more positive. A minuscule amount of information is available regarding employers' perceptions of learning disabilities and none is located relating to the leisure industry (e.g., hiring individuals or providing service). Attitudes from employers toward employees with learning disabilities were described as quite negative from 1980s surveys. Blalock and Johnson (1987) heard concerns from adults about maintaining their jobs:"Some adults found older people were kinder and more understanding of their difficulties, so they tried to look for jobs where the employers would accept them and not laugh at their mistakes" (p. 42). Other comments from employees with learning disabilities, whereby their employer was informed about the nature of their disabilities, follow below:

Jim   Jim was working at a fast food restaurant and had told his employer he was dyslexic before he was hired. Instead of letting him work full-time, the employer gave him part-time hours, which eliminated the chances of receiving benefits. His working hours continued to be shortened and he was working only one or two days a week. When he asked for more time, his employer told him that he was too slow. Jim also felt uncomfortable with his co-workers and decided to quit his job. He found a janitorial job; that employer told him he was not following his schedule and was not getting to work on time.

Mary   Mary was also dyslexic and informed her employer when she was hired. She was extremely talented in promoting ideas and overseeing others put her ideas into action. She also had strong skills in delegating and communication. She was unable to do other types of work that were required in the office. Her office manager did not believe she had dyslexia and requested she perform proofreading duties for him.

(Comments derived from Wisconsin's Division of Vocational Rehabilitation - Best Practices Project)

Gajar (1996) comments that employers are unaware of or are insensitive to the needs of adults with learning disabilities, or who lack experience in working with employees diagnosed learning disabled, might display a positive attitude toward a disability that they can see, and exhibit a limited knowledge base of learning disabilities.

With the passing of the Americans with Disabilities Act (ADA), along with providing access and modification of facilities and equipment, many business are incorporating sensitivity training with employees. It was determined important for the service industry to train employees about the needs of their customers and to eliminate any behaviors that might cause dissatisfaction to customers, thereby interfering with return business.

This type of training is taking place in the travel and tourism industry. In early 1992, Hyatt began a program called "Focus on Abilities," whereby all hotel employees underwent training about understanding the ADA, communications, and etiquette awareness, customer service, and supervision and promotion of the disabled. Marriott Corporation, Choice Hotels, Ritz-Carlton, Embassy Suites, Inc., and Super 8 Motels held sensitivity workshops and seminars about the ADA. Some of these hotels have been given awards by national organizations serving people with disabilities regarding their training of employees and service to those with disabilities. People with disabilities are recognizably vital to the travel and tourism industry. It is for those reasons that the lodging operators are very much concerned with developing and maintaining comfortable room accommodations, delivering quality service, and displaying hospitality to the satisfaction of all its guests. Service providers, education professional employers, and nondisabled persons could help decrease attitudinal barriers by adhering to the following tips:

1. Eliminate attitudinal barriers within the agency and between participants (e.g., hold workshops about effective human relations and communication skills).

2. Understand the person, not just the disability. For example, all persons with learning disabilities who wish to participate in a game of Scrabble® do not automatically need use of a dictionary.

3. Become empathetic to the individual's and family's beliefs and values regarding disability.

4. Provide a step-by-step process for smooth and successful community integration (i.e., proper transition planning through the individual's school years).

5. Do not force inclusion on the individual with a disability if he is not ready for it. If the individual would prefer private lessons

for skill building in a particular leisure activity before signing up for a course in this leisure activity, this is perfectly acceptable and should be communicated as so to the person with the learning disability.

6. Become aware of community resources to assist persons with disabilities.

Professionals and family members working with individuals having learning disabilities must continue to educate the public about the symptoms of learning disabilities, its impact on the learning process, and the ability for one to achieve success in society.

Multicultural Issues and Perceptions of Learning Disabilities

Hallahan et al. (1996) note that the beginning years of this field were dominated by the classification of learning disabilities for children living in white, middle-class communities. Demographics of the past decade suggest the situation has altered. Their evidence compiled from the U.S. Department of Education indicate the following racial breakdown for learning disabilities:

> 67.2% white, 21.6% black, and 8.4% Hispanic. In comparing these figures to secondary youth in general population: 70% white, 12% black, and 13% Hispanic, it demonstrates a disproportionately high prevalence of learning disabilities in African American students and a slightly disproportionately low prevalence of learning disabilities in white and Hispanic students. (p. 52)

The disproportionate placement of pupils of a particular group placed in special education programs means that this group is represented in such programs to a greater percentage than their percentage as a whole in the public school population. Harry and Anderson (1994) present the scenario:

> If African Americans account for 16% of the U.S. public school enrollment (U.S. Department of Education, 1994), then one would expect the special education enrollment to fall within a range of plus or minus 1.6% of the total enrollment; hence, any special

education placement percentage outside of the range from 14.4% to 17.6% would be considered disproportionate. (p. 602)

Educators and professionals have viewed this disproportionately high number of African American students in special education (e.g., 24.2% of all students in special education) as evidence of racial bias in referral and in the tests used to make diagnoses. The U.S. Congress Office of Technology Assessment in 1990, via a request from the Senate Select Committee on Indian Affairs, stressed concern about the prevalence of neurosensory disorders (reference of learning disabilities and dyslexia) and certain developmental disabilities appearing at a rate of 400 to 1300% greater among American Indians than other population groups. Again, is this due to environmental and health factors (e.g., childhood lead and mercury poisoning) or misdiagnosis due to cultural difference within examination process, biases in test measurement, and/or protocol of school systems?

A significant increase has also been noticed in the number of college athletes having learning disabilities. A large percentage of these athletes were identified during their junior and senior years of high school or early college years. MacDonald (1990) reports several factors that contribute to inappropriate assessment of student-athletes:

lack of agreement about adequate standardized testing instruments, inconsistency in the interpretation of the guidelines for determining a learning disability, and lack of diagnosticians at the postsecondary level who have experience with adults with learning disabilities and who are sensitive to multicultural issues in assessment. (p. 1)

Some colleges have noted that up to 25% of the student-athletes on specific teams have learning disabilities (Gup, 1989) and many of those students are in a minority category. Questions that need to be answered include, "Is the college student-athlete more susceptible to misclassification or overclassification due to acquired athletic talents, expectations placed on them by coaches and the student body, the stigma of being an athlete, and/or cultural test bias and incoming academic profiles?" or "Are postsecondary institutions experiencing an increase in the number of student-athletes with learning disabilities in proportion to an increase of individuals with learning disabilities attending colleges and universities?"

Data compiled by UCLA reports that 142,010 full-time college fresh-men nationwide reported having disabilities of some sort; of that number, 45,654 were reported to be learning disabilities (HEATH, 1995). The National Collegiate Athletic Association (NCAA), in an attempt to regulate incoming athletes with disabilities, has provided guidelines in its 1997-98 *NCAA Divisions I and II Manuals* regarding academic requirements and standardized tests reporting procedures for students with learning disabilities and other student-athletes with disabilities (see Appendix D).

Education is the key to understanding learning disabilities. The teleconference on "African Americans with Learning Disabilities" (October, 1995, Learning Disabilities Research and Training Center) focused on many issues surrounding diagnosis, eliminating negative perceptions about learning disabilities and utilizing support services. Primary, secondary, and post-secondary professionals, through this teleconference, have developed a clearer understanding about working with African American students having learning disabilities and will employ the strategies and techniques to effectively meet those students' needs, thus promoting success.

Another educational project addressing cultural needs of individuals with learning disabilities is the P'tach Program. This program is geared toward teaching Jewish children and teens with learning disabilities mainstream Jewish education. P'tach teachers are trained in special education and Jewish education, using different instructional approaches where necessary. These teachers realize Jewish subjects can pose extra problems for children with learning disabilities; therefore, they provide one-on-one instruction and a resource center to enhance learning. The program supplies academic instruction, counseling, and speech and language therapy within a Yeshiva setting. It encourages involvement in extracurricular activities and chosen interests in disciplines such as industrial arts, accounting, business math, and crafts. Parents whose children with learning disabilities attend this program comment that there should be more P'tach programs or similar programs available; there are many children out there struggling and they can benefit from such a program (Rapoport, 1994).

The goal to eliminate disparity is training professionals in the field of counseling, psychology, special education, and rehabilitation about cultural diversity and its impact in assessment and instruction. We need to develop cultural specific or integrated programs with cultural education themes promoting the social, emotional, and academic development of students with learning disabilities. Understand that children and adults of minority descent on school campuses feel they already stand out because they are different, and these individuals object to being seen as different and disabled. Yet, if one is legitimately diagnosed as having learning disabilities, it is important for professionals to encourage the individual to use campus and community support services, thereby heightening life skills.

References

American Psychiatric Association. (1994). *Diagnostic and statistical manual of mental disorders, Fourth ed., (DSM-IV)*. Washington, D.C.: Author.

Bauer, J.J. (1992). *The runaway learning machine: Growing up dyslexic*. Minneapolis, MN: Educational Media Corporation.

Blalock, J.W., & Johnson, D.J. (1987). *Adults with learning disabilities: Clinical studies*. Orlando: Grune & Stratton.

Brown, D. (1980). *Steps to independence for people with learning disabilities*. McLean, VA: NICHCY and Closer Look.

Cicci, R. (1995). *What's wrong with me? Learning disabilities at home and school.* Timonium, MD: York Press, Inc.

Council for Exceptional Children. (1994). Position statement on transition from the Division on Career Development and Transition. *CEC Policies for Delivery of Services to Exceptional Children.* Reston, VA: Author.

Davis, R.D., & Braun, E.M. (1994). *The gift of dyslexia: Why some of the smartest people can't read and how they can learn.* Burlingame, CA: Ability Workshop Press.

Edwards, J. (1994). *The scars of dyslexia: Eight case studies in emotional reactions.* New York: Cassell.

Faludy, T., & Faludy, A. (1996). *A little edge of darkness: A boy's triumph over dyslexia.* London: Jessica Kingsley Publishers, Ltd.

Gajar, A. (1996). Current and future research. In J.R. Patton & E.A. Polloway (Eds.), *Learning disabilities: The challenges of adulthood.* Austin, TX: Pro-Ed, Inc.

Gerber, J., & Ginsberg, R.J. (1990). *Identifying alterable patterns of success in highly successful adults with learning disabilities.* Richmond, VA: Virginia Commonwealth University.

Gerber, J., Ginsberg, R.J., & Reiff, H.B. (1992). Identifying alterable patterns in employment success for highly successful adults with learning disabilities. *Journal of Learning Disabilities,* 25, pp. 475-487.

Gup, T. (1989). Foul. *Time. 133*(14), pp. 54-60.

Hallahan, D.P., Kauffman, J.M., & Lloyd, J.W. (1996). *Introduction to learning disabilities.* Needham Heights, MA: Allyn & Bacon.

Hampshire, S. (1982). *Susan's story: An autobiographical account of my struggle with dyslexia.* New York: St. Martin's Press.

Harry, B., & Anderson, M.G. (1994). The disproportionate placement of African American males in special education programs: A critique of the process. *Journal of Negro Education, 63*(4), pp. 602-619.

Harwell, J.M. (1989). *Complete learning disabilities handbook.* West Nyack, NY: The Center for Applied Research in Education, Inc.

HEATH Resource Center. (1995). *College freshmen with disabilities: A triennial statistical profile.* Washington, D.C: Author, American Council on Education.

Hoy, C., & Gregg, M. (1986). The usefulness of the Woodcock-Johnson Psycho-Educational Battery Cognitive Cluster Scores for learning disabled college students. *Journal of Learning Disabilities,* vol. 19, No. 8, p. 489-91.

Kolb, D.A. (1985 Revised). *The learning style inventory: Technical manual.* Boston: Author.

Learning Disabilities Research and Training Center (October, 1995). In Noel Gregg (Chair) African Americans with Learning Disabilities: Issues and Assessment Teleconference conducted by the Learning Disabilities Research and Training Center at the University of Georgia on October 19, 1995. Taped off satellite with permission.

Leavitt, Sheffield, G. (1994). *The language of my soul: The anatomy of a dyslexic mind.* Okemos, MI: Erickson Learning Foundation.

Lelewer, N. (1994). *Something's not right: One family's struggle with learning disabilities, an autobiography.* Ecton, MA: Vander Wyk & Burnham.

MacDonald, T.M. (1990, Fall). Student-athletes with learning disabilities: Special issues. *Postsecondary Learning Disability Network News,* The University of Connecticut, A.J. Pappanikou Center on Special Education and Rehabilitation, 10, pp. 1-3.

Mangrum II, C.T., & Strichart, S.S. (1988). *College and the learning disabled student: Program development implementation and selection 2/E.* Needham Heights: Allyn & Bacon.

National Joint Committee on Learning Disabilities. (1988). *Letter to NJCLD member organizations.*

Rapoport, G. (1994). Maintaining focus: P'tach program for learning disabled teens helps them work into the mainstream. *The Jewish Week, 206*(45), p. 20.

Schleien, S.J., Meyer, L.H., Heyne, L.A., & Brandt, B.B. (1995). *Lifelong leisure skills and lifestyles for persons with developmental disabilities.* Baltimore: Paul H. Brookes.

Scuccimarra, D.J., & Speece, D.L. (1990). Employment outcomes and social integration of students with mild handicaps: The quality of life two years after high school. *Journal of Learning Disabilities, 23,* pp. 213-219.

Silver, L.B. (1990). Attention deficit-hyperactivity disorder: Is it a learning disability or a related disorder? *Journal of Learning Disabilities, 23*(7), pp. 394-397.

Smith, S.L. (1995). *No easy answers: The learning disabled child at home and at school.* New York: Bantam Books.

U.S. Department of Education. (1994). *Sixteenth annual report to Congress on the implementation of the Individuals with Disabilities Act.* Washington, D.C: Author.

Vogel, S.A. (Ed.). (1992). *Educational alternatives for students with learning disabilities.* New York: Springer-Verlag.

Vogel, S.A., & Forness, S.R. (1992). Social functioning in adults with learning disabilities. *School Psychology Review, 21*(3), pp. 375-386.

Weisgerber, R.A. (1991). *Quality of life for persons with disabilities: Skill development and transitions across life stages.* Gaithersburg, MD: Aspen Publishers, Inc.

Winbush, D.E. (1995). Myths, stereotypes: Higher education's learning disabled battle. *Black Issues in Higher Education, 12*(15), p. 22.

Testing Instruments

Wechlser Intelligence Scale
  for Children
The Psychological Corporation
San Antonio, Texas

Stanford-Benet Intelligence
  Test, 4th ed.
Riverside Publishing Company
Chicago, Illinois

Wechlser Adult Intelligence
  Scale-Revised
The Psychological Corporation
San Antonio, Texas

Test of Memory and Learning
  (TOMAL)
PRO-ED
Austin, Texas

Raven Standard Progressive
  Matrices (Standard Kit)
The Psychological Corporation
San Antonio, Texas

Wide Range Achievement
  Test-Revised Edition (WRAT-R)
Jastak Associates
Wilmington, Delware

Detroit Tests of Learning
  Aptitude - Adult (DTLA)
PRO-ED
Austin, Texas

Woodcock Reading Mastery
  Test-Revised
American Guidance Service, Inc.
Circle Pines, Minnesota

Test of Non-verbal
  Intelligence-2 (TONI)
PRO-ED
Austin, Texas

Peabody Individual Achievement
  Test-Revised (PIAT-R)
American Guidance Service, Inc.
Circle Pines, Minnesota

Woodcock-Johnson Psycho-
  educational Battery-Revised:
  Tests of Cognitive Ability
DLM Teaching Resources
Allen, Texas

Key Math Test
American Guidance Service, Inc.
Circle Pines, Minnesota

Nelson-Denny Reading Skills Test
Riverside Publishing Company
Chicago, Illinois

Scholastic Abilities Test for
  Adults (SATA)
PRO-ED
Austin, Texas

Diagnostic Spelling Potential Test
Academic Therapy
Novato, California

Bender-Gestalt Test for
  Young Children
American Guidance Service, Inc.
Circle Pines, Minnesota

Swanson Cognitive Processing Test
  (S-CPT)
PRO-ED
Austin, Texas

Bender Visual-Motor Gestalt Test
American Guidance Service
Circle Pines, Minnesota

Luria-Nebraska Neuropsycho-
  logical Battery
Western Psychological Services
Los Angeles, California

Test of Written Language-2 (TWS-2)
PRO-ED
Austin, Texas

Chapter Three

AWARENESS

Self-awareness

*He who knows not and knows
not that he knows not is a fool. Shun him.
He who knows not and knows
that he knows not is simple. Teach him.
He who knows and knows not that he knows,
is asleep. Wake him.
He who knows and knows that he knows
is wise. Follow him.*
— *Arab Proverb*

Self-awareness is simply an awareness of one's own actions, behaviors, and thought processes in a given situation in relation to others—being people, environment, or task. The awareness of others' perspectives sharpens the distinction between oneself and others. In the example of having a person talk to you, you let that person become a part of you for a moment. This is a suspension of awareness of oneself, after which you again become aware of yourself and either accept or reject what the other person said. If every individual has a particular perspective, then that perspective makes one unique. This accentuation of uniqueness heightens one's sense of self. With self-awareness, the person usually becomes aware of the distinction between inner, private feelings and outward, public behavior. Awareness of self flourishes from repeated experiences, whether the experiences are successful or not. The individual learns what works and what doesn't work, what he can and cannot do. What receives positive or negative reactions from people in that situation? How an individual perceives and understands everything that impacts his life is self-awareness.

One major part of self-awareness is acceptance of disability. Awareness of learning disabilities causes one to experience difficulties in a variety of areas and inconsistent occurrences. Once this awareness is present, then the person can ask himself the following questions: "What do I need to know and do to alleviate the problem or compensate to attain a solution?" "Why do I need to know what to do to alleviate the problem or to compensate to achieve a solution?" "How should I think and react in situations that cause distress to produce favorable outcomes in reaching solutions?" The importance of these questions relates to the attainment of competency in self-awareness. Inspirational speaker Bob Moawod developed "Five Levels of Competency" in his book *Increasing Human Effectiveness II* (1992). One portion of his training with employees of businesses is to have participants evaluate themselves to determine their level of competency functioning. A second portion teaches acquiring the skills that will enable them to reach level five, where decision making becomes advantageous to the person and situation. The "Five Levels of Competency" can be use when professionals evaluate the self-awareness levels of people with learning disabilities.

Self-awareness of Competency and Strategies to Improve Competency Skills

Five Levels of Competency

Level One: Unconsciously Incompetent

When you are unconsciously incompetent, you don't know, and you don't know that you don't know! People are held accountable for inappropriate actions and decisions—often made due to lack of awareness.

Level Two: Consciously Incompetent

When you are consciously incompetent, you know that you don't know, and therefore, you can begin to learn and change. Being aware of your incompetence creates a fever to improve, to know, to set and reach a goal.

Level Three: Unconsciously Competent

At this level of competency, you often make appropriate decisions and act accordingly. The challenge is that you aren't sure why you are competent or why things work out. This makes it difficult to repeat your success or to teach and share it.

Level Four: Consciously Competent

At this level you have learned how to be competent, develop skills, and determine appropriate behaviors and actions for success. But is it enough to know?

Level Five: Unconsciously Competent

Individuals turn their decision making over to their subconscious, where competency occurs naturally, free-flowingly, spontaneously, and consistently—at an automatic level.

(Adapted from Robert Moawod, *Increasing Human Effectiveness, 1992*)

Professionals working with individuals having learning disabilities often find their students' or clients' competency levels shifting between Levels One and Three. An individual at Level One lacks insight and, therefore, requires instruction about consequences of action. If this person is not approached with corrective criticism about the consequences of exhibiting inappropriate behavior, especially during social interactions, he can remain at this level. An example is provided about Joey.

Why is little Joey not selected to participate in the neighborhood kickball game on a regular basis? The overriding reason is not that Joey tends to foul out two out of the five times at kickoffs, but that Joey continuously displays immature antics, bosses his teammates, and laughs and talks excessively during the game (i.e., being the center of attention). This behavior irritates his teammates. They either do not invite Joey back to play with them or tell Joey to "shut up." He feels his teammates are just being mean, so he says "no," thereby continuing his antics. This is the time when a parent, coach, teacher, or recreation leader should inform Joey about his inappropriate social behavior. Depending upon Joey's attitude for change, comprehension ability, and insight, a simple reminder about poor sportsmanship and the importance of staying focused during a game might prove to be sufficient in making him aware of his behavior. Contrary to the previous suggestion, a role playing situation may be required by which another child acts out Joey's behavior and the group asks Joey his thoughts about this situation. This might provide some insight for Joey to change. In dealing with children and some adults having learning disabilities, supplying corrective criticism just once may not be enough. They might have to hear this corrective criticism many times to realize that they are actually doing something that is inappropriate or counterproductive in the situation. The realization of behavior is part of the self-awareness process, moving the person past Level One to Level Two. Parents or professionals would want Joey to begin questioning his behavior. He needs to ask himself these questions: "I know I play around too much, but why?" and "How can I stop this from happening?" When he can formulate these types of questions, he is now functioning at Level Two.

At Level Two the individual knows she is unable to perform a task at the same success rate as another person, so the individual needs to find out what she should do to improve skills. Mary, a young woman who enjoys assembling model airplanes, comments to her friends,

> I know I had problems throughout my life reading directions. I can watch someone put a model plane together and follow that person step by step. If I had to read the directions by myself, I could never put a model together. I just don't work on models by myself. I wait until my cousin has some free time and both of us work on the model together. Sometimes it will take two or three months to assemble one model; I wish I could do this by myself.

This individual has insight to what she can and cannot do and has accepted this as a way of life. She has offered no solutions to alleviating the problem of working an airplane model independently. When this occurs, a strategy needs to be implemented whereby the individual can consistently make her way through the levels and not fall back when difficult situations arise or depend on others to do the problem solving. One strategy that a person having problems like Mary can use is called Cognitive Behavior Management (CBM).

Cognitive Behavior Management, developed in the 1970s, based its premise on the fact that cognition plays a major role in shaping behavior, and that by modifying cognition, behavior can be shaped or changed. CBM is used to organize incoming information and to monitor one's responses. CBM is a self-instructional internal dialogue (see Figure 3.1) in which the person (being a student, participant, or client) asks questions about organizing information and making decisions. In order for the person to construct an internal dialogue she must see and hear the process demonstrated. The teacher, recreation leader, or therapist models this strategy. The person's role is to follow the examples set by the professional exhibiting the behavior. The professional needs to think out loud each step with the person. It is important for the professional to model mistakes and corrections, proving that it is "OK" to make a mistake.

Figure 3.1
Cognitive Behavior Management (CBM)

Six steps/self-statements modeled by the professional and rehearsed by the student:

1. **PROBLEM DEFINITION**
   "What do I have to do?"

2. **FOCUSING ATTENTION**
   "I have to think about this task."

3. **PLANNING AND GUIDING RESPONSES**
   "Be careful, look at only one problem at a time."

4. **SELF-REINFORCEMENT**
   "That's good; I got the right answer."

5. **SELF-EVALUATION**
   "Did I follow my plan and look at each problem?"

6. **COPING AND ERROR CORRECTION**
   "That's OK; if I make a mistake, I can backtrack and go slowly."

(Adapted from D. Meichenbaum, 1980 & 1983)

This self-instruction encourages the individual to "talk to himself" before, during, and after a social situation or recreation task, to analyze the thinking processes involved in a situation or task, and to identify the steps through which the person must proceed to attain a specific goal. Figure 3.2 displays an example of how CBM could be use to guide Mary in solving her problem.

Figure 3.2
Cognitive Behavior Management (CBM)
(A professional modeling behavior for Mary)

1.**PROBLEM DEFINITION**
   "I want to put this model airplane together by myself."

2.**FOCUSING ATTENTION**
   "I have to think about reading and understanding these directions."

3.**PLANNING AND GUIDING RESPONSES**
   "What causes me so much confusion?" (Looking at directions.) "Let's see. The instructions are on the back of the diagram. It would help if I saw them together. The diagram is too small. The number on the model pieces are too small and is the same color as the model."

4.**SELF-REINFORCEMENT**
   "That's what I find is the problem. Good, I figured that out."

5.**SELF-EVALUATION**
   "Did I locate all the problems I have assembling model airplanes?" (No.) "Well, I would like to see what the model looks like fully assembled, to hold and look at the model from all sides. I cannot get a clear picture of what the model should look like when I look at the picture on the box."

6.**COPING AND ERROR CORRECTION**
   "What can I do to correct these problems?" "I can attend a model airplane class." "Whom can I ask to help me with these problems?" "Maybe my cousin or someone who teaches a class in how to assemble models."

Another example of a strategy for guiding self-questioning in problem solving is called Visual Guiding (see Appendix E). Visual Guiding represents a schematic image that better serves individuals who have a visual learning style preference in understanding the steps of problem solving.

It is common for individuals with learning disabilities to declare a certain level of achievement in a situation as "definitive," just as Mary thought in her situation of assembling model airplanes. When this type of thinking is present, the professional should ask the individual if she has explored all possible solutions to this situation and then to employ the CBM or Visual Guiding strategies to assist in attacking problems, gaining knowledge, further developing skills, or having questions answered. By using the CBM or Visual Guiding strategies, Mary is moving up a level on the competency scale.

Teachers and coaches often have students who will perform the task successfully once, but the next time will perform it wrong. A common occurrence with students having learning disabilities, especially on the college level, is that they will receive a "B" on the first class test but a "D" on the next and yet swear that they used the same study techniques when studying for both exams. These students often approach tasks with the "hit and miss" approach. Awareness is lacking about what specifically enables these students to become successful at this task in the beginning and why.

In the "hit and miss" approach, students often do the following: use the wrong study techniques with the type of test that the instructor will give; use a different study method the second time, unsure of why this particular study method should be used to study information for the second test; decide to "shortcut" a strategy for time sake, thinking this would not affect test results; or eliminate use of an effective study skill strategy, falling back on old habits. At this point, the student has misjudged his ability of understanding the importance of using strategies correctly and consistently to improve performance. Assuaging the misjudgments that occur in the "hit and miss" type of individual requires self-monitoring. Figure 3.3 provides questions the individual can ask himself regarding knowledge and ability of strategy use. The understanding of why certain situations work out favorably on a relatively consistent basis moves the individual into Level Four.

Individuals become stuck at Level Four when they do not understand the theory behind making a particular decision. An

Figure 3.3
Strategy Monitoring (Self-questioning)

1. What type of strategies do I know that might help me perform this task effectively?

2. I need to list and review the content of each strategy. In performing this step, the person needs to ask, "What do I know about these strategies? When and where would I use this strategy?"

3. Select strategy—the question, e.g., "I feel this strategy is the best strategy to use and this is why."

4. I need to list steps in this strategy.

5. I now need to use this strategy with this situation or task.

6. I will perform all the steps described in the strategy.

7. Am I satisfied with the results I obtained in using this strategy? Why?

8. Is there more I need to know about using this strategy or applying this strategy in this situation?

9. Should I employ a different strategy to this situation or task?

example is the football player, e.g., quarterback, who is drilled on particular game plays and told to carry out those plays as instructed by the coach. The quarterback knows how to carry out those plays with efficiency but may not understand the coach's motives behind calling such a play. The quarterback knows he needs to get the ball in play by throwing or passing it to his teammate to move that ball closer to the goal. The quarterback may not understand that switching plays periodically from passing to throwing confuses the opposite team, hopefully throwing them off guard, thus helping his team get a touchdown. This might be the idea the coach has in mind. The coach has many more years of experience than his players, calling plays, seeing numerous variations of football plays, and predicting an array of outcomes based on one strategic move. This ability to outmaneuver the opponent comes from practice and constant involvement in a task or situation; this is what the coach has learned to do. This is the "enough to know" that moves the person from Level Four to Level Five. When that quarterback, through experience, begins to see the possible results of his passing and throwing plays, he is demonstrating awareness. He is learning the ability to analyze the situation from all sides and can predict possible reactions, based on his actions. Unfortunately, this is an area of difficulty with some individuals having learning disabilities.

The ability to analyze a situation from all angles, select a decision, predict possible responses from opponents and then respond (e.g., via a game move or play) to the opponent's moves are skills that require enhancing in individuals with learning disabilities. First, the individual must become aware that he has difficulties with this ability, especially after exposing himself to recreation activities. The individual can work with a teacher, coach, recreation therapist, or leader in using CBM or Visual Guiding in developing skills for analyzing situations. Level Four competency is essential to fully analyze a game or sport situation, thus enabling one to outwit his opponent.

Instructing individuals with learning disabilities in acquiring the skills to raise themselves from Level One to Level Four or the ultimate, Level Five, is imperative. There are many tasks and situations by which people with learning disabilities make decisions from their subconscious. This capability may be produced from many years of experience in a particular activity, continual corrective feedback from family and friends, practices of skills, trial and error in problem solving, and a constant search to improve oneself.

Why is self-awareness of competency important? To better improve the individual's skills. The person can communicate more effectively with people and come to understand one's own thinking process and learning style. The individual is in tune with his own likes and dislikes and develops strategies for dealing with a variety of life situations.

Parents' Awareness about their Children with Learning Disabilities

Cordoni (1990) states, "For most parents, the knowledge of the child's disability may have been only a faint suspicion before the child entered school" (p. 41). This suspicion could be based on the presence of older children in the home, providing characteristics and behaviors by which to compare the child. The conspicuousness of the characteristics displayed by the child, e.g., speech difficulties, slow to learn tasks, the repetition of an incorrect action after verbal correction, could provoke suspicion. It appears to be more common for parents to complain that schools do not recognize that their child has learning difficulties than for them to deny the existence of learning problems (Hallahan, Kauffman, & Lloyd, 1996). In the practice of parents going from one professional to another (e.g., physician, psychologist, or educator), they want to validate their suspicion that their child has learning disabilities. This process confirms their awareness that their child is in need of assistance.

A number of professionals in the field note that the mother seems to recognize the child's difficulties more often than the father, and that the mother is more accepting of the child having a diagnosis of learning disabilities than the father. This acknowledgment is based on reports that these mothers spend more time dealing with the children's education and life skills activities than the fathers. It is often the mother who deals with unexpected inappropriate behavior in public, questions her child's progress in school, encounters unsympathetic and resistant professionals, attends teacher conferences, takes the child to the pediatrician, and signs the child up for sports and recreational activities. It is most often the mother who is present when the child is participating in recreational activities. This is why understanding the feelings of a mother and her perceptions about her child's ability to participate in recreational activities is important for recreation leaders and therapists.

Parents of children with learning disabilities are very apt to catch their children's emotions—emotions of despair, anxiety, frustration, rage, anger, and happiness. Parents often know from the children's actions how well school went that day. Undiagnosed parents may notice similar characteristics in their own diagnosed child, thus the parents feel powerless to help their child cope with daily problems. These may very well be the same problems the parents are having problems coping with.

This is often a concern when a parent tries to help a child complete homework assignments. Some parents feel every one of their child's defeats, overlooking the accomplishments; this is especially true for parents who base their successes on their child's achievements. They usually experience inadequacy and bruised egos. An example is the mother hearing a co-worker talk about her son, the football star, and the number of points he scored in his last game. Or, the father whose boss has children who are always on the honor roll and who participate successfully in other extracurricular activities. Knowing that your child can't even catch a ball and continuously produces "C" work when putting in "A" quality study time can bring despair and hopelessness. The realization that the child with learning disabilities is not a replica of the parents, but an individual who has different interests, capabilities, and learning styles, and who has a distinctly different outlook on life and an ability to succeed, is the step to acceptance of disability.

Resourcefulness and planning are required from the parents of a child with learning disabilities. Perhaps the most important place they can begin is in their own attitudes. A self-assessment of their own attitudes regarding their child who has a learning disability can supply insight in how the parents are communicating with the child. What is the parent's primary area of focus on the child? What expectations do the parents have for this child? Two exercises can be used in providing awareness to parents about their perception of their child's personal values: the parent's own values and the communication of those values to each other.

The first exercise is called "I Learned That . . . ." The goal of this exercise is to increase the participant's awareness of personal values. In completing the form in Figure 3.4, parents answer the finished statements about their child; the statements should be short and clear.

The child completes the "I Learned That ..." exercise in the "I" form while the parents are completing their "I Learned That . . ." form. Both the parents' and child's responses are compared to determine awareness of the child's needs and the perception the parents have about the child's interest, abilities, and desires. The professional and family members conduct a discussion of answers in a small group. In completing the form in Figure 3.5, the child can have the form read and explained for clarification; finished statements should be short and clear.

The second exercise is called "Three Sides of Self." This exercise's goals are to assist participants in determining the negative and positive messages they received or are receiving during childhood; to decide whom the strongest messages came from (or are coming from); to have participants review how these messages affect their self-image in the physical, thinking, and social areas; and to help participants in overcoming or building upon other

Figure 3.4
I Learned That . . . (Parents)

1. I learned that my child _____.
2. I realized that my child _____.
3. I noticed that my child _____.
4. I discovered that my child _____.
5. I was surprised that my child _____.
6. I was pleased that my child _____.
7. I was unhappy that my child _____.
8. I found out that my child has a unique perspective on _____.
9. I could not believe that my child _____.
10. I would like to remember my child _____.
11. I want to tell somebody that my child _____.
12. I found out that my child could be better at _____.
13. My child really does not like to _____.
14. The best thing that happened to my child _____.
15. I would never have known that my child _____.
16. The thing I treasure most about my child _____.
17. My child is really good at _____.
18. If I had to do something over again with my child, I would _____.
19. My child is special because _____.
20. My child's desire is _____.

(Adapted from N.J. Stumbo, 1992, *Leisure Education II: More Activities and Resources*)

people's messages to improve self-esteem. The purpose of the activity is to explore messages parents send and children receive about themselves from one another. The messages come in three forms: physical, thinking, and social. All three become integrated into how we view ourselves.

The professional, serving as leader of this activity, hands out the "Three Sides of Self" form (see Figure 3.6). The leader should be very familiar with family members, able to intervene promptly in defusing conflicting matters. The parents are asked to recall negative messages or images they have said to their child on the top diagram of the form. The children are asked to recall negative messages or images they feel their parents have of them on the top diagram of the form. In each circle, the participants are placing

Figure 3.5
I Learned That . . . (Child)

1. I learned that _____.
2. I realized that _____.
3. I noticed that _____.
4. I discovered that _____.
5. I was surprised that _____.
6. I was pleased that _____.
7. I was unhappy that _____.
8. I found out that I have a unique perspective on _____.
9. I could not believe that _____.
10. I would like to remember that _____.
11. I want to tell somebody about _____.
12. I found out that I could be better at _____.
13. I really do not like to _____.
14. The best thing that happened was _____.
15. I would never have known that I _____.
16. The thing I treasure most is _____.
17. I am really good at _____.
18. If I had to do it over again, I would _____.
19. I am special because _____.
20. My desire is _____.

(Adapted from N.J. Stumbo, 1992, *Leisure Education II: More Activities and Resources*)

types of negative messages; for example, writing in the physical circle being called uncoordinated or clumsy; writing in the social circle not being invited to parties, recreation games, movies, or peers' houses; writing in the thinking circle not learning as fast as other students or being called "spacey." The second set of circles is for stating positive messages parents have given to children and positive messages children feel their parents have about them.

It will probably take about 15 to 20 minutes to complete both the diagrams. The leader asks the family members to share their circle diagrams. The professional should note comments on how different or similar the words in the circle relate to the parents' perception of their child and how the child feels his own parents' perceive him. The leader's discussion focuses on how an-

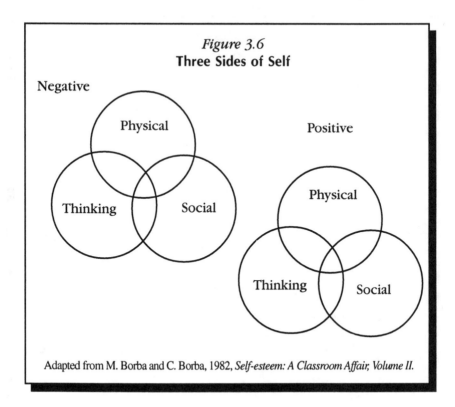

Figure 3.6
Three Sides of Self

Adapted from M. Borba and C. Borba, 1982, *Self-esteem: A Classroom Affair, Volume II.*

other person's perceptions have affected one and how this can be built upon or reversed when employing strategies to overcome negative messages.

Teachers, counselors, recreation leaders, and therapists working with these parents need to tap their own ingenuity to locate as many ways as possible to help parents feel better about themselves and their child having a learning disability. These professionals can work on building competency in parents and can encourage parents to trust their own observations and judgments. Parents need information, practical suggestions, and solid support. The aim of professionals should be to form a parent/professional alliance and to assist parents to be effective advocates for their children's social, emotional, physical, and educational concerns. They must become knowledgable in analyzing what the child does not know and discover ways to teach him, helping the child progress past Level Two of the Five Levels of Competency. Usually, parents know their own child better than anyone else does and, in the majority of cases, want to bring love, the best learning environment, and greatest opportunity to the child for him to experience.

Professionals could help the parents hold on to optimism regarding the child's strengths, building on whatever she likes to do best. These likes or interests can range from sports, art, dramatics, cooking, being a good friend, helping at home, recycling, community volunteer work, and even public speaking. Parents need to grab hold of the present and deal with it step-by-step, just as their child must. They need to learn not to set short-term and long-term goals too high for the child to achieve.

Parents should not feel obligated to be "perfect." Everyone in life makes mistakes, and parents should be encouraged to give themselves permission to make mistakes and to learn from them. This shows the child that people of all ages make mistakes, can employ corrections, and thus can survive a situation. The child sees that amends can be made for mistakes and things can be restored, perhaps not quite the same as before, but possibly better. Parents can point out to their child that they, too, have areas of difficulties. They would like to be talented in a particular endeavor, but lack of a certain ability or interest does not make them any less of a person. The child needs to understand that some people are naturally adept in some skills, while others have to work hard to accomplish the same goal. The child should also become aware that society needs people to contribute to it in many different ways, such as teachers, inventors, physicians, poets, builders, religious scholars, lawyers, writers, dancers, athletes, creators, thinkers and dreamers, and people who help us play.

Weisgerber (1991) points out that what professionals need to know about parents and their children with disabilities:

> Patience and support of the parents mean a great deal to children with a disability and play a major part in helping youngsters recognize the difference between what they cannot do and what they cannot yet do. They need to learn that with practice and persistence, they can improve on their present status. They will succeed if they are determined to succeed. (p. 48)

A Sibling with Learning Disabilities

A brother or sister with learning disabilities can provoke a broad range of emotional responses from a sibling. The following is an excerpt of a personal account involving a younger brother living with his older brother who has learning disabilities.

My Brother, My Friend - Anonymous

Having a learning/social disability affects not only your social life, but your school work and home life. Not only were these things affected in my brother's life, but in mine, too. Growing up in a house with an older sibling who has a learning disability is very difficult. My brother got a lot of special attention from both my parents. My mother was always at, or on the phone with, my brother's school trying to make things better for him. She would spend hours helping my brother with his homework. My parents were good about equaling out their time on both of us. I would get jealous of him for getting so much attention.

For me, the hardest part about living with him was coming to the realization that he wasn't like my friend's brother and that we may never have that "TV type" relationship. Until recently, I was never able to just go and talk to him about anything. Only a fellow sibling understands what goes on in the home, and it was hard not being able to really talk to him about these things. I felt as if I had been cheated out of something. I had been cheated out of a "normal" brother.

My bother went to special schools for his disability, but he felt ashamed going to them and was optimistic that he could succeed in a regular school. He started to attend public school in the fifth grade and continued until his senior high graduation. He did succeed, but the road was long and extremely difficult. At night I would watch him studying both alone and with my mom. He'd struggle for hours over a certain reading assignment that I could probably do in about half an hour. Sometimes he'd ask for my help, and, of course, I would help him, but often he'd get even more irritated because I could do it so easily. It was hard for me to watch him suffering like this. All I wanted to do was take his pain away. After he'd finished, however, the look of triumph on his face would put all my worries to rest.

Reading and writing came hard to him, so did making friends. Part of his disability affected his social life because he acted different compared to the other kids at school, and the others knew it. Growing up I always had a lot of friends around the house. He was jealous that I had so many because he always wanted what I had. Whenever they came over, he'd talk to them and invite himself to go out with us. This made me angry because these were my friends, not his. Sometimes I'd wish that he'd just disappear. As we each grew older, he became more respectful of my friends and me, and I became more tolerant of him. I now have him join us sometimes when my friends and I go out because I know it means a lot to him. He has become friends with some of my friends. I have realized that sharing them with my brother doesn't mean I have to lose them. He has been lucky enough to find a few special friends of his own who were able to see past his disability and see him for the wonderful person he really is. What is quite surprising, but wonderful, is that I have become friends with his friends and our friends are friends. Now that we each have put aside some of our jealousies, we are able to get along better together and as a group. My brother is very thankful for his friendships and they for him.

Even though we had some hard times, my brother has given me unconditional love and support. He has always taken care of me by making sure that I'm safe or happy. Even when I was mean to him and treated him badly, he still stood by me. A lot of it was because he looked up to me.

Just as my brother has gained a lot of strength and courage because of his disability, I have gained a better understanding for people that are not like myself. I love him because of who he is, and I would never want to change my brother in any way. He is not only my brother; he is my friend.

(Excerpts adapted from the 1993 issue of *Their World: A Publication of the National Center for Learning Disabilities, William* Ellis, Ed.)

Children who have siblings with learning problems need support to deal with their own feelings that arise as a consequence of their sibling's functional abilities. A sibling of a brother or sister having learning disabilities may encounter an unfavorable school environment. A teacher of children with learning disabilities expects these children's younger siblings not only to perform unsatisfactory on academic, perceptual, and memory tasks, but also to make less progress during the school year than younger siblings of nondisabled students (Dyson, 1996). Teachers, counselors, recreation leaders, and therapists must become cognizant of their prejudices. Just because Bob has a learning disability and has trouble playing baseball does not mean that his brother Joe will play poorly at the game, too.

Some of the same social characteristics children with learning disabilities exhibit toward their peers during school or at leisure are likely to also play a role in interactions with siblings. Poor impulse control, difficulties in reading social cues (e.g., facial expressions, tone of voice, mannerisms), and forgetfulness can make for a volatile sibling relationship. Feelings of anger and frustration can be displayed at a brother or sister who takes too long to complete tasks, demands continuous attention from parents for help with homework assignments, does not carry a fair share of household chores, and must be included in the sibling's play and leisure activities. Shame and embarrassment arise upon hearing a sibling being called names, such as "stupid" or "slow." These brothers or sisters may hold themselves responsible for their sibling's behavior. Reactions of fear, anger, and guilt that are directed toward that child with learning disabilities are the same feelings for both parents and siblings, but the siblings may have a more difficult time than the parents in coping with them.

To assist a sibling's understanding of his brother's or sister's learning disability characteristics, a teacher or recreation therapist can display and discuss examples of interpretation of street signs, pictures, cards, or familiar sayings. The following examples are displaying differences in perceiving information.

Look at the differences in viewing the road sign:

A person **without** learning disabilities	A person **with** learning disabilities

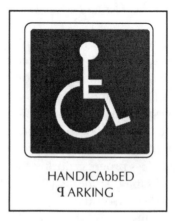

HANDICAPPED
PARKING

HANDICAbbED
ꟼ ARKING

Look at the differences in viewing the math problem:

A person **without** learning
disabilities

A person **with** learning
disabilities

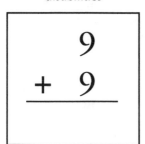

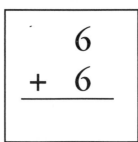

Look at the differences in viewing a playing card:

A person **without** learning
disabilities

A person **with** learning
disabilities

This gives the sibling without the learning disability a chance to visit the world of the brother or sister who is experiencing this kind of difficulty on a continuous basis. In the appendix section, Appendixes F, G, and H provide insight on how familiar sayings and activities are construed by those having learning disabilities in the areas of auditory discrimination, directionality, and visual figure-ground problems. Being aware of these discrepancies in interpretation allows for the sibling without learning disabilities to understand just how difficult life can be when this constantly occurs.

Relationships between siblings with and without learning disabilities is not always unfavorable. Dyson (1996) reports results from a study:

Relationships between siblings with and without learning disabilities were reported to be generally positive. Nearly half of the parents (46%) reported that nondisabled siblings were "understanding" and "displayed patience" with the sibling with learning disabilities . . . Nineteen percent of the parents reported various negative experiences among the siblings. (p. 283)

Siblings can develop intense feelings of joy and pride in the accomplishments of their brother or sister, or those feelings may fluctuate, depending on family experiences. In comparison to parents, some siblings have trouble adjusting, some adjust well, and some report that they actually benefit from the experience (Seligman & Darling, 1989; Senapati & Hayes, 1988).

A Spouse with Learning Disabilities

Not much information has been printed about understanding a spouse with learning disabilities. If circumstances are ideal, the individual with learning disabilities will have a mate who shows patience, supplies loving corrective criticism, recognizes attributes, encourages the development of skills, and gives support when needed. The opposite situation is a mate who furnishes constant comparative criticism (e.g., you did not do that last week so why are you doing it today); puts the spouse under unwarranted time pressures; never acknowledges successes, but instead accentuates failures; constantly does for the person; and is not accepting of disability characteristics.

With marriage comes the roles each mate is expected to fulfill. Although women have advanced in the professional arena, they are still expected to be good housekeepers, manage the household budget, raise the children, shop for food, and cook the meals. What household duties' wives who do not have learning disabilities take for granted (i.e., balancing the checkbook, determining essential versus unessential purchases, being aware of appointment times, judging temperatures and measurement when cooking, reading labels for cooking and washing, watering and feeding plants and animals, etc.) becomes an ongoing issue of concern for wives with learning disabilities. Because economics at this present time dictate that two incomes are needed to maintain an adequate family living, the wife with learning disabilities' duties are compounded with balancing family life and career, making life much more complex.

Organizational skills are critical for running a busy household. The wife always has to prepare for the next day's events ahead of time. One example is Jeanette, who, due to organizational and planning problems, could not estimate correctly how long it would take to prepare dinner upon arriving home from aerobics class. Every Monday, Tuesday, and Thursday, Jeanette would defrost frozen meat when she arrived home from her late afternoon aerobics class. Arriving home at about the same time as her husband, 6:00 p.m., she would then cook most of the night and they would usually eat dinner after 10:00 p.m. Unfortunately, this was one habit out of many that eventually caused the husband to divorce her. Jeanette was aware that she must bring her aerobics clothes to class, so she managed to pack her gym bag the night before class; her designated time for packing aerobics clothes was immediately before going to bed. However, she did not realize the importance of preparing dinner on her aerobics days. Perhaps if she had, she might have made a note to take frozen meat out to defrost in the morning or to transfer frozen meat from the freezer to the refrigerator the night before to thaw. Also, perceived designated roles in this marriage led the husband to think it was not his job to remove the frozen meat from the freezer in the morning before going to work. Together the couple did not ameliorate their problems through assuming other duties outside of their roles, and individually the husband did not encourage his wife to seek methods to improve her organizational abilities.

In relating this situation to the "Levels of Competency," Jeanette is functioning at Level One, lacking insight about organizational difficulties. If Jeanette is not approached with corrective criticism about the consequences of exhibiting nonproductive behavior, she could remain at this level in her organizational abilities. Marriage requires teamwork, not constant blame. Helping each other, adjusting to the other person's weakness, and supporting the other's strengths builds a better team.

The husband with learning disabilities is primarily concerned with his work and status on the job. Some of these husbands hold important executive positions; others work at occupations well beneath their abilities and are frustrated by this situation. Others hide their disabilities from co-workers and supervisors and use all their knowledge and abilities to perform each task to perfection. This pretense can be tiring, hindering the husband into not making any decisions or taking on any responsibilities at home. Often, the added responsibilities become part of the wife's job: making a list of household repairs, purchasing building materials, handling household expenses, paying car insurance, scheduling weekend chores or activities, and corresponding to all legal and business matters.

Other problems can plague the couple having a spouse with learning disabilities. If the spouse experiences difficulties in receptive and expressive language, the cause for frequent misunderstanding is surmountable. When the spouse is tactilely defensive, it presents problems in responding to a light touch, such as a caress. If attending to more than one stimulus at a time causes frustration, an evening of soft music, gourmet food, candlelight, and talk can be very distracting. The spouse with learning disabilities might turn off the music and turn on the lights when being attentive to the mate. This most likely ruins the romantic evening for the nonlearning disabled mate. How can the spouse without learning disabilities better understand what causes frustration for the spouse with learning disabilities? The following two exercises demonstrate difficulties with reading and fine motor control in the mate having learning disabilities.

This is a reading exercise designed to let others experience how frustrating reading is to the individual having learning disabilities. One suggestion for professionals using this exercise is to have the nonlearning disabled mates in a group read it together aloud, with a session leader assisting as needed. After the reading, the group discusses how they felt reading this passage and offers ideas they have about giving support and assistance to a spouse when reading is required.

A Reading Exercise Influenced by Learning Disabilities

In mobern soceity an inbivibual's ytiliba to be self-sufficient is usually Encouraqed fron childhool. By eht tine we are adults, we are uspposed to have learmed to debend upon ourselves, to de as puick on the ward as the next persom, and to be ready to dolh own own in a more or less ilesoht world.

Indeqenbence is also comsidered a civic virtue, for self-relaicme means pulling your own thgiew, paying your taxes, and not deing a durben on your hard-rpsseed fellow countrymen. The enphasis is almost lla bencial rehabilitaton is to retgrain the displaed person for probuctive work. If siht qroves unfeasible, they nay de considered useless and left to hsiugnal apart from the naimstrean.

This attiued quts tremendous pressure no the disabled norimyiit. Trying to keep threi self-respect im a society that equates inbequenbemce with physical well-being nakes an already tlucciffied situation almost elbarelotni, for the hamdicaqqed person is generally persuaded to think the sane way. Such emphsisover on paying ome's yaw seems to leave disabled qeoqle with only wot alternatives—to knock themselves uot trying to etepmoc om able-ddiebo terms or ot opt out entirely. This limited ccoihe would mot apply is society acknowledged other teriarc of worth.

It's inportamt to realize that on individual can really tsixe alone. Im a civilized society ew are all interbeqendent. And, at best, physical deinpendence is variable. Able-bodied or not, everyome experiences sdoirep of debenqence: illness and dlo age are undiscrinimating. Moral inqebendence, on the other hand, is elbitcurtsedni.

(Excerpts taken from Glorya Hale (Ed.), 1979, *Source Book for the Disabled, pp.40-41.* NY: Paddington Press. Recreated and printed as stated above in The Postsecondary Learning Disabilities Primer, Western Carolina University, 1989)

Translation

In modern society an individual's ability to be self-sufficient is usually encouraged from childhood. By the time we are adults, we are supposed to have learned to depend upon ourselves, to be as quick on the draw as the next person, and to be ready to hold our own in a more or less hostile world.

Independence is also considered a civic virtue, for self-reliance means pulling your own weight, paying your taxes, and not being a burden on your hard-pressed fellow countrymen. The emphasis in almost all medical rehabilitation is to retrain the displaced person for productive work. If this proves unfeasible, they may be considered useless and left to languish apart from the mainstream.

This attitude puts tremendous pressure on the disabled minority. Trying to keep their self-respect in a society that equates independence with physical well-being makes an already difficult situation almost intolerable, for the handicapped person is generally persuaded to think the same way. Such over emphasis on paying one's way seems to leave disabled people with only two alternatives—to knock themselves out trying to compete on able-bodied terms or to opt out entirely. This limited choice would not apply if society acknowledged other criteria of worth.

It's important to realize that an individual can really exist alone. In a civilized society we are all interdependent. And, at best, physical independence is variable. Able-bodied or not, everyone experiences periods of dependence: illness and old age are undiscriminating. Moral independence, on the other hand, is indestructible.

This next exercise can provide some insight as to why it takes a spouse so long to write names or copy text.

A Copying Exercise Depicting a Perceptual-Motor Learning Disability Characteristic

All tasks are to be completed with your NONDOMINANT hand.

1. Trace this design as you count from 978 to 1032.

2. Copy the design below with your neatest and quickest skill.

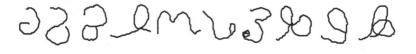

3. This is your name in manuscribble. Please learn to write it from memory. When you are ready, let the instructor know. You will be asked to demonstrate your skill.

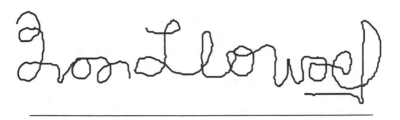

(Adapted from J. Jarrow, 1988, *AHSSPPE's Approach to Inservice Education from Faculty* and from the Learning Disabilities Training Project, 1989, *The Post Secondary Learing Disabilities Primer: A Training Manual for Service Providers*)

An illustration of the mate who has problems with direction-ality and figure-ground discrimination trying to learn embroidery is explored in Appendix I, "Drawn Fabric Embroidery." What is of particular importance with this illustration is the uncertainty the individual may exhibit in beginning a design pattern. In following the design pattern, this person could produce unwanted cross stitch-ing and have trouble distinguishing between warp fabric threads and cross fabric threads, creating an uneven embroidery design.

The increased public awareness of learning disabilities has enabled more adults to seek evaluation for the learning, reasoning, and coordination difficulties they have experienced all their lives. Support groups are available in many communities to serve fami-lies having a loved one with learning disabilities. When the support group is run by a professional knowledgeable in the field of learn-ing disabilities, the group ventures into areas of understanding and experiencing difficulties through activities; holding an open forum for expressing feelings; networking with community professionals; exposing members to successful people with learning disabilities; teaching compensation strategies; and involving members in group leisure activities. Involvement in a support group, couple/indi-vidual counseling, or just talking with another person who has a spouse with learning disabilities, can ease a mate's worries, reward the mate's patience, reveal a shoulder to lean on, and provide es-sential resources in case of an emergency (e.g., a spouse motiva-tion breakdown).

Advocacy

Now that the individual having learning disabilities and other family members are aware of the frustrations that take place with learning disabilities, how do these individuals go about seeking the services and assistance needed for managing their lives? Remem-ber the Biblical sayings, "Ask and it shall be opened unto you . . .," "Seek and ye shall find . . ."? It is difficult to get one's needs met when one does not seek or ask about services and assistance. The first step toward self-advocacy or advocacy for others is to inquire about what kind of service and assistance is available for the per-son with learning disabilities within the community.

Assertiveness

With advocacy comes assertiveness; assertiveness is the ability to express thoughts and feelings openly (e.g., concerns, opinions, affections). Assertiveness is important for a number of reasons:

1. It can give one the means for obtaining more positive responses from others.

2. It allows other people to better understand each other through exchange of thoughts and opinions.

3. It can assist in preventing aversive encounters and in enhancing problem solving.

4. It can facilitate developing close working and personal relationships.

Adults are expected to be self-advocates; therefore, they must display the assertiveness skills to get needs met. They must come to depend upon themselves to seek out information that can better their lives and the lives of their children. Many adults with learning disabilities know that they should ask for assistance or inquire about services, but they do not know how to do this. Individuals with learning disabilities who have always experienced difficulty with social encounters may exhibit behaviors of aggressiveness or passivity when asking for services. They may also have a misconception about what assertiveness actually means. It is common for all people to relate assertiveness to being aggressive, when in actuality, the two are different.

If advocacy requires one to be assertive, then what is being assertive? Table 3-1 can supply some insight on what behaviors are displayed when one is being passive, aggressive, or assertive. This table, along with a list for guiding assertive behavior (see Figure 3.7), can be used by professionals in teaching assertive skills in a group or individual session to adults with learning disabilities. It is these professionals' roles to educate adults in the appropriate way to inquire about services. Appendixes J, K, and L furnish additional materials in the form of three case scenarios that a group of adults can role play or discuss, internalizing the differences in one being passive, assertive, or aggressive. In instructing assertiveness skills, the professional must allege that being assertive does not guarantee all issues or conflicts will be resolved in the adult's favor. When this type of behavior is revealed, the adult will most likely receive positive results from future encounters with the same personnel delivering services.

Table 3-1
Passive, Aggressive, and Assertive Responses by People

Passive	Aggressive	Assertive
Indifferent	Attacks person verbally or physically	Speaks clearly and confidently
Lifeless	Hostile	Honest
Doesn't care	Sarcastic	Deals directly with anger
Avoids the problem	Blaming	Appropriate
"I'm not good enough"	Selfish	Considers the rights of the other person
"It doesn't matter"	Opinionated	Considers the rights of the other person
Builds anger	Acts out anger	Deals with the problem
Hopes that needs will be met	Demanding	Active
Lacks confidence	Fighting	Cares about self
Nonactive	Physical	Cares about results
Nonaggressive	Emotional	Cares about the situation

The professional conducting this group could use these words to provoke responses from group members about their perceptions of the meaning for each term.

(Adapted from Janis Johnson, 1992, *Facilitating an Academic Support Group for Students with Learning Disabilities: A Manual for Professionals*)

Figure 3.7
Guiding Assertive Behavior

1. I have a clear and reasonable goal in mind. Write it out!

2. I have decided that this encounter is one that is worth my risk-taking.

3. I choose an appropriate time to make sure the issue can be fully discussed.

4. I focus on the issue. (The issue is . . .)

5. I define my concerns in specific terms. (I see . . ., I hear . . .)

6. I communicate my feelings about the issue. (I feel . . .)

7. I express the fact that I want to explore the issue or solve the conflict cooperatively.

8. I maintain eye contact, good posture, and appropriate voice tone.

9. I am calm, I consider the other person, and I communicate clearly.

10. I will carry out these procedures again (1-9) to further explore the issue or resolve the problem.

(Adapted from Janis Johnson, 1992, Checklist for Assertive Behavior, Material Reference 7.3, *Facilitating an Academic Support Group for Students with Learning Disabilities: A Manual for Professionals*)

Parents and Siblings as Advocates

Parents become advocates for their children. This means that the parents having a child with learning disabilities must reveal quality assertiveness skills so their child can receive sufficient services. Parents who are advocates want to become well-informed about their child's progress at school and in other extracurricular activities. Parents play a key role in helping the teacher, counselor, recreation leader, and therapist to understand the special education needs of their children. Through reading and networking with national agencies, these are parents who may very well be more apprised about new techniques, trends and alternative instructional methods than the professional instructing the child. This is where the professional should display an open mind and be accepting to the parents' suggestions. If the professional has not heard of the technique or method, she must not become defensive, but ask the parent where one can find out more about the effectiveness of the particular technique or method. When the professional discusses the child's behaviors with parents, parents who are not as assertive should be encouraged to supply input about modifications to activities and the teaching format. The professional only sees the child for a very short period of time per week and does not have all the answers to create a "well-behaved, above-average performing child." Parents' input is greatly valued and important. The aim of professionals working with parents is to form a coalition that helps parents to be effective advocates for their children in all matters, not just the educational ones.

Siblings also become advocates for their brothers or sisters who have learning disabilities. Siblings who attend the same school together and/or participate in the same recreational activities are aware if changes should be made in how the sibling with learning disabilities is being treated. Children are not shy when it comes to speaking their minds and are often better advocates than their parents; but because children's opinions are not valued on the same level as an adult, they are often overlooked as not being important or exhibiting behavior that is "out of line."

To help parents become better advocates for the child with learning disabilities, it would be essential to recognize the comments of a sibling. Why should Johnny's brother Bill (who has learning disabilities) not be involved in the daily game of kickball during recess? Why is the teacher who is monitoring the recess period not aware that Bill is not playing with his brother and the other children? Johnny, sharing this observation with his parents, is advocating for the right to have his brother involved in the game of kickball. This may seem trivial to the teacher who has to monitor a large number of students during recess, but it would be more beneficial that the problem be resolved on this level than for it to continue. The parent may decide to call the school principal if the teacher does not solve the problem. Or, Johnny may decide himself to conduct a silent protest and not involve himself in any recreational activities that his brother is not involved in. Most likely, Johnny is going to conduct an overt protest and kick the ball out of the school yard into the street so no one gets to play kickball. In anger he will tell the teacher it is not fair that his brother does not get to play kickball like everyone else.

With children, and at times it is difficult to interpret, there are many kinds of protest for advocacy.

Disclosure

When a person has determined she is going to be an advocate for herself or others, she must disclose the nature of the disability. In disclosure, a person with a disability is telling another person about her particular disability. To enhance assertiveness skills, especially in adults with learning disabilities, that person would be instructed to inform others about her learning disability. When the individual who has the disability is notifying another, the purpose is to educate, inform about strengths and weaknesses, relate information about alternative teaching methods and services, explore modifications, and build a stronger understanding between the person with a disability and the person working with her.

Why should a person with learning disabilities disclose? The "why" will depend upon the individual. The benefits of disclosure to the professional consist of properly instructing the activity, knowing about skill level of the person having learning disabilities, and quicker institution of modifications to the session (e.g., different instruction of methods, equipment variation, purchases of modified equipment). Persons with learning disabilities might not choose to disclose due to fear of being embarrassed by peers or professionals for receiving special services, that information about the individual's disability will go beyond the initial contact person, and of consistently being given inferior task assignments or simplistic duties. Disclosure allows for the person and the professional to plan ahead and avoid possible confusion before it happens.

When should a person disclose? During registration of an activity, the parent or individual, when completing the activity registration form, can make a written note on the form about the context of the learning disability. The parent or individual can arrange a meeting with the activity or session leader before the activity begins to discuss characteristics and program modifications. Informing the leader before the activity begins allows ample time for the leader to prepare a variety of alternative materials and techniques for class. Also, a person should disclose when he notices difficulties in completing a task. Appendix L, "Case Scenario 3," portrays a situation where the individual did not disclose to his employer, after being hired, that his learning disability affects reading comprehension. When the individual noticed his difficulties with reading appearing and that his job required more reading than he thought, he sought help about disclosing from his college director of special services.

In disclosing, one should think about how much information one wants the other person to know. A parent who discloses during the registration of an activity might bring in an IEP (Individual Education Plan) for the recreation leader or therapist to review, especially if the IEP states recreation or recreation therapy within the plan. The IEP will state more information than just participation in a recreation program, thereby exposing the recreation leader to knowing more specifics about the child. Second, a parent may disclose the disability on the activity registration form but not state characteristics, leaving the responsibility to the professional to tailor the activity to the child's needs. Third, a parent may sit with the program supervisor for an hour explaining all of the child's idiocrasies and provide input about what a professional should do in case these behaviors occur. Most of this information should be kept confidential and not be mentioned in front of the child (e.g., "Your mother told me that you do . . ."); there are some things children do not want their teachers, coaches, or recreation leaders to know.

An adult can describe to a sailing instructor in detail what effects his auditory processing ability will have in a sailing class, or can just inform the instructor that he prefers to sit next to the instructor to assure understanding of sailing techniques. It is not mandatory during disclosure that a person mention he has a learning disability, especially if the adult feels major modification and equipment are not required for him to understand and perform the activity.

For example, a person does not have to state that he has a learning disability in order to view the sailing video a second time, because the activity leader allows anyone in the class to take home and view the video more than once. However, a person might have to disclose a learning disability, if, due to directionality problems and comprehension of oral instruction, the individual requires more than the three times allotted for actual sailing demonstrations. Basically, it is at the discretion of the adult to disclose the extent of his disability.

Regardless of how little or how much a professional knows about her participant's disability, it is important to exercise confidentiality of information. If a parent discloses information about a child, the professional should make sure that permission is obtained to relay this information to other professionals working with the child and that the child knows this. This can become a very uncomfortable situation when the child finds out that everyone knows she has learning disabilities and the child only expects that certain people will know this information.

Professionals should also use discretion and observation when acting to assist someone who does not wish to be helped. Just because a child requires extra drill sessions in soccer does not mean that in playing a game of cards she wants the recreation leader to add up her score. Overtly, this is not a breach of confidentiality, but covertly to the child a breach of confidentiality has occurred. She knows that the constant attention, frequent correction, and unasked assistance shown by the professional portrays someone who has a disability. Even though the professional did not talk about this person having a disability, the actions could be translated as so.

Never mention that an individual requires special equipment or accommodations to any other participant in the activity. The person having the disability is to explain the activity modification or accommodation to the inquisitive person if she wishes. This process helps in self-advocacy, explaining to another the justification for receiving assistance, and that this assistance, equipment, or service enables the person with learning disabilities to compete on the same level with others.

Impact of Advocacy

Advocacy is a vehicle for change, whether the change is on a singular level affecting one person or on a multiple level affecting an entire country; change generates progress. Weisgerber (1991) explains the effects of advocacy as:

> a proven mechanism for change. It is arguably an essential element in the quality of life of some lesser-abled persons. It focuses energy and attention in areas where energy and attention should be directed and provides a basis for monitoring progress toward needs. Advocacy is the result of voluntary action based on conviction and experience. (p. 120)

Gajar (1996) reports the current definition from NJCLD and other important issues about the individual having learning disabilities (e.g., professional and public awareness, appropriate education, vocational and employment training, transition programs, research on adults, curriculum development, awareness training for mental health professionals) arise from individuals, parents, teachers, and organizations advocating for the rights of adults with disabilities. Through self-advocacy, persons with learning disabilities received significant representation in local and national public policy arenas. Advocacy skills should be strengthened through innovative intervention and practice just like learning skills. Having a guide as a reference doesn't hurt either. Figure 3.8 is a guide to being your own advocate.

Figure 3.8
Ways To Be Your Own Advocate

1. Know your rights.
2. Remember that rights are not favors.
3. Be polite when you ask for help or share ideas.
4. Remember that your ideas are important.
5. Remember that you are a unique and special person.
6. Always ask "why" when you do not get the services you want.
7. Keep all important paper about services together in a safe place (e.g., notebook, file, etc.).
8. Never give your only copy of important papers to others. Let them make a copy if necessary.
9. Know that you have a right to have the records in your file explained to you.
10. Know who can help you get services (e.g., advocate, parent, teacher, therapist) and ask that person to attend meetings with you.
11. Do not give up asking for help until you have been helped.
12. If you call someone for help who does not return your call, call back.
13. Go to the next person in charge if you do not get the help you need from the first person.
14. Practice what you will say before a meeting.
15. Be ready to explain why you need a service.
16. Write down your most important points and questions before the meeting so you will not forget.
17. Follow up requests in writing and keep a copy of the letter.

Figure 3.8 Cont.

18. Listen to ideas shared by others.
19. Know what your body language is saying.
20. Dress neatly and be well-groomed.
21. Keep your cool.
22. Always show up for meetings and always be on time.

(Adapted from J.C. Galvin, & M.J. Scherer, 1996, *Evaluating, Selecting, and Using Appropriate Assistive Technology*, p. 335)

References

Borba, M., & Borba, C. (1982). *Self-esteem: A classroom affair, Volume 2*. Minneapolis, MN: Winston Press, Inc.

Cordoni, B. (1990). *Living with a learning disability: Revised edition*. Carbondale, IL: Southern Illinois University Press.

Dyson, L. (1996). The experiences of families of children with learning disabilities: Parental stress, family functioning and sibling self-concept. *Journal of Learning Disabilities, 29*(3), pp. 280-286.

Ellis, W. (Ed). (1993). My brother, my friend. *Their world: A publication of the National Center for Learning Disabilities*. New York: National Center for Learning Disabilities.

Gajar, A. (1996). Current and future research. In J.R. Patton & E.A. Polloway, (Eds.), *Learning disabilities: The challenges of adulthood*. Austin, TX: Pro-Ed, Inc.

Galvin, J.C., & Scherer, M.J. (1996). *Evaluating, selecting, and using appropriate assistive technology*. Gaitherburg, MD: Aspen Publication.

Hale, G. (Ed.) (1979). *Source book for the disabled*. New York: Paddington Press.

Hallahan, D.P., Kauffman, J. M., & Lloyd, J. (1996). *Introduction to Learning Disabilities*. Boston, MA: Allyn and Bacon.

Jarrow, J. (1988, July). *AHSSPPE's approach to inservice education for faculty*. New Orleans, LA: Association on Handicapped Student Service Programs in Postsecondary Education (AHSSPPE).

Johnson, J. (1992). *Facilitating an academic support group for students with learning disabilities: A manual for professionals.* Columbus, OH: Association on Handicapped Student Service Programs in Postsecondary Education (AHSSPPE).

Learning Disabilities Training Project. (1989). *The postsecondary learning disabilities primer: A training manual for service providers.* Cullowhee, NC: Western Carolina University.

Meichenbaum, D. (1980). Cognitive behavior modification with exceptional children: A promise yet unfulfilled. *Exceptional Education Quarterly,* 61(1), pp. 83-86.

Meichenbaum, D. (1983). Teaching thinking: A cognitive-behavioral approach. In Society for Learning Disabilities and Remedial Education (Ed.), *Interdisciplinary voices in learning disabilities and remedial education* (pp. 127-150). Austin, TX: Pro-Ed.

Moawod, R. (1992). *Increasing human effectiveness II: Managing the rapids of change.* Tacoma, WA: Edge Learning Institute.

Seligman, M., & Darling, R.B. (1989). *Ordinary families, special children: A systems approach to childhood disability.* New York: Guilford Press.

Senapati, R., & Hayes, A. (March, 1988). Sibling relationships of handicapped children: A review of conceptual and methodological issued. *International Journal of Behavioral Development* vol. 11, no.1, pp.89-115.

Stumbo, N.J. (1992). *Leisure education II: More activities and resources.* State College, PA: Venture Publishing, Inc.

Weisgerber, R.A. (1991). *Quality of life for persons with disabilities: Skill development and transitions across life stages.* Gaithersburg, MD: Aspen Publishers, Inc.

Chapter Four

LEISURE

Leisure and Its Importance to Persons with Learning Disabilities

LEISURE - Love for an activity, Equal access for enjoyment, Individualism of choice, Social integration, Unique approach to learning skills, Responsible for self-fulfillment, and Entering new horizons. These are all ideals within the acronym of leisure that persons with disabilities thrive to achieve. The process of explaining leisure to people with learning disabilities should encompass the "wh" questions. Each person needs to understand the following: what is leisure, when does leisure take place, why should a person with learning disabilities participate in recreational activities during leisure time, what are the person's interests in activities and why, and how can one become successful in his leisure time?

The word *leisure* possesses various definitions. These definitions contain two ideas: free time and release of participation from work or other obligations. *Merriam Webster's* states leisure as "freedom provided by the cessation of activities, especially time free from work or duties." *The American Heritage Dictionary* quotes, "leisure—freedom from time-consuming duties, responsibilities or activities." *Random House Unabridged Dictionary* reports leisure as "freedom from the demands of work or duty or unhurried ease." Researchers in the field of recreation and leisure formulated the definition of leisure as "an experience" that occurs within the context of time and activity (Henderson, Bialeschki, Shaw, & Freysinger, 1989).

As one explains these definitions of leisure based on one's own perceptions, the thought of leisure can evoke various images. These images could be any of the following: doing absolutely nothing, listening to music, driving a car, hiking, speech writing, or fixing a video cassette recorder (VCR) for a close friend. The determination as to what work, activities, duties, and responsibilities are, is up to the individual. One person may view fixing a VCR as work and would not want to engage in this type of activity during his or her free time, but another person who receives enjoyment out of assisting others and performing hands-on skills might consider fixing a VCR as a leisure time activity. In essence, free time is leisure time. It is during this time that an individual can choose how to use it (Talbot, 1979).

One factor in discovering whether one's leisure experience can be a rewarding adventure is to allow for choice in participation of an activity. The freedom of choice and participation, even for short times, can do wonders to build self-esteem. The process imparts responsibility toward decision making, motivation for involvement, and display of risk-taking ability. Along with choice in activity, the individual should also have choice in determining accommodations and modifications of activities to best ensure enjoyment. Persons with learning disabilities must be aware that participation in leisure activities is an important aspect of one's life in society. Leisure activities provide many opportunities for developing and nurturing, for example, social relationships between couples, siblings, and parents and their child and among friends (McConkey & McGinley, 1990).

Play within leisure activity stimulates problem-solving ability, giving individuals the specific skills to solve a variety of problems posed in life's circumstances. Some researchers speculate that by exploring and manipulating objects in play, individuals learn the properties of those objects as well as their potential for application to various other problem situations (Barnett, 1991). For example, when children roll balls on the floor, they learn the shape and feel of the ball, see where the ball is situated on the floor in relation to stationary objects, and with multiple throws they recognize the force they have to exert to knock items down or to position the ball close to other objects. The simple action of rolling a ball can prepare one to perform well in bowling, boccia, handball, and serving in kickball. Other benefits to having leisure are promoting physical health and conditioning, developing new skills, and integrating into the community environment (Schleien & Ray, 1988).

The words *leisure* and *recreation* have synonymous usage, although each word has its own distinct meaning. Recreation refers to particular activities done during free time. These activities range from active involvement in sports, crafts, socializing, and volunteering to art appreciation. Leisure, from the definitions above, is described as free time and involvement in activities during one's free time. To eliminate confusion, the word *leisure* will only pertain to free time. The words *recreation activity* or *leisure activities* will refer to involvement in any activities (e.g., sports, games, hobbies, social events, volunteering, etc.) of choice during free time.

Benefits of Recreation Participation

Why should a person with learning disabilities engage in recreation activities? Simply because they can derive many benefits from recreation participation. One benefit is learning from the experience. When the recreation activity experience has captivated the participant, this individual brings particular personality styles of learning, motivation, and expectations about the experience to the setting. The person faced with a specific environment, interpreted by the person or not, promotes one or more learning experiences. These learning experiences can be motor learning, understanding game directions, or performing a skill, all to meet the demands of that setting. These experiences may come from involvement in a structured recreation program and may be exhibited as part of the information outcomes of participation. Researchers in the field of learning and educational psychology have discovered a variety of learning outcomes. The following outcomes can be present because of participation in recreation activities: behavior change and skill learning, direct visual memory, information (factual) learning, concept learning, schemata learning, metacognition learning and attitude, and value learning (Roggenbuck, Loomis, & Dagostino, 1991).

The physiological benefits of recreation participation were derived from studies where people engage in physical activity of some kind (e.g., exercise, cycling, swimming, walking, jogging, running, hiking, weight lifting, etc). Specific results from involvement in a physical recreation activity are an increased lung capacity, reduced resting heart rate, and lower blood pressure levels. Other benefits consist of decreased body fat mass, increased lean body mass, increased muscle strength, and improved structure and function of connective tissues (ligaments, tendons, cartilage) and joints. Weight-bearing and strength-building activities help sustain bone mass and reduce the incidence of trauma-induced fractures (Paffenbarger, Hyde, & Dow, 1990). Moderate physical recreation activities are known to reduce the symptoms of mild or moderate depression and anxiety through improved self-image, social skills, and mental health (Taylor, Sallis, & Needle, 1985). Noted psychological benefits of recreation activity are as follows:

- perceived sense of freedom, independence, and autonomy,
- enhanced self-competence through improved sense of self-worth, self-reliance, and self-confidence,
- better ability to socialize with others, including greater tolerance and understanding,
- enriched capabilities for team membership,
- heightened creative ability,
- improved expressions of and reflection on personal spiritual ideals,
- greater adaptability and resiliency,
- better sense of humor,
- enhanced perceived quality of life,
- more balanced competitiveness and a more positive outlook on life (Academy of Leisure Sciences & Driver, 1994).

Involvement in recreation activities releases stress and tension from the perils of society. Braum (1991) recalls the findings of researchers that state, "relaxation tends to alleviate many of the symptoms of stress. Activities that fill leisure time, performed within a group, strengthen social support ties known to negate stress" (p. 407). The idea of choice in leisure presents opportunities where one can recreate.

One's environment can be a determinant to stress reduction. Natural environments can be pleasant, relaxing, and stress-reducing for many people, but large urban cities also provide the same experience. Having too much free time and limited access to various recreation activities of one's liking can produce stress. So, for those individuals living out in the country who have access to transportation, the joy of partaking in cultural events in the city on a weekly or monthly basis provides the opportunity for a stress-limited lifestyle. The same can be said for people living in the city who recreate in the country.

Social integration of children and adults with learning disabilities into community recreation programs offers the chance to develop a positive self-image through successful experiences and satisfying relationships with peers. McGill (1984) reports that integrated play opportunities are stimulating and highly motivating experiences for disabled children, offering them opportunities to imitate and model the play behavior of nondisabled peers. Social integration also enhances relationships between family members. We've all heard of the old adage, "The family that plays together stays together." This adage infers that leisure experiences promote family satisfaction and stability. Recreation activities provide opportunities for couples and families to interact and negotiate individual and collective interests. Orthner and Mancini (1991) state some benefits to the family:

> Leisure experiences promote opportunities for developing equity. Unlike many other environments within which people interact, leisure experiences promote opportunities for each individual to maximize her or his own interests and minimize competition. It is during leisure time when husbands and wives, and parents and children, are most apt to practice by negotiating family roles and reaching new definitions of consensuses. When individual interests are promoted over maximum joint interest, family bonds are weakened. Shared leisure experiences encourage opportunities to negotiations and improve the historical comparisons upon which subsequent negotiations are based. (p. 294)

Benefits of leisure in social integration are also noted in people without disabilities. The chance to learn from and to socialize with nondisabled peers has been cited as one benefit for individuals with disabilities participating in integrated and fully inclusive programs. Research in the 1980s determined that positive attitudes of children not having disabilities toward peers having disabilities were cultivated or increased when involved with an integrated recreation activity (Schleien & Ray, 1988). Recreation service providers also learn from this experience. Due to the Americans With Disabilities Act of 1990, all private, public, and nonprofit agencies delivering recreation services to the public must supply accommodations and modifications within their programs to persons with disabilities (as requested). These professionals may not have any knowledge of providing accommodations and/or modifications to participants with learning disabilities. The person with learning disabilities, upon disclosure, thus needs to educate the professional about what accommodations and/or program modifications should be arranged to enable full participation in recreation programs. This social interaction not only contributes awareness of this situation to another person but also demonstrates how important it is for individuals with disabilities to participate in a particular recreation activity like everyone else.

Discovering Recreation Interests

Most people in this world, regardless of race, creed, color, socioeconomic level, educational background, possession of a disability or not, display some interest in recreation activities. People have engaged in recreation activities throughout the centuries and will continue to do so. The "play" involved in recreation activities elicits feelings of enjoyment, contentment, or satisfaction. Play is not something that ends when one is no longer a child; it continues long into adulthood, usually making various changes throughout one's life cycle.

There are many ways to determine one's interest in recreation activities. The first area parents, teachers, counselors, recreation leaders, and therapists might explore is external influence. External influence pertains to advertisement in some form of media, for example, television, radio, computer search (Internet), magazines, books, or newspapers. These forms of media help promote games, sports, hobbies, and entertainment. Family, friends, and associates are another form of external influence: a husband describing to his wife how he enjoys playing golf and stating that he notices many women out on the course is probably encouraging his wife to play golf (in a subtle way); an employee reciting a sightseeing excursion during her cruise vacation to Europe with a co-worker who has never traveled out of the country; peers boasting about achieving high scores in video games to a child who does not own a computer; a person exhibiting an award won after a competition to her sister. These examples can influence one to become involved in that particular recreation activity. These "external influences" provide awareness to what types of recreation activities are out there in the world.

The second area of exploration is internal influence. What will give a person satisfaction during leisure time? Taking an inventory of one's personal leisure needs through self-questioning provides guidance to one's selection of recreation activities. An exercise taken from the book *Leisure Education: A Manual of Activities and Resources,* provides a simple checklist exercise to select and rank one's personal needs for satisfying leisure time (see Figure 4.1). Statements displayed in the exercise pertain to broad topics: physical activity, production, skill development, socialization, competition, organization, and relaxation. Separating the external and internal influences of recreation participation is difficult. Both are major factors in discovering recreation interests.

Figure 4.1

Meeting Personal Needs In Leisure
(Lady & Whipple)

It is important to me to:

_____ Do something meaningful	_____ Laugh and enjoy myself
_____ Be physically active	_____ Make use of my skills
_____ Be committed to something	_____ Improve my skills
_____ Keep busy	_____ Develop my skills
_____ Do lots of different things	_____ Have something to show for
_____ Relax and take it easy	my efforts
_____ Gain knowledge	_____ Get approval for what I do
_____ Enjoy some time to myself	_____ Be successful at what I do
_____ Be spontaneous	_____ Learn more about myself
_____ Organize something	_____ Experience new things
_____ Lead a group of people	_____ Develop friendships
_____ Compete with others	_____ Help others
_____ Compete with myself to do	_____ Try my own method of doing
better	things
_____ Meet new people	_____ Be part of a group/team member
_____ Be in attractive surroundings	_____ Have a feeling of personal worth

The purpose of this exercise is to improve self-awareness, leisure awareness, and leisure-related decision-making skills. The person completing this form is to read through the list and choose ten (10) statements that best describe his own individual needs. Then the person is to rank the chosen ten statements in order of importance (e.g., 1= most important; 10 = least important). If this activity is conducted in a group (e.g., family members, couple, friends, etc.), people should discuss the reasons behind their rankings, which needs are met through their present recreation activities, and which additional activities may meet their needs.

(Reprinted with permission from N.J. Stumbo & S.R. Thompson, (Eds.), 1986, *Leisure Education: A Manual of Activities and Resources*)

After one has examined his leisure satisfaction needs, the next step is to choose what type of activity would best fulfill leisure satisfaction needs and also to focus on the features or characteristics of different types of activity. Activity characteristics are categorized in a variety of ways. Table 4-1 illustrates one method of characterizing activity.

Table 4-1
Activity Characteristic Groups

Activity Characteristics	Description
Competitive/recreational	Does the person like to keep score (e.g., determine the winner/best performance) or is participating more important than the final result?
Creative/defined	Does the individual wish to have the freedom to pursue individual ideas and interpretations rather than being restricted to establish rules/expectations?
Individual/group	Are activities with a large group of people of interest, or are activities alone or with a partner preferred?
Organized/unstructured	Is a class or organized program at a particular time and place preferred, or is an activity that can be done fairly spontaneously when time permits more appealing?
Physically active/sedentary	Does the person wish to be involved in strenuous physical activity, moderate physical activity, or sedentary activities?

(Adapted from Galvin & Scherer, 1996, *Evaluating, Selecting, and Using Appropriate Assistive Technology*, p. 165)

If the person has some kind of knowledge about existing recreation activities, the person can just use a blank sheet of paper to create a list. One side of the paper would list leisure needs while the other side would list activities (see Figure 4.2).

Figure 4.2
Matching Leisure Needs with Recreation Activity

Leisure Needs	Recreation Activities
Releasing tension	Physical exercise
Being in aesthetic surroundings	Outdoor activities - green, mountainous, quiet
To do something productive	Crafts, fix-up work, writing, photography
Organizing something	Volleyball team tournaments for local leagues
Assuming a leadership role	Captain of a volleyball team
Socializing	Dining out with friends
Displaying creativity	Painting, drawing, composing music
Enjoying solitude	Reading, listening to music, hiking alone
Obtaining knowledge	Surfing the Internet, taking continuing education courses

---

The individual can assign a recreation activity to each of the leisure needs or discover that a particular recreation activity (e.g., volleyball) can satisfy a variety of leisure needs. One can also list more than one activity corresponding to leisure satisfaction needs.

Another suggestion could be to use a generic Recreation Interest Survey form as self-assessment (see Appendix M). This form is quite basic, separating activities into categories and supplying columns for "Have done" and "Will do." The reasons behind the creation of a "Have done" column is to first, recognize that the person has been involved in a particular kind of recreation activity in her life. And second, take note of the reasoning behind decreasing involvement in (or abandoning) this activity that once pleased the leisure satisfaction need. This Recreation Interest Survey can be expanded for additional activities and check columns. One may want to add columns on "Presently doing" and "Never do." Within the "Presently doing" column, one can specify frequency of participation, such as twice a week, weekly, weekends only, monthly, seasonal, and yearly. This would benefit the person who wishes to track her overall participation level in recreation activities.

Building and Maintaining Successful Leisure Relationships

When discovering one's recreation interests, the most important factor is being given the opportunity to find those recreation interests. In referring to the previously expressed adage, "A family that plays together stays together," we can say it is true, if everyone enjoys participating in that chosen recreation activity. Stress can occur within relationships when one person is deciding group recreation activities without the input of other people. This is particularly true with family leisure pursuits. When a person dominates the leisure activity planning by attending activities that only satisfies his leisure satisfaction needs, then the rest of the group could find leisure very dissatisfying. One way to alleviate this problem is for everyone in the family to create a list of what they would like to do during leisure time. Next, compare all of the lists to see which activities listed are similar and which are different (see Figure 4.3).

This leisure exploration activity was used during family recreation day at a substance abuse treatment center in the Southwest that included people having learning disabilities and substance abuse diagnoses. The results revealed that family members and couples had very little insight into each other's recreation interests. From this exercise many family members and couples expanded their choices of recreation activities. This allowed others to fulfill their leisure needs and to grant equal freedom to choose recreation activities.

Leisure time together between parents and children helps in understanding one's interest, strengthening family ties, and developing skills. Below is an adaptation from Cicci (1990); it's a created list on how parents can contribute to building a successful leisure relationship with their children having learning disabilities:

Figure 4.3
The "I" and "We" of Recreation Likes

Ten (10) recreation activities "I" like to do are as follows:

1. _____	6. _____
2. _____	7. _____
3. _____	8. _____
4. _____	9. _____
5. _____	10. _____

Recreation activities "We" have in common are as follows:
(if couple only, no need to list names)

1. _____	Names: _____
2. _____	Names: _____
3. _____	Names: _____
4. _____	Names: _____
5. _____	Names: _____

On the top half of this form the individual fills out recreation interests. The bottom half of the form compares recreation interests of each family member. One family member is assigned the task of comparing lists and writing the names of family members who have similar interests. Family members discuss similarities, then the family or couple plan how these recreation activities can be incorporated into a scheduled family recreation activity. If for some reason family members do not have similar recreation interest, one of two situations can occur: individual family members can invite each other to experience the other person's recreation activity (just because a family member did not write it down does not necessarily mean he will not like the activity); or the topic of discussion would focus on allowing family members the freedom to participate in the recreation activity of choice without bias from other family members or between the couple.

1. Spend time alone with child immersed in an activity of mutual enjoyment. Board games work quite well between child and adult; they are also a teaching tool. Board games allow for the child to learn rules, follow directions, develop strategies, enjoy winning, and accept losing.

2. Do not overschedule your child's time. Efficient amounts of free time provide for easier planning of its use. Organization of free time requires practice.

3. Provide the child with opportunities to play a variety of games and activities, giving him the option to choose recreation activities he can become successful in.

4. Encourage your child to participate in recreation activities with other children; extend invitations for play at your home. This exposure can help the child build socialization skills, become cognizant of a peer's problem-solving ability, and learn about competitive and cooperative interactions.

An important part of maintaining a successful relationship is sharing enjoying leisure experiences. A large amount of a couple's time spent together is during leisure. This is when the couple is dining out, watching television, reading, discussing the day's events, gardening, entertaining, playing cards, vacationing, attending spectator events, etc. Planning ahead, being aware of each other's likes and dislikes, and being knowledgeable about characteristics of learning disabilities and its effects on the person's ability to participate in certain recreation activities can help in achieving a successful leisure experience. **Couple Captivated Fun** is a guide to having a meaningful leisure experience:

- **Courtesy** (asking what someone needs);
- **Planning** (inquiring about an activity before it takes place);
- **Corrective criticism** (determining when it takes place);
- **Allowing choice** (planning group activities jointly or allowing individual pursuits);
- **Praising** (giving feedback for a good job);
- **Togetherness** (honor is in being with the other person and not the performance the other person is demonstrating;
- **Teaching** (passing skills to each other for involvement in new recreation experiences);
- **Evaluating** (activity for ongoing enjoyment);
- **Determining** (type of play; competitive versus cooperative; group versus solitary);
- **Flexibility** (bending the rules; making game accommodations or modifications).

The previous list and guide supply a family or couple with the tools to create a successful leisure relationship, the most important component of which is full dedication and participation from each family member to make a successful leisure relationship a reality.

Learning Disabilities' Effect on Recreation Participation

Chapter Two contributed in-depth information on the different types of learning disabilities and how learning disabilities cause difficulty in interpreting daily tasks. This section will focus on its interference with recreation activities. Often, the public and even some professionals who are knowledgeable about learning disabilities forget that everyone has a life after school and after work. Do not let the word *learning* impede any thinking that problems associated with learning disabilities will only surface during school or work. A person may read during leisure time, and that does not always mean a novel. A person reads directions to complete a craft project, instructions to play a computer game, a description of a recipe, and even the gate number on an airplane boarding pass. Dyslexia does not cease when one is playing Scrabble®. Auditory perceptual ability does not suddenly improve because a child receives lower amounts of verbal instruction on the baseball field than in the classroom. Dyscalculia does not go away when playing a card game. Learning disabilities can affect every area of one's life, including participation in recreation activities.

What occurs when learning disabilities interfere with participation in recreation activities? First, the person may only wish to participate in activities that reveal his attributes. For example, an individual who excels naturally in physical activities (e.g., basketball, volleyball, golf, tennis, etc.) may feel more comfortable playing in physical activities than a game of Scattergories®, which requires the ability to hold information in memory, process written text quickly, recall accurately, and spell precisely. Even when a person excels in physical recreation activities, unexpected obstacles can appear. A few of these obstacles are reading and interpreting written game plays or formations (e.g., basketball, football, gymnastics, marching band, water polo, hockey, etc.), keeping track of a score (e.g., golf), and outmaneuvering your opponent through pre-planned shots (e.g., racquetball, volleyball, tennis).

In referring to the types of learning disabilities listed in Chapter Two, shown is a compilation of illustrations that describes how specific types of learning disabilities affect performance in recreational activities:

Dyscalculia. This can cause one to produce a sum that is incorrect, resulting in losing a game or in misplacement of ranking in golf. This also can cause difficulty in playing games such as dominos; scoring bowling or in any type of card game; casino gambling; calculating dining charges, etc.

Dyslexia. This inability to understand written language poses a problem when reading craft instructions, theater programs, movie subtitles, travel itineraries, tour guide brochures, and interpreting the directions in learning a new game.

Auditory Acuity Difficulty. This may be the problem if, when playing a game of basketball, a player continually does not respond to a coach's directions from the bench or does not respond to a teammate's verbal play-making messages.

Auditory-Vocal Association Problems. The characteristic is displayed when a person hears what was said, is subsequently able to acknowledge the auditory stimuli in a correct manner, and yet proceeds to perform an incorrect or inappropriate action. In football, upon hearing the signal for an interception, a defensive back stop, turns, and begins to tackle opposing players rather than block (Yellen & Yellen, 1987, p. 51).

Auditory Memory Deficit. This could be the problem if a person finds difficulty remembering directions or instructions that have been previously explained (e.g., just before game or during halftime when new instructions were stated). In volleyball, a player does not remember alterations to a defense play made by the team captain at halftime.

Auditory Sequencing Problem. Here a student experiences the inability to recall a series of auditory instructions. During tap dance instruction the student performs a shuffle step beginning with her left foot instead of her right foot and before an eight-count circle to her left.

Catastrophic Response. This can occur anytime when the individual is overloaded with too much visual and/or auditory stimuli and results in high frustration. A scenario could be that the person misread or did not double check the time to return to the bus from an outing. This resulted in the person and accompanying friend missing the bus to return to their hotel. They are standing at the wrong bus station surrounded by hundreds of tourists. His friend is yelling, people are everywhere, and the person shuts down for approximately one minute.

Cognitive Disorganization. With cognitive disorganization, a person may often miss or forget steps in a sequence. During a cub scout weekly assignment, 10-year-old Bob never brings all of the materials required to complete a project, or he constantly confuses the steps taken to achieve merit awards.

Crossing the Midline and Directional Problems. These problems become quite apparent during aerobic exercise or dance class, roller or ice skating instruction, driving small motorized vehicles (e.g., scooter, go-cart racing, bumper cars, boats, etc.) and locating a room in a hotel. This individual is unable to smoothly mimic the movements of the aerobic or dance instructor and experiences difficulty mirroring responses. Controlling the steering wheel, judgement of turns on a course, and going in the correct direction may require many practice runs before exhibiting adequate skills.

Disinhibition. A person exhibiting this problem often finds complications with "fitting in" groups, especially team recreation activities. Constant laughing at a teammate when the ball is dropped, always retrieving a shot within someone else's playing zone (e.g., volleyball), and continually talking loudly when silence is expected (e.g., opponent is putting in golf) could lead to dismissal from the team, if the individual is unable to correct these types of behaviors, or could result in peers not inviting this person to accompany them in a recreation activity again.

Intersensory Problem. Trouble using two senses at once could interfere with designing a piece of pottery or hand painting a ceramic dish and holding a conversation with a talkative person who is sitting in the adjacent seat. Individuals exhibiting this dilemma may not complete the task or may make numerous mistakes during the process due to engagement in conversation.

Short-term Memory Problem. A person with a short-term memory problem does not remember the sequence of a turn taken during a table game, forgets to place a bet before the next poker round, and may not remember what he betted during the current poker round.

Visual Acuity Problem. A player does not exhibit the ability to see clearly and differentiate objects in his visual field. In bowling, the bowler experiences problems in lining the bowling ball up with the range finders on the runway.

Poor Visual Coordination and Pursuit. Here the task of following and tracking objects causes distress. A person has trouble positioning himself to catch a frisbee or misjudges the landing of a spin on a tennis shot.

Visual Figure-Ground Differentiation Problem. With this type of problem the person never identified where the object was from the beginning; she has an inability to distinguish between objects in the foreground and background. In soccer, a player has difficulty seeing her teammates when conducting a "throw-in" to continue the play of game.

Visual-Motor, Spatial-Form Manipulation Problems. An individual finds complications in successfully moving in space and manipulating three-dimensional objects with this problem. Examples are placing jigsaw puzzle pieces in their correct location within a puzzle, maneuvering one's bicycle through an obstacle course, and even parallel parking one's car.

It is common for persons with learning disabilities to employ survival strategies when learning a new skill or interacting in a group situation. Examples of these strategies are as follows:

1. ***Learn from doing:*** Jim cannot understand the chalkboard plays so his mind frequently "fades" out during those sessions. Jim feels since he will run that particular football play three times out on the field before the next game, he'll be fine in learning that game play.

2. ***Observe what others do:*** Sally is always one step behind when Coach Smith verbally explains new jumps she wants the cheerleading squad to try. Sally chooses to stand near the end of the cheerleading squad line. By the time her turn comes, she can successfully perform the jumps just like everyone else in the group.

3. ***Develop a buddy system:*** Keith has a problem interpreting what his college football offensive line coach, Coach Green, says during films. During the weekly viewing of football films,

Keith may only catch about a third of what Coach Green is explaining. Keith developed a close friendship with George, who is also a member of the offensive line. Keith and George would get together for about an hour after films to discuss what Coach Green wants the offensive team to accomplish for the next game.

4. ***Awareness of instructors' expectations:*** It is common in organized athletic teams that one person's wrongdoings or mistakes can jeopardize the entire team; youngsters and adolescents respond quickly to peer pressure. April immediately became aware of timeliness when the coach made her and her gymnastic teammates run 25 laps around the gym, twice in one week, due to April arriving late to practice sessions. This only occurred the first week of training, and throughout the 16-week training period April was never late again.

These are just a few of the strategies considered "compensation" strategies that individuals with learning disabilities acquire throughout their lives. Some individuals learn them through life experience (the school of hard knocks), while others are fortunate enough to have someone provide them with guidance. It does not matter how compensation strategies are obtained, as long as they are mastered and utilized to render effective participation in a recreation activity of choice. Determining *how* one can partake in a recreation activity that may demonstrate areas of difficulty is the solution to successful inclusive recreation involvement.

Determining Recreation Participation Ability

After discovering what recreation activities are of interest to the individual, the next step is to assess what abilities are necessary to complete the tasks required in these recreation activities. How does one know what one requires in a particular activity if he has never taken part in that activity before? Well, it is called doing a little research. A person needs to discover what is involved before spending some money. The previous statement might appear quite simplistic to many, but not for those children and adults whose learning disabilities interfere with remembering, sequential organization, and task planning. These people may sign-up for a recreation activity at a community center and not realize it is an advanced course. They might also forget to purchase materials (e.g., book and craft supplies). These individuals might also assume that the instructor will hold a sailing class at the center every week instead of at the lake, thus excusing the need for obtaining adequate outdoor clothing. These are kinds of problems that can occur when a person does not ask questions about the particular activity.

Ability as it pertains to participation in recreation activities is threefold. The first stage encompasses resources: Does the person meet the necessities of the program? Does she have the money, equipment, and transportation to attend the program? In the second stage one assesses her physical, cognitive, and social/emotional ability. Is the individual at the correct fitness level? What type of thinking takes place during this activity? Does the instructor want participants to problem-solve independently? Can a person work alone or does she choose a partner for this activity? Do members of the group have to act out a situation (e.g., role playing) or reveal private accounts of one's life experiences? The third stage is time. Can one realistically schedule time to participate in this activity of choice at this present date? With adults working, some simultaneously attending college and others as parents, the question becomes: "Can times be effectively arranged to ensure successful participation in the recreation activity of choice?"

Time Management Factor

Understanding that situations change and allowing for flexibility are good characteristics to possess for managing time. The following scenario illustrates solving a schedule conflict with a family's leisure pursuits:

> Mille, a mother with learning disabilities, could not complete her continuing education course in Spanish because her son's soccer game schedule interfered with her Spanish classes. Mille incurred this problem at the eighth week of a 16-week course. How could she look into ways of alleviating this dilemma? One, she might choose to drop the Spanish course to attend soccer games and continue with the course next semester. Two, she might choose to continue learning the information outside class since the book and audio tapes are already available to her. Three, she could explore attending a similar Spanish class on a different afternoon. Or, four, she could have used a week view schedule log before signing up for the Spanish course to detect conflicting times.

Using a Week View Schedule Log allows for an individual to know what her overall week looks like (see Figures 4.4A & B). This schedule log contains information that is considered "constant": events, tasks, and assignments the person would conduct on a steady weekly basis. A person would fill in information such as daily work schedule, school schedule, study time, daily living activities (e.g., eating, bathing, cooking, picking up children, driving time, etc.), and recreation schedule.

In looking at Mille's schedule, she has free time from 3-4 p.m. on Monday, Wednesday, and Friday for continuing to learn the Spanish course materials independently (e.g., listening to tapes, reading the textbook). The other alternative could be to take the Spanish course at night and hire a babysitter to watch the children during class times.

To plan ahead for next month's activities, Mille should look at scheduling upcoming events on a monthly calendar (see Figures 4.5A & B). The events planned for the coming months should coincide with the free time available on the Week View Schedule Log. This means that Mille would not schedule any activity or event during work, her already scheduled exercise period, or during the children's home time (Monday through Friday, 4:00 p.m. to 9:00 p.m.). Using a Week View Schedule Log and Monthly Calendar makes planning family leisure activities less complicated.

"What Does One Need to Know?" Factor

Now that one is aware of time and the importance of scheduling recreation activities into one's life, what is required of one for participating in the recreation activity program? Questions to ask of the instructor or agency personnel before entering the recreation activity program include the following:

In arts, crafts, and some physical recreation classes—
- Will the entrance fee cover all of the supplies needed for this class?
- If "no" is the answer to the previous question asked, do I need to purchase supplies on my own?
- Where is the best place to purchase supplies or equipment?
- How much do supplies usually cost?
- Can I rent equipment? If I can rent equipment, what is the cost?

Figure 4.4A
Week View Schedule Log

Name_____

Times	Monday	Tuesday	Wednesday	Thursday	Friday	Saturday	Sunday
6-7 a.m.							
7-8 a.m.							
8-9 a.m.							
9-10 a.m.							
10-11 a.m.							
11-12 p.m.							
12-1 p.m.							
1-2 p.m.							
2-3 p.m.							
3-4 p.m.							
4-5 p.m.							
5-6 p.m.							
6-7 p.m.							
7-8 p.m.							
8-9 p.m.							
9-10 p.m.							
10-11 p.m.							
11-12 a.m.							
12-6 a.m.							

Figure 4.4B
Mille's Completed Week View Schedule Log

Times	Monday	Tuesday	Wednesday	Thursday	Friday	Saturday	Sunday
6-7 a.m.	--WAKE	UP--	↑	↑	↑	SLEEP IN	↑
7-8 a.m.	--Make	Breakfast--	--Get kids	off to	school--		WAKE--Prepare for church
8-9 a.m.	Work		Work	Work	Work	WAKE UP	Church
9-10 a.m.	←→	Food shopping	←→	←→	←→	Breakfast	
10-11 a.m.		Dry cleaning				Open recreation	
11-12 p.m.							
12-1 p.m.	LUNCH	↑	↑	↑	↑	↑	↑
1-2 p.m.	Going to exercise		Going to exercise		Going to exercise		
2-3 p.m.	Exercise	--Cleaning	Exercise	←→	Exercise	--Prepare	
3-4 p.m.		house--		←→			dinner--
4-5 p.m.	--Prepare	dinner--	↑	↑	↑	--Eat	dinner--
5-6 p.m.	--Eat	dinner--	↑	↑	↑	Free	time
6-7 p.m.	Help	children ■	with	homework ■	--	←→	↔
7-8 p.m.	◄ --Relax,	watch	T.V., or	read	--	↑	↑
8-9 p.m.	--Put kids	to bed--	↑	↑	↑	↑	↑
9-10 p.m.	--Continue	with T.V.	or reading--			↑	↑
10-11 p.m.	↔	↔	↔	↔	↔	↔	↔
11-12 a.m.	--Prepare	for bed--	↑	↑	↑	↑	↑
12-6 a.m.	SLEEP	SLEEP	SLEEP	SLEEP	SLEEP	SLEEP	SLEEP

◄ Rose Society Meeting - 2nd & 4th Monday of each month at 7 p.m.

■ Jill's Ballet Lessons - Tuesday & Thursday from 6-7 p.m.

● Next month is Mike's soccer practice - Monday, Wednesday, & Thursday from 4-5:30 p.m. Add to next month's weekview schedule log.

★ Next month is Mike's soccer games - 1st & 3rd Saturday from 2-4 p.m. Add to next month's weekview schedule log.

Figure 4.5A
Monthly Calendar

19_____   Month:_____

Notes:

Sun	Mon	Tue	Wed	Thu	Fri	Sat

Figure 4.5B
Mille's Monthly Calendar for October

19_____   Month: ____October____

Notes:● Mike's soccer practice - Monday, Wednesday, & Thursday 4-5:30 p.m. (Thursday - babysitter takes Mike to practice.)

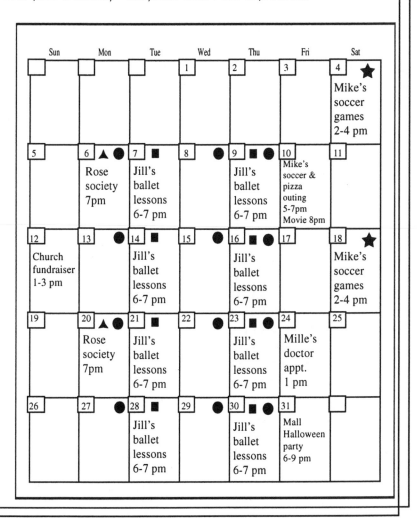

- Can an older edition of this book be used for this class?

In tours and recreation classes that dictate site visits -
- How many times during the recreation course will we attend this site?
- Will the agency supply transportation for the class to the tour site?
- If "no" is the answer to the previous question asked, will I receive directions on how to get there?
- Will we travel to the site as a group? or individually?
- Will there be a fee once I arrive at the site? If "yes" is the answer to the previous question asked, what will the charge be? Is this a "one time" fee or do I need to pay every time we go?

In general recreation classes, concerns about time and conduct in class—
- If I miss one or two classes, how can I make them up?
- Can I attend the class instructor's other class during the week to learn more about the subject or catch up with lecture information?
- Will the class instructor teach this class next month, season, semester, year, etc.?
- Whom would the class instructor recommend as a teacher I should take for the second part of this class?
- Do I have to work in groups?
- Do I have to work alone?
- Do I have to talk or present information in front of a group?
- Will homework assignments be required for the class?
- How often do I need to practice per week to become proficient at this task or sport?
- Do I have specific duties to perform during this activity?
- What type of skills should I possess before joining in this activity?
- Will I be ordered to reveal personal things about myself during class?
- Do students have to correct other class members about their performance in a task?

One strategy is to organize your thoughts first and make brief notes on paper before posing statements to the recreation instructor or agency personnel.

Assessment Instruments

Professionals can assess recreation participation ability through observations of the participant or by providing the participant with a formalized assessment self-survey instrument. Assessment is a means by which a professional can establish a meaningful baseline of the individual's abilities, aptitude, social/emotional outlook, and leisure-related interests. For school or behavioral center programs, prescription and implementation of a special recreation plan and/or a leisure counseling program cannot be targeted for a specific participant's outcomes unless a baseline is first obtained to decide the current level of participant functioning (Stumbo, 1992).

Professionals who most likely are interested in determining one's recreation ability are therapeutic recreation specialists, occupational therapists, adapted physical education teachers, recreation leaders, counselors, special education teachers, and counseling social workers. There are many instruments available to rate one's recreational ability, but most of these instruments were not developed for individuals having mild cognitive impairments and self-evaluation reporting. The following instruments are used by professionals in schools and clinical settings when the individual is observed during a recreation activity to rate his/her functional cognitive ability level: Functional Assessment of Characteristics for Therapeutic Recreation (FACTR) (Peterson, Dunn, & Carruthers, 1983), Ohio Leisure Skills Scales on Normal Functioning (OLSSON) (Olsson, 1988), General Recreation Screening Tool (GRST) (Burlingame, 1988), and Recreation Behavior Inventory (RBI) (Berryman & Lefebvre, 1981). These instruments are discussed in more detail in Appendix N.

The Cognitive Leisure Indicator instrument was developed to determine if one's cognitive ability has an effect on one's ability to participate in leisure activities. It is a three-page, forced-item Likert score, self-report instrument intended to measure perceived cognitive ability and perceived leisure participation ability. The author created the instrument through awareness that individuals who report having cognitive difficulties may not be aware of its effects on ability to participate effectively in leisure activities. The statistical data from the indicator form determines which area of cognitive functioning most affects leisure participation ability. The instrument has been tested with people having cognitive impairments (e.g., stroke, traumatic brain injury, learning disabilities) and people not having cognitive impairments. Its findings determined that this instrument can detect differences in functional ability and recreation participation ability between those having cognitive impairments and those not displaying cognitive impairments. A sample of this self-report inventory is in Appendix O, labeled "Cognitive Leisure Indicator Form," and provides directions, validity, and reliability reports. An abbreviated checklist of the Cognitive Leisure Indicator Form is also available; see Appendix P, "Cognitive Leisure Checklist," for a specific explanation.

The professionals listed in this section—caregivers, parents, spouses, or persons with learning disabilities—can review this chapter's appendix section to see what instruments would best suit one's particular situation. Assessment determines one's present abilities and skills and is used as a guideline, not a permanent diagnosis. Through the ability to question recreation participants, the professional can realistically determine recreation competency.

Steps in Recreation Participation

Early federal laws addressed the need for persons with disabilities to receive equal opportunities within the community. Public Law 94 -142, the *Education for All Handicapped Children Act*, and PL 101-476, the *Individuals with Disabilities Education Act* (IDEA), requires that a free appropriate public education, which includes special education and related services (recreation and recreation therapy), be available to children and youth with disabilities in mandated age ranges (3 to 21). These laws implemented the *least restrictive environment* (LRE) concept. LRE suggests that children with disabilities are to be educated, to the maximum extent possible, alongside their nondisabled peers. This also includes participation in community recreation programs.

Integration provides the opportunity to learn from and to socialize with nondisabled peers. Participation in integrated environments is also believed to be beneficial for the nondisabled participants, as explored by Schleien and Ray (1988). Attitudes of nondisabled individuals toward their peers having a disability have been extensively studied, resulting in better acceptance and understanding of the individual having the disability by the nondisabled peer. Full inclusion of people with disabilities into community recreation programs is essential in the process of living a normal life. An effective integration program requires that general program staff, teachers, coaches, recreation specialists, parents, and spouses work collaboratively. Private and public community recreation service providers should network to exchange ideas, offer solutions to problems, and share resources, making their environments as accessible as possible. The main goal is for the individual with a disability to have enjoyable and successful leisure experiences, just as nondisabled persons do, in community recreation programs.

Basic Steps for Community Recreation Participation

The following steps assure active involvement in community recreation programs for a person with learning disabilities.

1. *Identify a preferred recreation activity.*
   - Become aware of a community recreation setting/activity through yellow pages, newspaper, radio, and television advertisements.
   - Become motivated in visiting community recreation settings/activities.
   - Request information about location of and directions to facilities; obtain a program brochure for specific information on activity schedules and fees.

2. *Arrange to attend recreation activities.*
   - Complete program registration procedures.
   - If under an age restriction, obtain guardian permission.
   - Ascertain cost of the program.
   - Arrange transportation to the facility.
   - Inquire about appropriate attire and any necessary materials/equipment for the activity.
   - If one does not own appropriate attire and materials/equipment required for activity, then purchase it.
   - Ask other questions (see the section "Determining Recreation Participation Ability"—questions to ask an instructor or agency personnel before entering recreation activity programs).
   - Determine what kinds of accommodations or modifications the agency can arrange for one's participation in the activity.
   - Drive to the program site before the first class session (if the activity is not held at the recreation facility where registered or if you experience directionality problems).

3. *Commute to recreation activity programs.*
   - Prepare before leaving home: bring required funds, clothing, and materials/equipment.
   - Travel via selected mode of transportation.
   - If using own vehicle, park in designated area.
   - Take funds, clothing, and materials/equipment into facility and locate activity or program area (if experiencing difficulty finding program area, ask staff in facility for assistance).

4. *Participate in targeted recreation activity.*
   - Complete sign-in and equipment/materials checkout procedures (if necessary).
   - Locate appropriate area to engage in activity.
   - Engage in activity; exhibit questioning to assure understanding of tasks involved in an activity.
   - Sign out (if required) and return any equipment/materials following the end of an activity.
   - If you brought your own equipment, double check to make sure you are taking your own equipment home.
   - If aware of additional modifications or accommodations needed to improve involvement in the activity, discuss this matter with the instructor so staff can make arrangements before the next activity session.

5. *Leaving recreation facilities.*
   - Leave program area with clothing and equipment/materials brought.
   - If activity ends at night, ask a peer to escort you to your vehicle to assure safety.
   - Leave program area to return home or to prearranged location.

(Excerpts adapted from Schleien & Ray, 1988, *Community Recreation and Persons with Disabilities: Strategies for Integration,* pp. 54-55)

This brief outline covers the basic steps an individual would take when participating in a community recreation activity. This outline may seem simplistic to some, but for those who would experience organizational problems, memory impairments, attention deficit to details, or directionality deficits, this outline is beneficial.

   Persons having learning disabilities should be exposed to leisure education. The teaching of leisure skills, awareness of satisfaction during leisure time, perception of leisure, inquiring about leisure activities, enhancing leisure skills, appropriate conduct in leisure activities, and location of leisure resources are some of the topics that can be addressed when teaching leisure education. Murphy, Niepoth, Jamieson, & Williams (1991) explained various models of leisure education that instruct individuals in the process of enjoying leisure activities:

> The authors cite the Peterson and Gunn (1984) model that focuses on awareness of leisure and leisure resources, and activity and social interaction skills. The Mundy (1987) model adds attention to self-awareness and decision-making processes. The Howe and Carpenter (1985) model suggests a continuum of leisure education based on needs of the individual .... some people only need information that tells them what activities are available and where to find them at one end; other people with psychological or attitudinal problems related to leisure requiring more complex intervention (leisure counseling) are at the opposite end. In between these two ends of the continuum, leisure education may take the form of experiences that increase awareness, clarify values, or develop skills. (p. 230)

For the child with learning disabilities in a special education program, leisure education is a valid component of that child's transition plan. The main emphasis of PL 101-476 is the requirement that by age 16 young adults with disabilities must have included in their Individual Education Program (IEP) "a statement of needed transition services" (Lichtenstein & Michaelides, 1993, p. 183). Transition pertains to

> a change in status from behaving primarily as a student to assuming emergent adult roles in the community. These roles include employment, participation in post-secondary education, maintaining a home, becoming appropriately involved in the community, and experiencing satisfactory personal and social relationships. The process of enhancing transition involves the participation and coordination of school programs, adult agency services, and natural supports within the community. (Halpern, 1994, p. 117)

Leisure is incorporated in the roles of "community involvement" and "developing satisfactory personal and social relationships." The previous section "Basic Steps to Community Recreation Participation" outlines how one can become involved in community recreation, an important component to teaching leisure within the school system. The individual with learning disabilities having a network of friends or associates can aid in the continuation and exploration of community recreation. The development of short-term and long-term leisure goals, introducing the student to community recreation agencies, and creating a follow-up plan including leisure monitoring by community agency personnel (e.g., college support services, social services, vocational rehabilitation, or developmental disabilities agencies) provide one with the skills to construct organized leisure time. Teaching the tools vital for successful participation in a recreation activity would certainly help deter any major problems involved with planning and participating in recreation activities of choice in the future.

References

Academy of Leisure Sciences & Driver, B.L. (1994). *The benefits to leisure*. Academy white papers on leisure, recreation, and tourism. Internet address: http://www.georg.ualberta.ca/als1.html.

Barnett, L.A. (1991). Developmental benefits of play for children. In B.L. Driver, P.J. Brown, & G. L. Peterson (Eds.), *Benefits of leisure*. State College, PA: Venture Publishing, Inc.

Baum, A. (1991). A psychophysical perspective, with emphasis on relationships between leisure, stress, and well-being. In B.L. Driver, P.J. Brown, & G.L. Peterson (Eds.), *Benefits of leisure*. State College, PA: Venture Publishing, Inc.

Cicci, R. (1990). What's wrong with me? Learning disabilities at home and school. Baltimore, MD: York Press.

Galvin, J.C., & Scherer, M.J. (1996). *Evaluating, selecting, and using appropriate assistive technology*. Gaithersburg, MD: Aspen Publishing.

Halpern, A.S. (1994). The transition of youth with disabilities to adult life: A position statement of the Division on Career Development and Transition. *Career Development for Exceptional Individuals*, 17(2), p. 117.

Henderson, K.A., Bialeschki, D.M., Shaw, S.M., & Freysinger, V.J. (1989). *A leisure of one's own: A feminist perspective on women's leisure*. State College, PA: Venture Publishing, Inc.

Howe, C.Z., & Carpenter, G.M. (1985). *Programming leisure experiences*. Englewood Cliffs, NJ: Prentice-Hall.

Lichtenstein, S., & Michaelides, N. (1993, Fall). Transition from school to young adulthood: Four case studies of young adults labelled mentally retarded. *Career Development for Exceptional Individuals*, 16(2), p. 183.

McConkey, R., & McGinley, P. (Eds.). (1990). *Innovations in leisure and recreation for people with a mental handicap*. Lancashire, Eng.: Lisieux Hall, Whittle-le-Woods.

McGill, J. (1984). Training for integration: Are blindfolds really enough? *Journal of Leisurability, 11(2)*, pp. 12-15.

Merriam Webster's Collegiate Dictionary, 10th ed. (1995). Springfield, MA: Merriam-Webster, Inc. (p. 665).

Mundy, J. (1987). Leisure education. In A. Graefe & S. Parker (Eds.), *Recreation and leisure: An introductory handbook*. State College, PA: Venture Publishing, Inc.

Murphy, J.F., Niepoth, E.W., Jamieson, L.M., & Williams, J.G. (1991). *Leisure systems: Critical concepts and applications*. Champaign, IL: Sagamore Publishing.

Orthner, D.K., & Mancini, J.A. (1991). Benefits of leisure for family bonding. In B.L. Driver, P.J. Brown, & G.L. Peterson (Eds.), *Benefits of leisure*. State College, PA: Venture Publishing, Inc.

Paffenbarger, Jr., R.S., Hyde, R.T., & Dow, A. (1991). Health Benefits of Physical Activities. In B.L. Driver, P.J. Brown, & G.L. Peterson (Eds.), *Benefits of leisure*. State College, PA: Venture Publishing, Inc.

Peterson, C.A., & Gunn, S.L. (1984). *Therapeutic recreation program design: Principles and procedures*. Englewood Cliffs, NJ: Prentice-Hall.

Random House Unabridged Dictionary, Second ed. (1993). New York: Random House. (p. 1100).

Roggenbuck, J.W., Loomis, R.J., & Dagostino, J.V. (1991) .The learning benefits of leisure. In B.L. Driver, P.J. Brown, & G.L. Peterson (Eds.), *Benefits of leisure*. State College, PA: Venture Publishing, Inc.

Schleien, S.J., & Ray, T.M. (1988). *Community recreation and persons with disabilities: Strategies for integration*. Baltimore: Paul H. Brookes.

Stumbo, N.J. (1992) *Leisure education II: More activities and resources*. State College, PA: Venture Publishing, Inc.

Stumbo, N.J., & Thompson, S.R. (Eds.). (1986). *Leisure education: A manual of activities and resources*. Illinois: Central Illinois Center for Independent Living and Easter Seal Leisure Resource Center.

Talbot, M. (1979). *Women and leisure*. A review for the Sports Council/SSRC. Joint Panel on Recreation and Leisure Research.

Taylor, C.B., Sallis, J.F., & Needle, R. (1985). *The relation of physical activity and exercise to mental health*. Public Health Reports, 100, pp. 195-202.

The American Heritage Dictionary of the English Language, Third ed. (1992). Boston: Houghton Mifflin Co. (p. 1029).

Yellen, A.G., & Yellen, H. (1987). *Understanding the learning disabled athlete: A guide for parents, coaches, and professionals*. Boston: C.C. Thomas.

Resources on Functional Assessment Instruments

Functional Assessment of Characteristics for Therapeutic Recreation (FACTR) (Peterson, Dunn, & Carruthers, 1983) Developed 1983, published 1984.

Burlingame, J., & Blaschko, T.M. (1990). *Assessment tools for recreational therapy*. Redbook #1. Seattle, WA: Frontier Publishing.

Dunn, J.K. (1984). Assessment. In C.A. Peterson & S.L. Gunn (Eds.), *Therapeutic recreation program design: Principles and procedures* (2nd ed.).

Ohio Leisure Skills Scales on Normal Functioning (OLSSON) Olsson, R.H. (1988). The effectiveness of a computerized leisure.

Burlingame, J., & Blaschko, T.M. (1990). *Assessment tools for recreational therapy*. Redbook #1. Seattle, WA: Frontier Publishing.

Olsson, R.H. (1990). The Ohio leisure skills scales for normal-functioning: A systems approach to clinical assessment. In G.L. Hitzhusen & J.O. Neil (Eds.), *Expanding horizons in therapeutic recreation XIII*, (pp. 132-145). Columbia, MO: University of Missouri.

General Recreation Screening Tool (GRST) (Burlingame, 1988)

Burlingame, J., & Blaschko, T.M. (1990). *Assessment tools for recreational therapy*. Redbook #1. Seattle, WA: Frontier Publishing.

Recreation Behavior Inventory (RBI) (Berryman & Lefebvre, 1984)

Berryman, D., & Lefebvre, C. (1984). *Recreation behavior inventory*. Denton, TX: Leisure Learning Systems.

Chapter Five

DELIVERY OF RECREATION PROGRAMS TO PERSONS WITH LEARNING DISABILITIES

The previous chapter centered on persons with learning disabilities becoming involved in recreation activities. This chapter examines how recreation service providers can assist in securing a satisfactory leisure experience for individuals with learning disabilities. Public and private recreation agencies and departments, through knowledge of federal laws, proper staff training, understanding usage of special equipment and activity modification, can effectively deliver high quality recreation programs to individuals having learning disabilities.

Federal Legislation's Influence on Inclusive Community Recreation Programming

A number of legislative measures were created to guarantee equal opportunity for people with disabilities. These measures were Public Law 99-457, the *Handicapped Children's Early Education Programs;* PL 94-142, the *Education for All Handicapped Children Act;* PL 93-112, the *Rehabilitation Act of 1973;* PL 101-476, the *Individuals With Disabilities Education Act;* and PL 101-336, the *Americans With Disabilities Act.* The first four laws mandate equal access to public education, diagnostic assessment, allied health services, and physical entities (buildings where federally-funded programs are housed), and encourages parents of a person with disabilities to contribute to education plans. The last law, the Americans with Disabilities Act (ADA), is to "provide a clear and comprehensive national mandate for the elimination of discrimination against persons with disabilities."

The ADA prohibits discrimination on the basis of disability in employment, public services, and public accommodations. This law contains five main sections—Title I: Employment, Title II: Public Services, Title III: Public Accommodations, Title IV: Telecommunications Relays, and Title V: Miscellaneous. Individuals with learning disabilities are covered under all five titles of the law. With this book's interest in equal and fair participation of people with learning disabilities in recreation activities, Title II: Public Services (*A. Government Services*) and Title III: Public Accommodations would most appropriately address this area.

Title II: Public Services—*A: Government Services*—Any unit of state or local government, or any extension, department, or instrument thereof, in delivering local government services, is prohibited from discriminating on the basis of disability against an individual who, with or without a reasonable accommodation, meets essential eligibility requirements for receipt of that service. State and local government services are broadly interpreted to include every program, service, and activity of such an entity. A reasonable accommodation shall include, but is not limited to, the changing of rules, policies, and practices; the removal of architectural, transportation, and communication barriers; and the provision of auxiliary aids and services. A city or county recreation department offering a community program is under the auspices of Title II.

Title III: Public Accommodations—Any private, nonprofit business that provides goods, services, or facilities for the public is prohibited from discriminating on the basis of disability in the provision of those public accommodations. Entities must provide reasonable accommodations for individuals with disabilities who meet essential eligibility requirements (e.g., basic requirements for program entry or participation: fees, equipment or materials, conduct, capacity limit, etc.) for public accommodations provided by that entity.

(Excerpts adapted from J. McGovern, 1991, *the Americans with Disabilities Act: Implications for Change in Recreation and Park Agencies*.)

Title III: Public Accommodations—This defines *public accommodations* as the following:

1. privately operated entities whose operations affect commerce, including inns, hotels, motels, or other places of lodging (exempting establishments located within an owner-occupied residence and contains no more than five rooms for rent or hire—bed and breakfast places);
2. restaurants, bars, or other establishments serving food or drink;
3. movie theaters, other theaters, concert halls, stadiums, or other places of exhibition or entertainment;
4. auditoriums, convention centers, lecture halls, or other places of public gathering;
5. retail sales establishments, including bakeries, grocery stores, clothing stores, hardware stores, and shopping centers;
6. service establishments, including laundromats, dry cleaners, banks, barber shops, beauty shops, travel services, shoe repair services, funeral parlors, gas stations, accounts' or lawyers' offices, pharmacies, insurance offices, doctors' and other health providers' offices, and hospitals;
7. terminals, depots, or other stations used for specified public transportation;
8. museums, libraries, galleries, and other places of public display or collection;
9. parks, zoos, amusement parks, or other places of recreation;
10. schools of all levels;
11. social service centers, including day-care and senior citizen centers, homeless shelters, food banks, and adoption agencies;
12. places of exercise or recreation, including gyms, health spas, bowling alleys, and golf courses.

(Rovner, July 1990, "For the Record—Provisions: Americans with Disabilities Act." *Congressional Quarterly*, p. 2440)

This law paves the way for inclusive community programming. If an individual with learning disabilities chooses to participate in a Monday and Thursday, 6-7 p.m., six-week model airplane class with 25 other participants, instead of the Monday and Thursday, 5-6 p.m., eight-week model airplane class with a participant limit of 15, then he has the right to do so. The eight-week class might be better suited for a person who experiences difficulties reading instructions (especially diagrams and directions); the class instructor may spend more individual instruction time with her students and tasks might be demonstrated in more steps. This is something that the program director can suggest to the individual if he discloses about the nature of learning disabilities during registration for the activity, but the individual cannot be forced or prohibited from attending the selected recreation activity of choice. If this person does experience difficulty with reading model instructions, the instructor for this class, as in any other class this individual attends, must provide the person with certain accommodations or modifications. The modification could be additional explanations about model construction, the use of paint or fingernail polish to color code numbers on models for easy identification, or enlarged Xerox copy of directions. An accommodation could be using a Visualtek machine (for the enlargement of reading materials), a Kurzweil Reading Edge (a machine for synthesizing speech from printed text), or a colored overhead projection sheet (placed over instructions to eliminate the "floating or 3-D effect" of text) for clearer reading of text on class handouts.

Some programs held by community recreation agencies will have stipulations for participation, which under the ADA is called *eligibility criteria.*This means that

> A public entity may not impose eligibility criteria for participation in its programs, services, or activities that either screen out or tend to screen out persons with disabilities, unless it can show that such requirements are necessary for the provision of the service, program, or activity. (ADA Title II Technical Assistance Manual, 1996, p.12)

Eligibility criteria can consist of health and safety requirements, cost of service, knowledge or experience in activity, equipment and material usage, and training guidelines. Examples of eligibility criteria are as follows:

1. Requirement of a county recreation program that all participates registered to partake in the scuba program must pass the agency's swimming test. This test demonstrates that being able to swim is necessary for safe participation in the class. This test is permitted even if it unfortunately screens out people having particular kinds of disabilities.

2. All persons (regardless of disabilities or not) interested in en-
    rolling in the Stained Glass: Intermediate course held at the
    continuing education center of a local college must pay a fee
    of $170 and have basic knowledge of cutting glass and assem-
    bly in both copper foil and lead. Even if a person meets these
    requirements, entry to class is not guaranteed due to the class
    enrollment limit of six.

3. A beginning photography class provides an in-depth introduc-
    tion to 35mm camera operation—the function of F-stops, proper
    use of shutter speeds, and metering techniques, along with other
    important photography topics. A 35mm SLR camera with shut-
    ter speed and F-stop controls is required for use in this class,
    and four rolls of color slide film will be used as well. Purchase
    of film and the cost of film development will be approximately
    $75. Enrollment is limited to 12 and the cost of this five-week
    class is $100. Regardless of a disability or not, the person must
    use the designated equipment and materials and pay the re-
    quired fees as stated in the agency's brochure description of
    class in order to participant in this class.

Examples of ADA's Impact on Recreation and Parks Departments

Problem: Programs for people with disabilities that are not
equal to programs available for people without disabilities.

*   A state recreation facility that offers 80 seasonal programs
    for people without disabilities, but has only 20 programs
    for those with disabilities.
*   A camping facility that has a six-week summer camp for
    children without disabilities and a two-week summer camp
    session for children with disabilities and requires that chil-
    dren with disabilities must enroll in the two-week summer
    camp specified for children with disabilities.

Solution: All department programs must be open to people
having disabilities and must provide modifications as needed.

Problem: Agencies inflexible to changing staffing patterns to accommodate a participant's need for additional attention, enabling him to learn and enjoy the recreation activity.

- A city community center refuses to provide additional staff or supervision when necessary for a person with a disability to enjoy the activity (e.g., one-on-one golf lessons for a person with physical or cognitive impairment during or after the instruction class; a sign language interpreter for hearing impaired people in a ceramics class, etc.)
- An indoor golf center charging the participant with a disability additional fees for requiring extra assistance in an activity (e.g., use of a second staff member or activity leader spending more time with the participant before or after an activity session).

Solution: The recreation leader carefully reads all of the participant's registration information. If an individual discloses, call or meet with this potential participant to discuss the need for accommodations or possible program modifications. The professional may also need to consult with professionals in the community, such as special education teachers, adapted physical education teachers, or therapeutic recreation specialists for alternative teaching approaches to an activity. If the solution warrants an additional staff person to provide the accommodations (e.g., five extra one-on-one lessons) then the recreation leader makes those arrangements). Unless it is stated within the guidelines of the department and advertised in the brochure (e.g., a beginning 10-week golf class is $80, but if anyone would like to receive extra lessons the price is $10 per hour) the agency cannot charge participants with disabilities additional fees for requiring extra assistance. Persons with learning disabilities do not wish to have freebies, charity, or handouts bestowed upon them. What may happen is that either the adult having the learning disability or a parent of a child with a learning disability will offer the recreation leader or supervisor a fee for extra one-on-one instruction of an activity, despite whether an additional fee is warranted. Accepting money for this arrangement is based on the department's or agency's policies and procedures handling such a matter. What is important to remember about this situation is consistency and fairness of policies and procedures with all participants.

Problem: Registration for recreation programs by persons with disabilities only at certain times and places.

- Limiting racquetball lesson registrations for people with disabilities to Friday at 10:00 a.m. because the staff person who is knowledgable about disabilities will be working at that time.
- A parent signing up his child for baseball requested to talk with someone about his child's special needs and is told he must come back later in the week to personally speak with the league director.

Solution: All staff members should be exposed to knowledge about disabilities within their staff training or job orientation. Staff members are not expected to become "experts" in the field of disabilities, but should be able to exercise sufficient communication ability. The staff person could pose the questions in such a way that they receive appropriate answers that would further assist the recreation leader in preparing her sessions to accommodate the person having disabilities. Individuals with disabilities lead busy lives like everyone else; informing someone to return later could result in the agency or department losing a potential customer. This customer may not see the agency as competent or friendly (does not exhibit the ability or interest to inquire about the customer's needs). The proper response from a staff person is to relay a message from this customer to the league director and inform the individual that the league director would call him to talk about this matter. Agencies and departments must allow persons with disabilities to register at the same times as persons who do not have disabilities.

Undue Hardship and Reasonable Accommodations Terminology in ADA

The purpose of ADA is to prohibit discrimination and ensure equal access. Equal access can be achieved in many different ways that will not cause hardship on the entity supplying the accommodation. An establishment conducts business to successfully serve many people; checks of credits and debits are part of a balance sheet permitting the establishment to run efficiently. The question for establishments is how to deliver good services or products at the most effective cost. The answers to this question deviate from establishment to establishment. Undue hardship and reasonable accommodation evaluate what type of situation is best for each business and customer. Businesses are always eager to have return customers. It is a way to rate customer satisfaction.

The ADA states *reasonable accommodation* as changing policies, practices, or procedures; removing architectural barriers; removing communication barriers; removing transportation barriers; and providing auxiliary aids or services. *Undue hardship* under the ADA means action requiring significant difficulty or expense. This stipulates factors to be considered in determining whether a specific accommodation would impose an undue hardship—nature and cost of the accommodation needed, overall financial resources of the agency involved in the accommodation (impact of agency operation), and type of operation covered in an entity. The following scenarios depict agencies experiencing undue hardship with requested accommodations and the solution—reasonable accommodations—to deter that hardship from occurring.

John: John, who has severe dyslexia, attends an after-school program. One hour of activities often consists of table games such as Scrabble®, Scattergories®, Skip-Bo®, Monopoly®, Life®, etc. John is very hesitant about participating in table games where the game instructions require spelling. He has access to a computer at school for checking his spelling and he is wondering why he can't use a computer to check his spelling before entering an answer in the game. He informed the after-school program director about this matter and asked that a computer be purchased for him to check spelling during a word game.

The after-school program is housed in a community center. Presently, the community center has two computers used by staff during after-school program hours to input the day's attendance data. The center would have to rearrange staff hours to later that evening for data input. It would be nice for the after-school program to purchase a computer, but due to budget constraints and staff cutbacks there is no money to purchase a computer. Even delaying the hours of staff because of shift-differential pay and added cost of building utilities for long operating hours would present a hardship to the after-school program. The director suggested other accommodations such as teaming with a peer to act as "editor" of the student's word answers, as with Scrabble®, and to allow the use of a dictionary and cooperative play (e.g., assisting each other in creating and spelling words) or the use of a small electronic spell checker. John said he never thought about asking a friend, but then remembered that Bob always helps him with his spelling in homework and Bob wouldn't mind being his "editor." The director explained the program could purchase an electronic spell checker for under $50. This equipment can also be utilized by other students completing their homework during the program's homework period. There is no need to spend $1,000 or more on a computer or add an additional $3 more per hour to a staff salary plus extra building utility expenses each week when a reasonable accommodation could cost between $0 and $50.

Jill: Jill is an adult with reading comprehension difficulty, slow processing speed, and Scotopic Sensitivity Syndrome (visual perceptual problem plagued with perceiving printed text differently, restricted span of recognition, sustained attention difficulty, and poor depth perception, often found to coexist with learning disabilities). She is taking a drawing course at the local high school's continuing education program. Part of the course requirement is to read short-stories about a presented artist's works before drawing a rendition of that artist's works. Jill is not comfortable reading or drawing in this classroom; the text and picture details in the book look fuzzy, giving a 3-D type of effect, and images are distorted. The walls of the room are cinder box white. The tile on the floor is white with light blue specks. The tables where students work are bright white, and the lighting in the room is too bright. She is also having trouble completing the reading and drawing before class concludes. The instructor expects all of his students to have their drawing completed by the end of class. Jill, who is knowledgable about her visual-perceptual, reading, and processing problems, informs the instructor that he needs to move his class to another room; she cannot read or draw in that room and needs extra time to complete her drawings.

The instructor informs Jill that this is the only room available in this building, but there is space at the Northside Community Center, which is approximately ten miles away. The instructor polls the class to see if they would like to move the class to the Northside Community Center; the majority rule "no." The reason they stated is that they chose this facility because it is close to their home or work. The instructor agrees with the majority to keep the class in its present location, but grants Jill extra time to complete her drawings. He allows her to finish her drawings at home, then submit them to him during the next class period. She would not be penalized for a late submission. Jill is still upset about the classroom not being changed. "If the class can't move, how am I going to read and draw? Everything is too bright," Jill complained.

The instructor thought about ways to darken the room. He asked the maintenance man if he could unscrew two florescent ceiling light bulbs every Tuesday and Thursday evening for the next eight weeks. The maintenance man stated it would be no problem, just to write a work order for this request. Her classmates did not object to less light in the class; in fact, they thought it would make the environment more conducive to drawing. The instructor, along with help from Jill, decided to bring large rolls of butcher block (brown) paper to class to cover the tables. This would serve two purposes, prevent permanent stains on the table and decrease the glare from the ceiling florescent light onto her book. She also would use beige drawing paper to create her renditions, which would provide an easier visual focus of drawn images. These accommodations made the classroom environment conducive to learning for Jill.

What would have caused *undue hardship*? Having all class members relocate 10 miles to another facility. The *reasonable accommodation* was adjusting lighting, using the butcher block paper to cover tables, and allowing extra time to complete drawings. The accommodation could have been taken a step further by having Jill place a colored (blue to purple tones) transparency (used for overhead projectors) on top of the page she was reading. Reading text through the colored transparency decreases the glare on the white paper, thus making the text clearer and helping to extend reading time.

Marcia: Marcia wants to enroll in a tennis course. In reviewing her work and personal schedule, the only agency that has classes that match her schedule is the Brenton-Wooden Tennis Club. This private tennis club advertises tennis lessons to the general public. The classes are small, approximately 4 to 6 participants, at a cost of $220 for 16 lessons.

Marcia has always had problems with following objects in space (visual figure-ground difficulties), positioning self correctly to hit a moving object (depth perception, coordination problems), and directing objects to a specific target. With a small class, she felt her problems would be minimal.

The tennis instructor, Dennis, a former tennis professional, teaches class in a high-pressured, rigorous, fast-paced manner. This presented difficulty for Marcia. The instructor told her she was too slow, he could not repeat instructions three or four times, and she was wasting her time being in his class. His comments also mentioned how her slowness would hold the group behind, therefore, impinging on the next group's lesson. He claims, "if the lessons continue to run beyond their scheduled times my next group will cancel their lessons, making the club lose money!"

Marcia, tearful and frustrated, informed the tennis supervisor about the difficulties she was having in the tennis class. The supervisor empathizes with her concerns, but states that the lessons cannot run any later than the provided allotment of time; the club must adhere to its schedule. He allows her to receive extra lessons at other times during the week with a slower-paced instructor and informs her to try using an oversized racket at all her class lessons. The supervisor will also instruct the tennis professional to wrap her right hand with athletic tape or an Ace bandage to secure her grip during forehand practice and to allow a double bounce return of balls in practice games. Marcia agreed in trying these accommodations and within two weeks noticed improvements in her tennis skills.

The possible *undue hardship* would have been for her class to extend its lesson time, interfering with the next scheduled class. This meant the students in her class and the next class would have to change their overall schedule for the day to accommodate Marcia receiving extra time. This could have resulted in many students leaving the tennis program. But the *reasonable accommodation* suitable to all parties was scheduling extra lessons and acquiring different equipment and practice game modifications; this enabled Marcia to continue on a successful note with her tennis lessons. It would be beneficial to this club to implement disability sensitivity training within its employee training program to assure that problems like this do not occur again. What the previous agencies in the scenario displayed was *good faith effort*; making arrangements of accommodations for the individuals having disabilities, so they could enjoy participation in that program alongside nondisabled peers. When the agency knows the laws that promote and protect the rights of persons having disabilities, respects the requests for accommodations or program modifications from persons having disabilities, and displays a caring and professional attitude toward arranging accommodations, the risk of inequality is nonexistent.

Establishing Recreation Opportunities for Individuals with Disabilities

The following advice can assist an agency or department in reaching that ideal "Inclusive Community Recreation Program."

1. Adhere to ADA guidelines regarding employment, public access, available/accessible transportation, and communication devices. Conduct an ADA self-evaluation of your agency to determine compliance and ability to accommodate needs of individuals with disabilities (see ADA Self-evaluation Guide reference in Chapter 7).

2. Allow adults with disabilities or parents of children with disabilities the opportunity to participate as members of community recreation advisory boards. The transition to inclusive community recreation is much smoother when a person having a disability is represented when partaking in the development

and implementation of services beneficial to the well-being of people having disabilities. When agencies and departments form advisory boards, they should actively publicize the philosophy and duties of that advisory board, being an "equal opportunity employer" and that "individuals with disabilities are encouraged to apply." Some advisory board members are appointed by government officials. Educate your government officials to the importance of appointing one or more members who have disabilities to the board. Also, take advantage of the knowledge community experts have in programming and delivering services to individuals with disabilities (mental health counselors; social workers; physical, occupational, art, and music therapists; special education teachers; therapeutic recreation specialists; physicians; nurses) as potential advisory board members.

3. Advertise programs or events through the media (print, television, radio, etc.) about facilities and programs being accessible, for example, providing recorded tour descriptions; programs in large type or Braille; reserved front row seating; wheelchair accessibility; one-on-one instruction; and volunteers to assist those with special needs, etc. During an agency's television or magazine advertisement, illustrate the universal symbol for disabilities or feature a person having a disability. Send the agency a schedule of events and activities to public and private social/cultural associations that serve persons having disabilities or contains members having disabilities.

4. Involve persons with disabilities in the planning and evaluation process of agency programming, public relations, and facility construction. This matter will often be addressed in agencies having advisory members with disabilities, but not in some private agencies (e.g., bowling alley, billiard hall, restaurant, nightclub, etc.). Directors or supervisors of private agencies can contact a community recreation department to inquire about seeking the skills of a person having a disability (e.g., advisory board member, employee, member of an association, etc.) in assisting the commercial agency to develop a more accessible program. The directors or supervisors can also meet with the director of an association serving individuals with disabilities to ask about the skills and interest levels of its members for participating in the development and evaluation of a private commercial recreation agency.

5. Maintain persons with disabilities in agency programs. It requires that the session instructor, tour guide, concessionaire, driver, agency director, or owner and employees are empathic to the needs of the individual with a disability. Important points in assuring return business is being courteous, exercise patience, ask the person about needs (accommodation), provide accommodation in ample time, treat each customer as an individual, and be knowledgeable about job duties, and agency policies and procedures.

Relating the Purposes and Philosophy of Leisure Services to Persons with Disabilities

A variety of leisure services exist, primarily, to provide opportunities for people, individually and collectively, to engage in leisure pursuits that satisfy their personal goals. People can fulfill their leisure desires through partaking in recreation activities located within three major subdivisions under leisure services. These major subdivisions are as follows:

1. *Public subsystem*—this consists of city recreation and parks departments, city recreation commissions, and school-sponsored recreation.

2. *Private Non-profit subsystem*—this contains organizations such as the youth serving agencies (YMCA, Girls/Boys Clubs, church-sponsored recreation, social and fraternal organizations, country clubs, Kiwanis).

3. *Commercial subsystem*—this houses facilities such as amusement parks, theaters, tennis, golf, marinas, and hotels and resorts (Murphy, Niepoth, Jamieson, & Williams, 1991, pp. 100-01).

Each major subdivision promotes its own philosophies and purposes for providing recreation opportunities to the general public. Depending upon how one wishes to satisfy his leisure time, the philosophy and purpose behind a particular type of organization can help navigate one toward a direction of meeting leisure needs.

Murphy et al. (1991) explain Howard and Crompton's (1980, pp. 209-227) interpretation of dissimilar facets within the public, private, and commercial divisions of leisure services:

Leisure Services—Philosophy

Public agency   Enrichment of the life of the total community by providing opportunities for the worthy use of leisure. Nonprofit in nature.

Private agency   Enrichment of the life of participation members by offering opportunities for worthy use of leisure, frequently with emphasis on the group and the individual. Nonprofit in nature.

Commercial agency   Attempt to satisfy public demands in an effort to produce profit. Dollars from, as well as for, recreation.

Leisure Services—Purpose

Public agency   To provide leisure opportunities that contribute to the social, physical, educational, cultural, and general well-being of the community and its people.

Private agency   Similar to public, but limited by membership, race, religion, sex, socioeconomic level, etc. To provide opportunities for close group association with emphasis on citizenship, behavior, and life philosophy values. To provide activities that appeal to members.

Commercial agency   To provide activities or programs that will appeal to customers. To meet competition. To net profit. To service the public (p.103).

Leisure Services—Program design

Public agency   Designed to provide a wide variety of activities, year-round, for all groups, regardless of age, sex, race, creed, social, or economic status.

Private agency   Designed to provide programs of a specialized nature for group members, keeping within the aims and objectives of the agency.

Commercial agency   Program designed to tap spending power in compliance with state and local laws (p.105).

At one time or another, people will engage in all three types of leisure services. The choice may be due to preference—individuals who spent a great deal of time in their youth as members of a country club (private agency) might favor attending activities in a private club rather than a public agency. The choice may pertain to availability—a person might choose to participate in a commercial bowling league because it offers more leagues than the city recreation department's bowling program. Another factor could be cost—a person might choose to attend a group outing to a Six Flags Amusement Park sponsored by the city recreation department (which includes transportation to park) because it is less expensive than going with a small group independently. Personal, social, and political views may dictate where one chooses to participate in recreation activities. One favors attending a carnival co-sponsored by a community recreation center and nonprofit organization raising funds for the homeless, involvement in ethnic-American clubs located within the city, or participation in recreation activities conducted by self-help groups (e.g., pot lucks, picnics, crafts shows, etc.).

Let's not forget all the important considerations that seem to attract people to recreation activities, i.e., "special perks and discounts," that can be offered by any of the three types of leisure services. A parent might think that purchasing a Summer Super Movie Pass at the Mall Cinema for a child is a better deal than the weekly movies shown at the community center. Or, a mother might enroll her child at the local YMCA after-school program because it promotes discounts with renewal of registration instead of choosing the private day-care center program without discounts and less activities available for children.

Being apprised of the three types of leisure services enables participants with disabilities to investigate the best options for selecting recreation activities. Knowing about leisure services imparts to the individual a large choice level of where to recreate, more opportunities for engagement in various forms of recreation, increased social interaction and community involvement, development of a network through community departments and agencies, and the using of problem-solving skills by way of exploring community recreation options. Agencies located within each of the subdivisions must serve persons with disabilities, therefore, these potential customers will be examining the following:

- which agency provides the most efficient and effective services for the price;
- which agency offers a wide variety of activities and events to enhance personal growth and development;
- which agency has staff who are friendly and knowledgeable about teaching activities and the agency's operation;
- which agency offers the best instruction or implementation of a particular activity (e.g., participant suggestions regarding direction of class, choices within activity, available skill levels of activities);
- which agency will assist the participant in meeting personal needs when they arise (e.g., allowing creativity or alternative instructions within class, advocating advice to participants, and networking—having connections with other community organizations and being knowledgeable about their services for participant referral).

When individuals evaluate leisure services based on the previously–stated criteria, simply providing recreation programs is not good enough. The services need to extend from planning the leisure activities to selecting competent personnel and organizing the leisure activities with the following:

Information-Referral	This is supplying information about various topics outside of the realm of the program (e.g., community center aerobic class providing handouts about the local hospital cardiovascular program), co-sponsoring leisure services programs with other agencies (e.g., a health club and Arthritis Foundation co-sponsoring a weekly "Exercise Swim Bash"), and referring participants to other community agencies (e.g., after-school program networking with a private tutoring agency for possible reading tutor referrals). This process connects leisure to other aspects of a person's life and promotes an inclusive manner of community.
Enabler	This is where the recreation professional guides the participants to freedom of choice, encouraging self-directed choices and responsibility for leisure planning, for example, a commercial

travel agency hosting "Cruise Nights." After attending one or a couple of sessions, the person contemplates if a cruise is what he would like to take. He could ask himself the question: "In what I just learned about a cruise, would it satisfy my personal needs?" If the participant is interested in a cruise, other questions to self-examine are, "Where would I like to go and on what type of cruise?"

Advocacy   This is where a leisure service agency or recreation personnel are involved in changing what the agency or staff professional views as inadequate or inefficient conditions obstructing freedom of participation, enjoyment, and inclusion of people. For example, a private agency located on a main street, housing a large after-school program, feels a "child crossing sign" should be erected at the four-way intersection to slow down traffic, preventing any casualties with children attending its facility. The agency director will attend city planning committee meetings to resolve the problem. Other examples of advocacy involvement are when local recreation commissioners are board members of associations (e.g., Learning Disabilities Association, Literacy Coalition, etc.) or when members of associations or area professionals are on community recreation advisory boards, and commercial recreation agencies sponsor social organizations fundraisers (Murphy & Howard, 1977).

Leisure agencies that incorporate the full range of service delivery approaches are more likely to successfully intervene and enhance opportunities for leisure expression among all members of the community (Murphy et al., 1991, p. 131). This holistic method of delivering leisure services to participants, especially participants with disabilities, connects the multifaceted domains (e.g., physical, social, emotional, intellectual, spiritual needs) that exist in the person's life with the multidivisional community service system network in utilizing the resources to maintain or achieve a state of wellness.

Registration Process: Acquiring Knowledge about Abilities and Needs of Participants

How do community recreation service providers best serve the adults and children in their communities with learning disabilities? The first step is to understand the needs of the individual. It is easy to put people into particular categories because of the characteristics they present. The difficult part is separating the individual from the category, then being objective in determining the best delivery of services to the person.

The recreation leader will encounter some individuals who previously participated in only designated community therapeutic recreation programs (no integration), in community recreation programs without the use of accommodations (achieving little success in activity), in community recreation programs not requiring accommodations (achieving success), or never participated in community recreation programs (only school-based or family-centered recreation activities). The recreation leader having knowledge of this must deal with the person at his level of previous community recreation involvement experience.

For the individual who only attended community therapeutic recreation programs, introduction and interaction with peers who do not have disabilities might be the issue of concern. The recreation leader must provide support and assurance to this individual, always communicating (verbally or nonverbally) that she has the ability and right to participate equally in community recreation. The person who tried community recreation programs in the past that resulted in a negative experience needs to know that he can be successful in a community recreation activity. Together, the recreation leader, participant, family member (if child participant), and professional (if needed) will determine what type of accommodations or program modifications would best help the participant to accomplish the tasks required in completing the activity. For the person who participated in community recreation activities successfully without accommodations, the recreation leader must respect the participant's choice for not requesting accommodations and remember the person's need for accommodations is determined in conjunction with the person having the disability, not solely by the recreation leader. A person's first-time exposure to community recreation programs might comprise of inviting child and parent or adult participants to view activities in progress, tour the facility, discuss activities represented in age groups (including family-oriented activities), or provide a one-time free pass to social/spectator events.

The registration process consists of acquiring vital information from the participant. This usually is name, address, age, gender, sex, emergency contact person, experience in recreation activities, selection of an activity or program, special needs during activity, etc. Figure 5.1A presents an example of a generic recreation agency registration form. Figure 5.1B shows the generic recreation agency registration form completed by an individual with learning disabilities (person disclosed disability on form). Information obtained during the registration process will supply the recreation leader with basic facts about the potential participant's interest and needs regarding recreation pursuits.

Figure 5.1A
Generic Recreation Agency Registration Form

Angel City Community Recreation Center
1404 18th Street
Angel City, (State) 21345

Registration Data

Name: _____ Date: _____

Address: _____

City: _____ State: _____ Zip code: _____

Home number: _____ Work number: _____

Age: _____ Date of birth: _____ Sex: _____ Marital status: _____

Ethnicity: (optional) _____ Social Security number: _____

If under 18, parent/guardian name: _____

Address (city, state, zip code): _____

_____

Job title & Work address: _____

_____

In case of emergency call (person's name): _____

Phone number: _____

Figure 5.1A Cont.

Program Information

Programs of interest (you can circle more than one category):

Creative expression	Sports (adult or youth)	Social events
Personal growth (educational)	Field trips	Health & Fitness
Hobby clubs (adult or youth)	Senior activities	Aquatic
Community service (volunteering)	Outdoor activities	Crafts

Enrollment in program: _____ Program section: _____

Schedule of program: _____

Program location: _____ Program fee: _____

Equipment/Material rental (what & price): _____

Payment of fee (please circle one):   Cash   Check   Money order

Special considerations to assist you in program?   Yes_____ No _____

If yes, please state what that need would be: _____

_____

If not certain about special need, would you welcome a brief meeting with program leader to discuss special considerations? Yes_____ No _____

(If yes, program leader will contact you for meeting.)

Is there anything else you would like to inform the agency about yourself or family? _____

Participant Information

Have you ever participated in a community center recreation program?

Yes_____ No _____

If no, would you like to know more about the center?

Yes_____ No _____

How did you find out about this agency? (please circle one)

Family	Friend	Newspapers
T.V.	Radio	School
Other _____		

Please list recreation interests: _____

_____

Please provide us with suggestions on activities or events you would like to see at the center: _____

_____

Would you like to be on our mailing list? Yes_____ No _____

Figure 5.1B
An Individual's Recreation Agency Registration Form

Angel City Community Recreation Center
1404 18th Street
Angel City, (State) 21345

Registration Data

Name: _____ John F. Smith _____   Date: _____ March 10, 1997 _____
Address: __ 9216 South Wales Rd. _____
City: __ Angel City __   State: __ State __   Zip code:__ 21345 __
Home number:__ (002) 354-8296 __   Work number: __ (002) 824-3968 __
Age: _35_ Date of Birth:_ 10/14/61 _ Sex:_ M _ Marital status:_ S _
Ethnicity: (optional) _____   Social security number:_ 444-22-3333 _
If under 18, parent/guardian name: _____
Address (city, state, zip code): _____
_____

Job title & Work address:_ Graphic Design Technician - _____
_ Mike Graphic Design, 442 Jardin St., Angel City, (State) 21345 _
In case of emergency call (person's name): __ Cecil Beaver - brother _
Phone number: __ (002) 354-6262 _____

Program Information
Programs of interest (can circle more than one category):

Greative expression   (Sports (adult or youth)) Social events
Personal growth (educational)   (Field trips)   Health & Fitness
(Hobby clubs (adult or youth))   Senior activities   (Aquatic)
Community service (volunteering) (Outdoor activities)   Crafts

Enrollment in program: Photography   Program section:__ A __
Schedule of program:__ Monday & Wednesday 5:30-6:30 p.m., _
_ April 2-June 4 _____
Program location:_ Angel City Community Center _ Program fee:_$55_
Equipment/Material rental (what & price):_ Film developing materials - _
_ $20 _____
Payment of fee (please circle one):   Cash (Check) Money order

---

Figure 5.21B Continued

Special considerations to assist you in program: Yes__X__ No_____
If yes, please state what that needs would be:__I am dyslexic and____
__require more time to read written materials._____
If not certain about special needs, would you welcome a brief meeting
with program leader to discuss special considerations? Yes___ No _X_
(If yes, program leader will contact you for meeting.)
Is there anything else you would like to inform the agency about yourself
or family?__No_____

Participant Information
Have you ever participated in a community center recreation program?
Yes__X__ No_____
If no, would you like to know more about the center?
Yes_____ No_____
How did you find out about this agency? (please circle one)

Family	Friend	Newspapers
T.V.	Radio	School

(Other) girlfriend_____

Please list recreation interests: hunting, fishing, boating, fixing cars,
__and hiking_____
Please provide us with suggestions on activities or events you would like
to see at the center:__Season fishing trips_____
Would you like to be on our mailing list? Yes _X_ No ____

The profile obtained from this registration form states that
John Smith is a single, 35-year-old white male, graphic design technician having previous experience with community recreational
activities. He has dyslexia, states specific difficulties, and would not
like to have a meeting with a program leader to discuss his needs
within that activity. His interests are in sports, outdoor activities,
aquatics, field trips, and hobby clubs. It is possible John might need
some sort of accommodation if the photography instructor requires
reading of all its participants. This is a question that John should
ask a staff member during the registration process. If the staff member at registration does not know the answer, the question can be

passed on to the photography instructor, so he can contact John about specifics of the course. John stated he did not wish to discuss his needs with the program leader, so during the class the photography instructor might want to observe John's progress in class and allow John to initiate the accommodation when the time arises. The photography class instructor's knowledge about John's difficulty in reading helps the instructor to prepare alternative teaching formats for that class.

The professionals conducting, organizing, and implementing sports and recreation activities, through their specialized training, possess the following: a systematic body of knowledge within their field, achieved professional recognition based on specialized training, designated credentials for professional practice, and adherence to a code of professional ethics. From the information obtained during the registration process, there may be specific skills and knowledge areas that recreation leaders, program supervisors, activity instructors, and league coaches should possess for working with and understanding participants who have disabilities, especially learning disabilities, within a particular agency or department. These specific skills and areas are as follows:

- *Processes involved in learning*—ways to teach information the participants will learn.
- *Effective communication skills*—are participants understanding what is being said?
- *Knowledge about disabilities*—facts, etiquette, perceptions, and awareness of rights.
- *Accommodations and modifications*—individual, group, program, or facility.
- *Location of resources*—within the agency or community.
- *Leadership and group function*—efficiency, support, and problem solving.

The teaching of additional skills and knowledge become part of the agency's staff training when the agency has determined that all of its employees should impart the same level of skill and ability when performing their job. Ascertaining this training curriculum is based on the agency's service scope, its philosophy, purpose, and goals.

All facets of the recreation agency are interconnected. The community needs assessment (e.g., process of identifying and gathering information about the community for making appropriate decisions regarding planning recreation programs and serving the population's leisure needs) determines selection of program content and implementation and management of the program. The program dictates hiring staff, staff development and training, creating and maintaining documentation and record keeping procedures, promoting the program, determining and acquiring the budget, and selecting equipment/materials to be purchased. Program evaluation informs an agency about the progress of programs, adjustments to the budget, satisfaction of participants, efficiency of agency operations and record keeping, quality of staff performance, and the delivery of programs and services. Along with the staff learning about the philosophy, purpose, goals and objectives, and daily agency operations, staff training should also include those agency-designated skills and knowledge base deemed essential for all employees to master.

Staff Training and Education about Disabilities

A staff training program is intended to satisfy a variety of staff needs. The program's goal is to increase employees' understanding of job responsibilities; to strengthen job-related skills; to assure continued progress relevant to both employer and employees' needs; to encourage employee involvement and support of agency; to promote education to keep abreast of trends and issues concerning the agency, participants, and staff; and to foster a positive and productive work attitude.

When employees are hired to work in leisure services, they are exposed to four types of training:

1. **Orientation to the agency**—This occurs within the first few weeks of employment.

2. **Training related specifically to the position for which the employee was selected (on-the-job training)**—This encompasses acquiring specific competency in agency-designated matters that personnel are required to know and demonstrate and also keeping abreast of the latest techniques and informa-

tion in one's profession on what impacts the agency, so personnel and agency can deliver service more efficiently.

3. **Training to keep the worker abreast of changes in agency operation**—This is a continual process, usually conducted through periodic scheduled inter- or intra-departmental meetings within the agency by agency staff.

4. **Continuing education**—This is to enhance professional knowledge and skills that often take place when staff attend specialized institutes, conferences, or professional meetings.

The specific skills and knowledge areas (e.g., processes involved in learning; effective communication skills; knowledge about disabilities, leadership, and group function; accommodations and modifications; location of resources) an agency would want its staff to understand in working with participants having learning disabilities are taught within the training type of "on-the-job training" and "continuing education." Most often, training is conducted by staff already equipped with the skills and knowledge area of the agency's recommendations. To continue enhancing the knowledge base and professional growth of employees, suggestions include attending workshops led by disability specialists obtained from the community; attending credit or continuing education courses in therapeutic recreation, special education, or social work; and participating in periodic training sessions held by local advocacy organizations serving persons with disabilities. All these keep employees apprised of the concerns, issues, and trends of serving participants having disabilities (Schleien, McAvoy, Lais, & Rynders, 1993).

A brief overview of the specific skills and knowledge areas (e.g., processes involved in learning; effective communication skills; knowledge about disabilities, accommodations, and modifications; location of resources; leadership and group function) an agency wants its staff to understand when working with participants having learning disabilities will be discussed as a guide for staff training on the following topics.

What basic information should any leisure professional teaching participants having learning disabilities know about the "processes involved in learning?"

1. **Learning is an experience.** It is the experience of being in an environment and interacting with the elements of that environment. An individual present in the activity will learn something about that activity. The instructor or leader should provide equal opportunity for participation in each task contained in the activity; interact with the participant to determine if the individual is learning what she set out to learn about the activity. The instructors should recognize the difference between their expectations about what is learned in this particular activity and what the participants learned from the activity. In the beginning of the session, goals and objectives of the activity should be stated, informing participants about what is important for them to learn.

2. **Problem solving is involved in learning.** The learner is expected to draw generalizations from specific information—to apply principles, interpret results, and provide logical conclusions based on specific results (critical thinking). The purpose here is to foster independent decision making and analyze why the participant came to that decision. This is the skill required for stumping the opponent in sports and passive recreation activities, in determining correct materials (e.g., amount, shape, texture, combination, weight, directions, etc.), in designing art, making travel arrangements, completing crossword puzzles, etc. Teach the why, how, when, and where it occurs within an activity, not just "what it is."

3. **Attitudes influence learning.** As the individual perceives the information, his feelings influence his behavior. The child might have the feeling that the program leader cannot be trusted; he's concerned that the leader will tell other children at the center about his difficulty in reading and following directions. This child's behavior toward the leader is distant; he prefers to ask peers for extra help and clarification instead of the program leader. Instructors and leaders should become aware of their own attitudes and behaviors, encourage participants to talk and ask questions, and welcome an open-door policy. Also, instructors and leaders need to observe participants' behaviors and talk with them about their attitudes before difficulty occurs. This difficulty can result in failing class assignments, fighting with teammates, increasing frustration with mastering tasks, and increasing truancy and isolation within the activity. In-

struct the participant in tips that people employ when asking for help (e.g., identifying the problem and teaching the appropriate approaches to asking someone for help; displaying appropriate attitudes or mannerisms to receive help, and thanking the person for giving assistance).

4. **Learning takes place through different modalities: movement, discussion, visualization, reasoning, and values.** Everyone does not learn in the same way; people have preferences for learning and these preferences can change throughout one's life. Human beings perceive and process experiences and information in different ways. The combinations formed by our own perceiving and processing techniques form our unique learning styles (McCarthy & Morris, 1994). Instructors and leaders will have participants who want information seen (visual), heard (auditory), manipulated (kinesthetic), and touchable (tactile). Some of these participants also might be extrovert vs. introvert, intuitive vs. sensing, thinking vs. feeling, or perceiving vs. judging, as indicated on the Myers-Briggs Type Indicator. Even within this same group of participants, some learn by listening and sharing ideas; a few will learn through forming theories and integrating observations from facts or experts; others learn by testing theories and applying common sense; and the last few will integrate an experience then apply that experience for change or improvement (McCarthy & Morris, 1994). Instructors should create a learning environment that presents information to all the sensory modalities (e.g., visual, auditory, tactile, kinesthetic, and even olfactory, if applicable; for more information, see Chapter Six on Multisensory Instruction), allows group discussion for exchange of ideas and experiences, provides hands-on application to understanding the working of an activity, presents facts and background information about their activity, and encourages development and exploration within the activity.

5. **Learning occurs through set goals, objectives, and perceptions that an individual employs.** It does not matter how vague or explicit the idea the participant has on learning something about the activity, the participant enters the activity on the expectations that she will learn more about the activity after attending it. Goals and objectives for the class could be

predetermined by the instructor or created jointly by the instructor with comments from participants. The goals and objectives in learning serve the purpose of guiding the learning experience and providing the criteria for evaluating the effectiveness of the learning experience; it is recognizing the participants' purposes for attending the activity (Niepoth, 1983).

The importance of effective communication between leisure professionals and participants with learning disabilities.

Participants having language processing deficits incur difficulties organizing and retrieving information. Incoming stimuli is stored haphazardly, rather than in meaningful units, so this makes language retrieval inefficient and often frustrating. A useful strategy to employ for improving language processing skills is compensatory cueing. Compensatory cueing expedites organization and retrieval of language by encouraging the storage of associated language stimuli together. The goal of cueing is to provide as much information as necessary for the student to retrieve a target word. Within compensatory cueing, there are five cueing techniques to facilitate retrieval of information (Richard & Honner, 1987).

1. **Additional Time**—This allows more response time for the participant to ask questions, answer questions, and state opinions about a topic; this time span can range from 15 seconds to 30 seconds or more. The average classroom response time ranges from five to seven seconds. This time difference seems like an eternity to the instructor, but it is something that must become accustomed to. The instructor or leader is not to put words into the participant's mouth (e.g., "you want to say …"), finish the sentence the person began, or interrupt the participant during expression of the thought process.

2. **Stimulus Repetition**—When the participant is taking additional time to process information, that person may lose focus of the question or topic of discussion. The instructor can repeat the question or last sentence spoken on the topic to assist the student in refocusing on the original task. This technique allows the participant to process independently without relying on additional external information.

3. **Question Prompts**—Questions are asked to prompt information the participant is trying to retrieve. The who, what, when, where, why, and how questions are typical prompts. In the initial stages of this technique, the instructor generates the questions, then the participant is instructed to use this self-questioning method independently. Some examples of question prompts are, "Who made that statement? What letter does it start with? How does it look? When did this incident occur? Where did you locate that information in your book? Why did you choose this? Which topic does it belong in?"

4. **Additional Information**—This is a technique of providing supplemental information in assisting a participant to recall a specific word. Various types of additional information cues consist of using gestures (e.g., pantomime or a hand demonstrating specific word); describing the function of specific words; describing; categorizing (e.g., it is an article of clothing); figuring the beginning sound; rhyming or similar sounding words; differing between meaning (e.g., it can be used to dig dirt) and context (e.g., "In tennis, you toss the ball up in the air with your left hand, before you swing your right arm up and forward for a _____."); employing multiple choice (e.g., supplying several word choices with the target word included), and using other information that could help in retrieving the target word, such as location, sounds, smell, and environment.

5. **Naming**—The procedure of presenting a target word to the participant in a written or verbal manner and then having the participant repeat the target word overtly or covertly to herself is naming (Richard & Honner, 1987).

The instructor or leader must become cognizant of participants who misinterpret auditory instructions, for example, "Turn to the right" translates as "Turn and write." In a discussion about attending a child's birthday party, a person asks, "She is six today?" and the response from the listener is, "Who is sick?" Another example is when asking an individual to explain safety measures. The question: "What would be the thing to do if, while playing beach volleyball, you noticed a person yelling help in the ocean?" gains this response: "I would tell my friends I played beach volleyball this past weekend." When these following types of miscommunication patterns occur, restate the information, making sure pronunciation is clear, and (if needed) use a different context or category example to deduce the correct meaning of explained ideas from the participant.

Understanding persons with disabilities

What has been taking place in the public and private business sector since the passing of the Americans with Disabilities Act is how service providers interact and meet the needs of persons with disabilities. A number of leisure service providers, especially in the tourism industry, have implemented "Disability Sensitivity Training" within staff training for their employees. The curriculum is most often designed and sometimes conducted by persons having disabilities. Sensitivity training programs vary in content, but general training components consist of understanding the ADA, overviewing disabilities (see Appendix Q, "Overview of Disabilities"), gaining communications and etiquette awareness, working on customer service, and supervising and promoting the disabled. The following is general information assisting employees in displaying proper etiquette when serving participants with disabilities:

Disability Etiquette
Basic Guidelines

- Make reference to the person first, then the disability. Say "a person with a disability" rather than a disabled person. However, the latter is acceptable in the interest of conserving print space or saving announcing time.
- The term *handicapped* is derived from the image of a person standing on the corner with a cap in hand, begging for money. People with disabilities do not want to be recipients of charity. They want to participate equally with the rest of the community. A disability is a functional limitation that interferes with a person's ability to walk, hear, talk, learn, etc. Use handicap to describe a situation or barrier imposed by society, the environment, or oneself.
- If the disability isn't germane to the story or conversation, don't mention it. Remember—a person who has a disability isn't necessarily chronically sick or unhealthy. He is often just disabled.
- Just because a person does not appear to have a disability does not mean the person is without one. A person with dyslexia clearly appears to be reading a menu like other nonvisually im-

paired persons, but the interpretation is not the same. An individual with an auditory processing deficiency does not wear hearing aids and gives the appearance to hear like someone without a hearing impairment, but the information is not clearly understood. If a person asks to have something read, orally restated, re-explained or graphically depicted, honor the request by doing so. *

- Because a person is not a condition, avoid describing a person in such a manner. Don't present someone as an "epileptic" or "post polio." Say instead, "a person with epilepsy" or "person who has had polio."

Common Courtesies

- Don't feel obligated to act as a caregiver to people with disabilities. It is all right to offer assistance to a person with a disability, but wait until your offer is accepted *before* you help. Listen to instructions the person may give.
- Leaning on a person's wheelchair is similar to leaning or hanging on a person and is usually considered annoying and rude. The chair is a part of one's body space. Don't hang on it!
- Share the same social courtesies with people with disabilities that you would share with anyone else. If you shake hands with people you meet, offer your hand to everyone you meet, whether or not they are disabled. If the person with a disability is unable to shake your hand, he will tell you.
- When offering assistance to a person with a visual impairment, allow that person to take your arm. This will enable you to guide, rather than propel or lead, the person. Use specific directions, such as "left one hundred feet" or "right two yards," when directing a person with a visual impairment.
- When planning events that involve persons with disabilities, consider their needs before choosing a location. Even if people with disabilities will not attend, select an accessible spot. You wouldn't think of holding an event where other minorities could not attend, so don't exclude people with disabilities.

Conversation

- When speaking about people with disabilities, emphasize achievements, abilities, and individual qualities. Portray them as they are in real life: as parents, employees, business owners, etc.
- When talking to a person who has a disability, speak directly to that person, not through a companion.
- Exercise patience and clearly explain directions or procedures with individuals having cognitive impairments, providing writ-

ten materials (handouts, brochures, or schedules) and names of contact personnel to assist in clarifying any needs or concerns. *

- Relax, don't be embarrassed if you use common expressions such as, "See ya later" or "Gotta run," that seem to relate to a person's disability.

- To get the attention of a person who has a hearing impairment, tap him on the shoulder or wave. Look directly at the person and speak clearly, slowly, and expressively to establish if they read lips. Not all people with hearing impairments can read lips. Those who do rely on facial expressions and body language for understanding. Stay in the light and keep food, hands, and other objects away from your mouth. Shouting won't help. Written notes will. (***Note***: individuals having receptive language difficulties also prefer being spoken to clearly and directly, reading lips, and facial expression.)

- When talking to a person in a wheelchair for more than a few minutes, place yourself at eye level with that person. This will spare both of you a sore neck.

- When greeting a person with a severe loss of vision, always identify yourself and others. For example say, "On my right is John Smith." Remember to identify persons with whom you are speaking. Speak in a normal tone of voice and indicate when the conversation is over. Let them know when you move from one place to another.

(Reprint of Disability Etiquette from *PARAQUAD*, 1993) Asterisk (*) and **Note** inserts are provided by the author.

Accommodations and modifications enabling equal access and opportunity for persons with learning disabilities

The first area of knowledge leisure service personnel should become familiar with is, "What is meant by accommodations and modifications?" *Accommodation* means making some kind of arrangement or change for the individual with a disability within the program by introducing materials, policies and procedures, or equipment so that the individual can have an equal opportunity to fully participate in program like nondisabled participants. Examples of accommodations for persons having learning disabilities would be giving extra individual lessons to review instructions taught in class; giving extra time for in-class written or reading assignments; allowing an audio recorder to tape class lectures; re-explaining directions or supplying enlarged, color-coded written directions; and using different equipment, such as an oversized racket or a brighter colored ball. Accommodations are individually selected (by the person with a disability and staff personnel), most often only affecting the individual requesting the accommodation.

The *ADA Title II Technical Assistance Manual* explains *reasonable modifications* as "a public entity must reasonably modify its policies, practices, or procedures to avoid discrimination. If the public entity can demonstrate, however, that the modifications would fundamentally alter the nature of its service, program, or activity, it is not required to make the modification" (p. 13). This manual also states guidelines to "modifications in the regular program." The passing of ADA did not abolish special program designated for particular clientele having disabilities; these programs can still be offered and are quite appropriate for persons with disabilities wanting to participate in such programs. If the person with a disability decides to take part in the regular program the following guideline should be observed:

> When a public entity offers a special program for individuals with a particular disability, but an individual with that disability elects to participate in the regular program rather than in the separate program, the public entity may still have obligations to provide an opportunity for that individual to benefit from the regular program. The fact that a separate program is offered may be a factor in determining the extent of the obligations under the regular program, but only if the separate program is appropriate to the needs of the particular individual with a disability. (The Department of Justice's *ADA Title II Technical Assistance Manual*, 1992, p.12)

An illustration is a special crafts program designed for children 12-15 with cognitive impairments. A 13-year-old child with severe dyslexia enters the program. She discovers that the instructions were too simplistic and very little reading and writing was involved, so she becomes bored with the class and asks her mother if she could attend the regular group craft program. The child is placed in the regular children's craft program, but she now requires someone to read the directions out loud to her and spend five minutes each session reviewing the progress of her project after class. The instructor for this regular craft program did not feel these modifications would present hardship on the class. The instructor would read the instructions out loud for the class and the child was teamed with a peer who did not mind rereading the craft project instructions (i.e., accommodation). The class would end five minutes early so the instructor could spend time reviewing the child's project before teaching the next scheduled craft class.

Modifications usually impact others to some extent, and can affect the design, implementation, and conduct of the program. For example, having the class leave five minutes early required everyone in the class to adjust to this arrangement, but no one thought it was detrimental in learning about the craft projects. Another example of a class modification was presented earlier in this chapter under the subheading "Undue Hardship and Reasonable Accommodations" section. Remember Jill, the student in the drawing class who exhibited reading comprehension difficulties, slow processing speed, and Scotopic Sensitivity Syndrome? She requested a different classroom, but the only one available was at a community center 10 miles from the present facility, and her classmates voted "no" due to inconvenience. That request was considered a *modification* affecting the entire class. The alternative modification that she, her classmates, and instructor deemed "reasonable" was having the maintenance man unscrew two florescent ceiling light bulbs before each class session and covering the tables with brown butcher block paper. Her peers, the instructor, and school administration did not object to the use of these modifications, which must have had very little or no affect on them.

There are many resources available to assist leisure service staff in acquiring the knowledge about accommodating and modifying programs for persons with disabilities. Specific information on this topic follows in Chapter Six, "Specific Accommodations and Modifications of Recreation Activities for Persons with Learning Disabilities." Resources on this topic are listed in Chapter Seven of this book.

Location of resources to assist the agency and participants with learning disabilities

Training in this area refers to the "Information-Referral" portion of leisure services where the agency supplies information about various topics outside the realm of the program (refer to section "Relating the Purposes and Philosophy of Leisure Service to Persons with Disabilities" of this chapter). Staff must become aware of what information and assistance community social service agencies, educational agencies or institutions, health care agencies, and recreation agencies can provide participants who partake in the community recreation agency program. For example, a community recreation agency conducting an after-school program might have brochures in its department on immunization, parenting classes, little league sports, nutrition, education (e.g., private schools, home schooling, tutoring programs), financial support (e.g., food stamps, low-cost child care, Aid to Families with Dependent Children, child abuse, etc.) and commercial recreation (e.g., Putt-Putt Golf, carnivals, bowling, movies, video establishments, etc.). The after-school program could offer monthly workshops for the family; experts would talk about topics of "What is Attention Deficit Disorder?" "Childhood allergies," or "Planning that summer vacation with the children."

It would be ideal for the agency to create a "resource book" and place it in an accessible area where staff can review its contents at anytime and also become involved in updating the resource book on a regular basis. An important part of this training is to encourage staff to use community resources and invite area professionals to the center to discuss a staff-requested topic. If a recreation leader notices that a large number of children with learning disabilities are signing-up for sports activities and the staff presently employed have very little knowledge about learning disabilities, that staff person should bring this issue to the attention of his supervisor and suggest next month's in-service training focus on working with children having learning disabilities.

This in-service training could be conducted by a teacher or educational therapist connected with the state branch of the International Dyslexia Association, special education teachers specialized in learning disabilities, or college professors of special education departments. Parents and participants are always good candidates for obtaining referrals; take note of their job title, place of employment, and listed recreation interests on the registration form. Inputting this information into an agency computer system can assist in networking opportunities for the future.

Facilitating effective leadership and group function to assure equal participation and learning opportunities for participants with learning disabilities

Leadership is the ability of an individual to motivate, guide, and direct a group of people toward a desired goal or objective. The effective leader has the capacity and desire to rally individuals to a common purpose. Being an effective leader means one must "behave in such a way that she comes to be perceived almost as another group member; at the same time she must help all group members feel as free as the leader to make contributions and perform needed functions in the group" (Gordon, 1977, pp. 42-43).

To elaborate on the last statement, the leader must foster an environment allowing subordinates and participants to present ideas, supply feedback to the leader, and partake in problem solving. Effective leaders accept accountability for the groups they lead. In evaluating one's performance in leading a group, one would ask oneself these questions: "Did I teach this group the important information in acquiring this skill?" or "In the way that I conducted the group, do they have the basic background knowledge to continue in learning more about this activity?" An effective leader must understand the characteristics of a group. Members of a group interact with one another and share common goals and sets of standards; they also develop a set of roles and a network of interpersonal attractions which serve to differentiate the group from another group (Niepoth, 1983, p. 155).

Individuals with learning disabilities have a similar goal for participating in a particular activity, just as those participants who have no disabilities. These participants expect to learn skills, rules, and procedures of an activity, just as nondisabled participants, and these participants expect to fulfill their role and handle responsibility within the activity on an equal basis to their peers not having learning disabilities. Appropriate accommodations or program modifications assist in providing the participant with equal participation within an activity. The leader, having clearly stated goals, objectives, and expectations for the group at the beginning of the session, aids participants with learning disabilities in determining what behaviors are expected of them during this activity. An illustration of this is shown in the Hula Hoop Roll activity.

The goal of this activity is to get your hula hoop to the opposite end of the gymnasium. When the hula hoop gets to the opposite end of the gym, the person receives 10 points. A maximum of 100 points wins the game. The objectives: 1) everyone must roll their hula hoop by placing their hand on the top of the hoop, palm down, pulling the hoop back and then forward to release; 2) the hula hoop must roll past the black line in the middle of the gym; 3) each participant must follow in order of turn; and 4) each participant must maintain her own score.

All participants, including those having learning disabilities, are expected to roll the hula hoop as instructed. The hula hoop must roll past the black line in the middle of the gymnasium, and the participant must be aware of order of turn and keep her own score. If any difficulty occurs with the execution of tasks within this activity, that is when accommodations or program modifications should be addressed.

Also, understanding the way a participant with learning disabilities reacts to displayed instruction in one activity class is not the way that same person will react to displayed instructions in another activity class, even if the same information is being presented. In using the "Hula Hoop Roll" activity, due to the leader's style of instructing participants, a person may feel one class is more competitive than the other or a stricter adherence to rules is expected in one class more than the other; for example, everyone might have a second chance at rerolling the hula hoop when a bad roll occurs in one class and not have that chance in another. Different teaching styles are needed to enhance the many different qualities of an individual. During in–service training, if a number of leaders are conducting the same activity, it is important to discuss each's style in teaching the activity, not to achieve sameness, but to look at ways of promoting motivation within the group, encouraging competitiveness or cooperative skills, relating this activity to similar activities, properly placing participants, and exchanging new techniques helpful in participant success.

Active Participation in Program Evaluation

Evaluation is the means of collecting information in order to make a decision on how to improve service delivery. Administration, staff, and program participants are asked to evaluate service delivery. Program participants and recreation leaders conducting the class or activity evaluate its content, delivery, and format after completion of the class or activity. The facility supervisor might evaluate all of the activity classes and programs at the end of a season or the administration may evaluate the overall program at the end of a fiscal year. The program session, season, or year evaluation results can determine if the individual or overall program was run efficiently. Results from an evaluation can help answer the following questions:

- What changes need to be made in existing programs to improve them?
- Should some programs be combined or eliminated based on staff and participants' evaluation input?
- Can staff be utilized more effectively to deliver a wider variety of programming throughout the community?
- Is staff knowledgeable about activities taught
- Is staff knowledgeable about agency operations?
- Were participants treated in a courteous and respectful manner?
- Was equipment or material used during the program in satisfactory condition?
- Did the staff provide assistance when requested?

The agency or department must be willing to make changes in order to improve the operation of its services, thus, viewing change as "good."

The first step in the evaluation process begins with the participant—the customer. Having the participant complete a program evaluation form at the cessation of the activity assists management in better meeting the participant's needs. The participant evaluation form is distributed by the recreation leader or instructor. This generic form should be available in large print, audio recording, or Braille (if necessary). If the recreation leader or instructor feels uncomfortable assisting a person in evaluating her class, another agency staff member or classmate can be assigned to help the participant with learning disabilities to complete the form, if so requested by the participant. Participants can remain anonymous during the evaluation process or elect to write names on the evaluation form. Parents of children having learning disabilities should be encouraged to complete an agency evaluation form and make comments about the registration process, professionalism of the staff, delivery of services, child's satisfaction of services, etc.

The purpose of evaluating programs and agency operations is to supply corrective criticism to the agency staff; it should not be used to vent personal frustrations, explain life stories, make legal accusations, discuss personal matters about other participants, or state gossip about staff or agency operations. Active participation in the evaluation process does not necessarily begin at the end of the program. If a participant feels a particular matter is pertinent for the recreation leader or other agency staff to know, then that matter should be addressed at that time.

Some examples of matters that require immediate attention are as follows: unsatisfactory condition of equipment, materials, or playing surfaces; the use of illegal substances during activities or in the facility; incurring health problems while participating in activities; a change in a personal schedule that interferes with participating in an activity; inappropriate conduct by staff or peers within an activity; and difficulty understanding and accomplishing tasks required during an activity.

If the participant or a family member voices concerns about a particular situation occurring within an activity, then that concern should be quickly addressed by the staff, and if that problem was not solved by the end of the activity, then this incident needs to be addressed again on the participant or agency evaluation form. Staff members should inform the participant or person who brought the problem to the staff's attention that the agency is looking into solving this problem and then thank that person for bringing this problem to the management's attention. Too often leisure service employees do not inform the participant or person about the agency's attempts to elucidate a problem, only to hear at a later date or read on an evaluation form that a particular problem was not resolved, when in fact it had been resolved or is in the process of being resolved. Most people can understand some problems not being solved to their satisfaction, especially when due to uncontrollable or unforeseeable circumstances (e.g., money, delivery of equipment, absent staff, time, etc.), but ignoring their concerns adds insult to injury.

The participants' evaluations of a program and/or agency operations are combined with the staff's evaluations in order to achieve optimal quality satisfaction between the staff's and the participants' ideals. The evaluation form asks questions that the staff feels the participants would want to answer, but this is not always the case. For example, participants using community recreation agencies view facility dressing rooms and shower facilities as important, especially regarding safety and hygiene, but this is a question that is often absent from many agency evaluation forms. An agency may assume that having an efficient program leader and top quality equipment will draw participants to its program, but when people stopped attending this center's program, it was because the showers were dirty and lacking hot water and lockers were always broken. To make sure an agency is asking the questions the participants want to answer, at the end of the evaluation form have participants list what additional questions they wished the agency would have asked them—what they feel is important when participating in the agency's program (see Appendix R, "Participant Evaluation Form").

References

Department of Justice. (1992). *ADA Title II technical assistance manual.* Http://gopher.usdoj.gov/crt/ada/taman2.html

Gordon, T. (1977). *Leader effectiveness training, L.E.T.: The no-lose way to release the productive potential of people.* New York: Wyden Books.

Howard, D. R., & Crompton, J. (1980). *Financing, managing and marketing recreation and park resources.* Dubuque, IA: Wm. C. Brown Co.

McCarthy, B., & Morris, S. (1994). *The 4MAT course book, Volume 1: Fundamental training.* Barrington, IL: Excel, Inc.

McGovern, J. (1991). *The Americans with Disabilities Act: Implications for change in recreation and park agencies.* Paper presented at the 1991 NRPA Congress held at the Baltimore Convention Center, Baltimore, MD.

Murphy, J. F., & Howard, D.R. (1977) *Delivery of community leisure services.* Philadelphia, PA: Lea & Febiger.

Murphy, J. F., Niepoth, E. W., Jamieson, L.M., & Williams, J.G. (1991). *Leisure systems: Critical concepts and applications.* Champaign, IL: Sagamore Publishing, Inc.

Niepoth, E. W. (1983). *Leisure leadership: Working with people in recreation and parks settings.* Englewood Cliffs, NJ: Prentice-Hall, Inc.

PARAQUAD. (1993). *Disability etiquette*. St. Louis, MO: Author.

Richard, G.J., & Honner, M. (1987). *Language, processing, and remediation*. LinguiSystems, Inc.

Rovner, J. (1990, July) For the Record—Provisions: Americans with Disabilities Act. *Congressional Quarterly Weekly Review*, 48 (30), pp. 2437-2444.

Schleien, J.S., McAvoy, L., Lais, G.J., & Rynders, J.E. (1993). *Integrated outdoor education and adventure program*. Champaign, IL: Sagamore Publishing, Inc.

Chapter Six

SPECIFIC ACCOMMODATIONS AND MODIFICATIONS OF RECREATION ACTIVITIES FOR PERSONS WITH LEARNING DISABILITIES

Provision of Accommodations and Modifications

One approach for one answer produces some successes.
Many approaches for one answer produces many successes.
A variety of approaches for one answer establishes new approaches to new answers.

What is an *accommodation*? Accommodation means making some kind of arrangement or change for the individual with a disability within the program by introducing materials, policies and procedures, or equipment so that individual can have an equal opportunity to fully participate in the program like nondisabled participants. An accommodation is person specific, only affecting the individual using the accommodation. Most literature available discussing accommodations usually relates this term overwhelmingly to job duties and employment environment or educational setting (e.g., elementary, secondary, post-secondary, or trade schools); that focal point was influenced by the wording contained in some federal laws (e.g., the Rehabilitation Act of 1973, the Education of All Handicapped Children Act of 1975, and the Carl Perkins

Vocational Education Act of 1984).With the passing of the Americans with Disabilities Act, accommodations in the area of recreation is equally as important as employment and education.

The cost of an accommodation will depend upon the individual's disability and the circumstances of the accommodation within the program. Because learning disabilities, at times, manifest themselves as "inconsistent," the occurrence for use of accommodations will vary, but opportunity for its use must always be available. For example, a person taking a karate class might feel he requires assistance with karate stances and moves. The student notifies the instructor about this concern. Because the student is not certain about the amount of extra assistance needed, future provisions were arranged within this 12-week course for the instructor to provide one-on-one sessions to the student when requested. This accommodation can cost the agency anywhere between $0 to $256. This price is based on one-on-one sessions at $8.00 per hour, the same hourly salary the agency pays the karate instructor for teaching the class. The student does not have to pay for the additional lessons; the agency absorbs the cost. What's important about this accommodation is that an arrangement was made in advance so that when the student felt he needed the accommodation, it would be available and provided in a timely manner.

Surveys evaluating the cost of accommodations for persons having disabilities is most prominent in the area of employment. The results indicated that 50% to 80% of accommodations cost less than $500 (United States General Accounting Office (GAO), 1990; Job Accommodation Network, 1995) and within that percentage range, 19% to 51% of the accommodations cost nothing. So with a little creativity, use of presently used equipment, materials, and dual brain power (e.g., staff member and person with a disability) there is no need for the agency to worry about going over budget to accommodate persons with disabilities.

What is a *modification?* This is where an agency reasonably modifies its policies, practices, or procedures to avoid discrimination, thereby, including persons with disabilities to equal program access and participation. However, if the agency can demonstrate that the modifications would fundamentally alter the nature of its service, program, or activity, it is not required to make the modification. Unlike accommodation, modification affects others within the program. For example, Jane, a participant in a leisure education program, has a visual impairment in addition to her learning disabilities. Within the leisure education sessions, slides are used to depict examples of recreation activities and equipment. Modifications to this program include moving the slide projector as far away from the screen or wall as possible to create a larger image of the slide and employing sound effects of game in play (e.g., bat striking a ball, racket hitting a shuttlecock, etc.) or environmental sounds (e.g., cheers of the crowd, silence between golf club strokes, echoes of shouts from the coach in the arena). The latter modification introduces "sensory awareness" and the many variables involved in a leisure activity to Jane and the other participants. Modifications can serve as an innovative teaching techniques for the entire class, not just for the person(s) requiring a different presentation.

Inviting assistance is another way of promoting accommodations and making disclosure more comfortable for the person having a disability. Remember, one must disclose the nature of the disability to determine and receive an accommodation or modification. The following statement printed on a college syllabus has opened doors for many students with learning disabilities: *"Students who have any disability which might affect their performance are encouraged to speak with the instructor at the beginning of the term"* (Schuck, 1992, p. 2).

A slight variation of the previous statement can be used with instructors teaching leisure-oriented classes. The only disadvantage to this invitation is the student who is not able to predict whether she will experience any difficulty; therefore, this type of student will not speak up at the start of class. If this type of student encounters difficulty half-way through the class term , she may feel it is too late to receive help and perceive embarrassment in asking for help. An open invitation for assistance should be encouraged throughout the term of the class or league season.

Response to an open invitation is verified with proof of a disability. The student must present some evidence documenting that a learning disability exists from a certified professional (see Chapter Two, Guidelines in Assessing Learning Disabilities, for professionals and diagnostic test information). The acceptance of this documentation depends upon the policies of the agency, department, or institution.

Determining Accommodations and Modifications for Children

A child having learning disabilities usually experiences some difficulties explaining how he best learns a new activity. The child may be reluctant to mention having a disability for possible fear of being singled out or separated from the group, thus avoiding the situation of being "special," similar to the experiences the child has in school when attending special education classes. A parent may disclose the disability on the recreation program registration form hoping that this might aid the recreation professional in understanding the child, but just stating the facts does not guarantee optimal teaching directives from the recreation leader. The leader should be made aware of the characteristics and learning styles of the child.

Determining an accommodation for a child's needs entails a variety of approaches: observing (acquiring awareness), questioning (obtaining information), and determining resources (skills and materials). These activities can be accomplished in the following ways:

1. If a parent discloses, ask questions using the abbreviated Cognitive Leisure Indicator Form (see Appendix P, "Cognitive Leisure Checklist"). This self-reporting form enables the recreation leader to determine if assistance and accommodations are essential to this person performing adequately within a particular activity.

2. Observe the behavior of a child over a period of time (approximately three sessions) to determine consistency of behavior. For example, noticing that Johnny (playing shortstop) always forgets who to throw the ball to after he catches it or that Bob (pitcher) experiences difficult reading hand signals from the catcher.

3. If a child experiences continuous difficulties learning a task, approach in a caring manner. Questions to ask the child could be, "You appear to be having some trouble keeping the ball inbound" or "I see you do not like to keep score in the bowling game." Ask questions about behaviors exhibited pertaining to completing the task.

4. Determine together (child and recreation leader), with parent (s) and, if necessary, a professional (adapted physical education professional, special education teacher, or recreation therapist who is familiar with learning disabilities) about appropriate accommodations for both the child and the situation.

5. The provision for accommodations will depend on the joint decision made between parties, availability and cost of alternative equipment, and skills/resources of the recreation department.

What happens when given all the accommodations and skill enhancements, Johnny still appears to forget who to throw the baseball to while playing the shortstop position? Suggest an alternative position within the same sport, for example, playing an outfield position that requires a limited number of throwing plays (e.g., return ball to second baseman, third baseman, or shortstop) or becoming the referee at first base. The point stressed here is to keep the child involved with the sport or activity that brings enjoyment.

To provide appropriate assistance to a child struggling with a specific task, the recreation leader must become aware of that child's needs through observation, questioning, and correct comprehension to ascertain resources. The recreation leader's awareness assists in promoting continual involvement in active and passive leisure pursuits. She can teach the child how to use compensation skills and can promote the idea that participating in recreational activities can result in building camaraderie and having fun.

Determining Accommodations and Modifications for Adults

An adult having learning disabilities who is not in denial will have some insight as to what type of situation or task will present difficulties. The concern is whether the adult chooses to disclose these difficulties to the recreation leader or select to solve the problem by himself. A recreation leader can use some of the following approaches to determine accommodations for adult participants:

*   if the adult discloses, ask questions using the abbreviated Cognitive Leisure Indicator Form;
*   if the adult does not disclose, but the leader notices the participant having difficulty mastering a task, observe for

details in completing tasks (e.g., frequently using incorrect measurements or missing steps in cooking, ceramic, or other craft activities);

- ask questions about behaviors displayed during activity or class sessions;
- discuss accommodations with the adult participant (and, if necessary, a professional);
- research to determine reasonable accommodations, availability and cost of equipment, and resources within agency (e.g., knowledgeable staff, funding, or obtaining assistance from other community agencies).

In determining accommodations based on information received (via verbal or written) or observed, it is best to decide on more than one accommodation, if possible, for a particular situation. Also, the use of a professional knowledgeable about learning disabilities makes the process of finding many solutions much easier.

Fundamental Principles in Providing Accommodations

The following are important fundamental principles in trying to provide appropriate and reasonable accommodations for persons with learning disabilities.

1. Develop a partnership between the service provider and the individual having learning disabilities (or parents of child with learning disabilities) to be accommodated. The most successful accommodations transpire when the individual with learning disabilities is involved in the process from the start.

2. Focus on the person's ability, not disability. Service providers, including recreation leaders, supervisors, or coaches who look at the person's disability, possibly down-rate skills and abilities based on disability. These speculations are often based on uniformed judgements about a certain type of disability.

3. Realize solutions must be individualized. As was stated in Chapter Two of this book, the characteristics of learning disabilities are numerous; everyone who has learning disabilities does not possess all of the characteristics and there is even a range of distress within the characteristics. In this being the case, solutions for persons with learning disabilities will not be the same.

4. Always look at keeping the accommodation simple; this calls for being creative with materials the service provider has at its disposal or realistically can acquire. Simplicity minimizes the cost, facilitates repairs, and does not disrupt the facilities' operations.

5. Apply the least invasive approach, depending upon the request of accommodation from the person with the disability. A recreation leader or activity teacher may encounter a participant who does not mind receiving enlarged directions, one-on-one instructions, or using a tape recorder in class to tape the session's instructions, but another person may feel these accommodations draw too much attention to the person. Accommodations can be arranged so as not to be so overt—the tape recorder can be placed in the front of the class where the teacher is talking instead of at the person's desk; the individual and teacher can arrange for a convenient time for additional instructions, not in class where others are working on individual projects, but directly after class where the participate remains seated until everyone leaves the room to receive extra instructions. Consider the preference of the individual with the disability.

6. Develop a holistic approach. It is best to look at the entire picture when considering an accommodation, including how a specific accommodation will affect the rest of an activity or agency operation (e.g., Who is responsible for ordering requested equipment? How will staff scheduling be rearranged? What type of training is needed?).

7. If the accommodation requires purchasing equipment, whenever possible, have the person being accommodated use the equipment before purchasing it, preferably within the environment where it will be operated. Try to purchase equipment from companies that have a 30-day trial period or 30-day return policy.

The significance of this section is to realize that just and reasonable accommodations result in customer satisfaction. All recreation participants are customers. When satisfied with the service, they come back to use the service again and again. In fact, these satisfied individuals tell others about the agency's services. As a supervisor, employee, or owner, your purpose is to deliver a service that imparts to the customer a pleased or contented feeling. Having agency supervisors and employees listen and act upon the needs of someone having a disability in the way of a suitable accommodation or program modification can result in a very satisfied customer and perhaps an increase of use of services by the community.

If the participant wishes to continue involvement in a particular activity despite problems accomplishing tasks, enhancing skills through small group instruction or one-on-one sessions may prove to be beneficial, along with employing alternative teaching methods. The recreation leader should try to present the instructional task in many different formats, utilizing a multisensory approach. This means that the person should receive handouts about game procedures, become active in role play (especially after demonstration of the task was provided), view a video about the task, talk about the technique with peers, and participate in practice of the task. It also is helpful to eliminate time constraints and not compare this individual's performance with that of the others in his group.

Providing an Effective Teaching Environment through Multisensory Techniques

Everyone possesses a preference, at one time or another in one's life, to a style of learning. Learning appears to be most effective when the information is presented in the style that is most conducive to that person's mode of learning. Because learning involves being attentive to incoming information and applying recognition, registration, and understanding of information (processing), instructors who employ a multisensory teaching method try to present information through the student's strongest perceptual channel. The primary channels are visual, auditory, kinesthetic, and tactile. Konstant (1992) notes that "Visual learners can best process and remember information that they see, be it in the form of charts, diagrams, pictures, or printed text. Auditory learners learn more efficiently with verbal explanations or discussions. Kinesthetic learners need to move or do things" (p. 6). Some writings on sensory learning style preferences will group kinesthetic together with tactile. Even though movement can be associated with a tactile experience, the event of actually touching (e.g., texture, pattern, depth, shape, solid mass or minute particles, hardness or softness, etc.) the object registers the learning experience. A simple example of this is petting zoos and interactive museum exhibits. These recreation environments provide the tactile learner with the opportunity to learn through touch and not be penalized for touching something. Sensory learning preferences are not dictated by age. Unfortunately, tactile and kinesthetic recreation environments are mostly created and advertised for children; however, many adults with the same learning style preference also enjoy these environments.

To help all participants learn new information, the recreation leader or activity instructor should utilize a multisensory approach. This means using a combination of visual, auditory, kinesthetic, and tactile techniques in teaching a task. For example, in a class of 25 people learning to ski, the instructor will have students who are visual, auditory, kinesthetic, and tactile learners. In order to meet the learning style preferences of the students in the class, the instructor might have students talking about what they know about skiing, then present their experience about skiing to the class. This discussion session can clear up any misconceptions, conclusions, thoughts, or concerns the class might have about skiing. The instructor, in addressing correct skiing form, might show a video or still pictures of championship skiers demonstrating correct downhill skiing form. The next session might focus on viewing the type of skis a person can purchase. Students would have the opportunity to feel the skis (e.g., instructor points out difference in weight, length, width, and shape). These students would have the opportunity to wear the skis, experience movement, or glide the skis on the ground (e.g., the class could participate in a sports store demonstration on a simulated downhill ski slope), while the teacher narrates what the skier is experiencing going downhill.

In using the previous suggestions, each sensory learning style preference is conveyed to classroom participants learning how to ski. Often, the only complaint the instructor might receive from students is not demonstrating a sensory style learning preference long enough for certain students; these may be student experiencing difficulty comprehending information in the class. Because recreation is considered a "show and do" activity, the styles most covered during instruction are the visual and kinesthetic. Recreation leaders and activity instructors must be careful to incorporate the auditory and tactile examples within instruction. In auditory instruction, the instructor or students read information aloud, the instructor allows students to audio record classroom topics, or the class is divided into small groups and group members discuss how to solve a particular problem. With tactile instruction the instructor presents tactile wrongs and rights, for instance, placement of hands on equipment (e.g., tennis racket, golf club, baseball bat, rowing paddle, etc.) and the feel of tension, spacing, and form. For the latter tactile demonstration, have students close their eyes while feeling the warp and cross yarn threads in weaving, use participants' fingers to determine spacing in tile work, and run finger tips across the edge of sewing or quilting projects for judging spacing and size of stitches. Konstant (1992) provides a list of multisensory techniques that can be employed when teaching different types of subject matter:

♦ Present information in as many ways as possible; say it and write it, draw it and discuss it, show it and touch it, talk about it and act it out.

♦ Develop color, abbreviation, sound, or gesture systems for concepts that the student understands but cannot remember names for.

♦ Combine techniques whenever and to whatever extent possible. For example, have the student read something aloud while pointing to or highlighting it; thus, the student is getting visual, auditory, and kinesthetic input.

♦ Be animated; involve the student in the session and encourage active participation.

♦ Be creative. Try to think of new ways to convey what you are expressing. Do not repeat the same explanation two or three or seven times; the student is no more likely to understand it the seventh time than the first. Find ways of communicating through the student's strongest perceptual channels (p. 8).

If the instructor is interested in learning about the class sensory learning style preference or of one participant, the Learning Styles Sensory Modality Inventory (see Appendix B) can be used. Along with employing a multisensory teaching approach, other beneficial techniques are used when teaching participants about specific sports and recreational activities.

Teaching Tips to Use with Participants Having Learning Disabilities

1. Provide an overview of the purpose and goal of the learning activity, then break down tasks into small increments of learning and teach the student in a paced, sequential manner.

2. Select books carefully; review for organization and progress from simple to complex, including subheadings, graphics, chapter summaries, glossaries, indexes, and appendices. Also, instruct students on how to read the book, locating information in the table of contents, index, chapter summary, graphs and table sections, and glossary.

3. Make sure the student has acquired one skill before presenting the next skill in the sequence of learning tasks.

4. Relate new material to everyday life whenever possible. Using role-playing techniques or real-life assignments to back up those concepts taught can make abstract concepts more understandable.

5. Provide structured repetition by allowing for brief, 5-minute reviews at the beginning and end of each session and asking questions of your students so you will get a feel of their understanding.

6. Present a variety of short assignments. Structure assignments for the student and provide frequent feedback about the quality and appropriateness of work completed.

7. Provide activities that allow the student to experience small successes on the way to a larger goal to enhance his self-concept.

8. Capitalize on the student's strengths. For example, if the student is a good listener and can follow oral directions well, present material orally. Teaching through the student's strengths helps to remediate weak areas.

9. Control the complexity of directions. Many students with learning disabilities benefit from having directions broken down into steps with one step presented at a time.

10. If possible, provide the student an opportunity to repeat verbally what has been taught as a check for accuracy. This can take place during the session or after class.

11. Use a directed-reading approach for all assignments involving reading. Review vocabulary and state the purpose for reading.

12. Make eye contact frequently. This is important for maintaining attention and encouraging participation. Invite students to sit in the front of the classroom where they can hear well and have a clear view of the board.

13. Teach mnemonic strategies such as RAP (Read paragraph, Ask yourself what you have just read, Paraphrase it in your own words) or other memory tricks to assist in learning information.

14. Use the board or overhead projector with groups whenever possible, assisting students in visualizing material. The more a student can visualize (if the student has a visual sensory learning style preference) and hear what is presented, the better the material will be understood. Visual aids can include an overhead projector, videos, a slide projector, flip charts, computer graphics, and other large illustrations. Using color within the visual presentation aids learning.

(Adapted from *GED Items,* September/October 1992)

Compensation Strategies in Sports and Recreation

Some persons having learning disabilities experience difficulty with self-regulating mechanisms such as checking, planning, monitoring, testing, revising, and evaluating during an attempt to learn or solve problems. Also, those with deficits in mental operations, such as logically organizing and coordinating incoming information, produce poor performance on tasks that require the use of general control processes or strategies for solution. Swanson (1989) notes that strategy intervention is a possible instructional goal that is directed at the executive processing or monitoring of various components to ensure a smooth coordination of information processing during task performance (p. 10).

What is meant by compensation strategies? It is the use of techniques and/or methods to do the following: more effectively solve problems, approach mastering a task efficiently, learn procedures within an activity more elaborately, and understand a concept when integration and assimilation are required. Compensation strategies are useful with visual, auditory, perceptual-motor, language, and memory disorders within learning disabilities.

Difficulties with auditory recognition and processing lend emphasis to visual or motor compensation techniques or behaviors. The participant must be trained to pay closer attention to the game officials' or coach's instructions (e.g., before, during, and after the game), and other lead players in the game or activity. The phrase "pay closer attention" means establish eye contact with the person who is speaking, become aware of regular body gestures or facial expressions exhibited by lead players, and notice when the coach repeats a name or phrase. The repetition of a term, signal, or play signifies "importance"; this is something the listener must remember to act upon. With team competitive play, the player with the auditory disorder is attentive to his opponent's eyes and body movements since this player has difficulty interpreting oral signals from teammates.

Strategies of repetition include the coach or activity instructor asking the player to repeat back the directions he just administered. Or, the player can physically demonstrate those directions to assure that the player is being focused and understanding the directions correctly. This strategy, as well as all of the strategies presented in this section, should be demonstrated daily. The overall goal is to transfer this technique from an external occurrence to an internal occurrence, evoking the internal locus of control. Instead of the coach asking the player, "What is meant by making a zone move (basketball)?" The player should be asking herself, "What is meant by making a zone move?" The person responding to this question should be able to either describe these series of plays orally, in written form, or with kinesthetic demonstration (e.g., movement).

With deficiencies in visual coordination, directionality, and tracking, the use of computer games is beneficial in improving these skills. The computer game could be as simple as Nintendo or sophisticated as NBA, NFL, or NHL Sony Play Station. Below is a list given by *Next Generation Magazine* (February 1997, pp.137-138) on selected console (e.g., play station type) sport games.

NGM Rating of Selected Console Sport Games

Title	Publisher	Rating
Play Station		
Bases Loaded	Jaleco	Poor - simple to use
FIFA Soccer	EA Sports	Excellent
Madden '97	EA Sports	Excellent
NBA Shoot Out	Sony	Good
NBA in the Zone	Konami	Average
NCAA Gamebreaker	Sony	Excellent
NFL Full Contact	Konami	Average
NFL Game Day	Sony	Excellent
NHL Face Off '98	Sony	Excellent
Olympic Soccer	U.S. Gold	Good

Title	Publisher	Rating
Saturn		
Bases Loaded '96: DoubleHeader	Jaleco	Poor
Frank Thomas Big Hurt Baseball	Acclaim	Good
NBA Action '96	Sega	Average
NBA Jam TE	Acclaim	Average
NFL Quarterback Club '96	Acclaim	Average
NFL Quarterback Club '97	Acclaim	Good
NHL All-Star Hockey	Sega	Average
NHL Powerplay '96	Virgin	Revolutionary
Olympic Soccer	U.S. Gold	Good
Pebble Beach Golf Links	U.S. Gold	Good
Quarterback Club '97	Acclaim	Good
3D Baseball	Crystal Dynamics	Good
World Cup Golf: Pro Edition	U.S. Gold	Good
World Series Baseball	Sega	Excellent
World Series Baseball II	Sega	Revolutionary
Worldwide Soccer	Sega	Good
Worldwide Soccer 2	Sega	Revolutionary

This rating is based on program features (e.g., levels of difficulty, control and manipulation of characteristics, scoring capabilities, etc.), graphic depiction, and operating usage.

When visual memory is a problem, the use of color, especially coding different stages and phrases of plays on paper, overhead transparencies, or chalk talks is one strategy to assist the athlete in visualizing the plays. Converting the plays into manipulative symbols and reconstructing and manipulating these visual symbols and pictures help with imprinting the information into memory (Yellen & Yellen, 1987, p.77). Figure 6.1 depicts a reference key that players can use to understand and manipulate basketball diagrams.

Figure 6.1
Key to Basketball Diagrams

All diagrams

→	=	Path of player
- - - →	=	Path of ball
~~→	=	Dribble
——⊣	=	Screen

Offensive diagrams

① = Point guard
② = Shooting guard
③ = Small forward
④ = Power forward
∞ = Center
≈ = Point with ball
X = Defensive player

Defensive diagrams

X1 = Player assigned to 1
X2 = Player assigned to 2
X3 = Player assigned to 3
X4 = Player assigned to 4
X5 = Player assigned to 5
⊗ = Offensive player with the ball
O = Offensive player

Drill diagrams

C = Coach
M = Manager
General situations:
O = Offensive player
X = Defensive player

Specific situations:
Numbers used when perimeter vs post distinction is made
Example:
② = Perimeter offensive player, perhaps the shooting guard
X4 = Post defensive player, perhaps the power forward

(Adapted from *Coaching Basketball Successfully* by Morgan Wootten, 1992, p. 70)

This key informs the players of what is being demonstrated and discussed. Color can be added to the key—offensive diagrams outlined in red and defensive diagrams outlined in green. The symbols on this key could be printed on cardstock paper and cut out so that the player has an opportunity to manipulate the pieces on her basketball board just as the coach can manipulate pieces on his basketball board. Below is a generic basketball court to manipulate ball pieces.

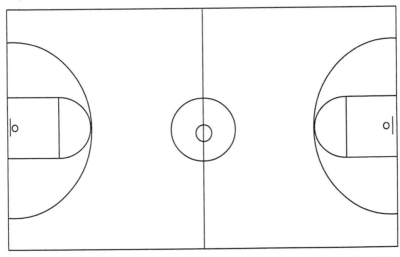

(Basketball court graphic adapted from *Coaching Basketball Successfully,* Wooten, 1992).

The same procedure used in making basketball plays easier to visually remember can also be applied to football. Both players and coaches can use the manipulative symbols in figure 6.2, applying them to the football diagram (figure 6.2a) to create a visualization of a particular football play.

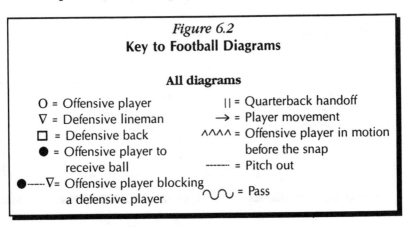

Figure 6.2
Key to Football Diagrams

All diagrams

O = Offensive player
∇ = Defensive lineman
□ = Defensive back
● = Offensive player to receive ball
●-----∇= Offensive player blocking a defensive player

|| = Quarterback handoff
→ = Player movement
∧∧∧∧ = Offensive player in motion before the snap
------ = Pitch out
∿∿ = Pass

Figure 6.2 Cont.

Basic defensive positions

∇N = Nose tackle

∇T = Tackle

∇E = Defensive end

⬚S⬚ = Safety

⬚R⬚ = Rover

⬚H⬚ = Halfback

⬚LB⬚ = Linebacker

⬚CB⬚ = Cornerback

Basic offensive positions

Ⓣ Ⓔ = Tight end

Ⓣ = Tackle

Ⓖ = Guard

Ⓒ = Center

Ⓔ = End

Ⓢ Ⓔ = Split end

Ⓠ Ⓑ = Quarterback

Ⓦ Ⓑ = Wingback (or slot)

Ⓕ Ⓑ = Fullback

Ⓣ Ⓑ = Tailback

Ⓗ = Holder

Ⓟ = Punter

Ⓚ = Kicker

(Adapted from *Coaching Football Successfully* by Bob Reade, 1994, pp. 74, 95, 112)

The coach or activity instructor should teach play options separately and break down the steps within each play. For example, in teaching the running game in football, review the type of plays: Wishbone, I-formation, Split-back Veer, and Wing-T. Discussion within each particular type of play should focus on the "what" of the play, "why" of the play, "when and where" the play is implemented, "who" is involved in the play, and "how" the play is carried out. The use of the "wh" questions covers all aspects of the topic. It also helps the participant relate the detail parts or steps to the overall purpose of the task.

Figure 6.2a

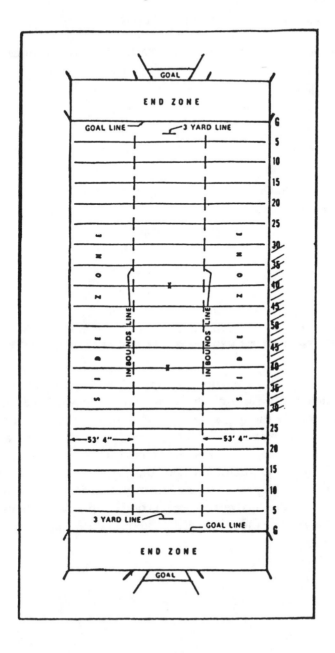

(Football field graphic adapted from *The Parent's Guide to Coaching Football,* 2nd ed. by John P. McCarthy, Jr. 1995).

Players who experience difficulties in calculating game strategies such as reasoning, outmaneuvering the opponent, and predicting a number of possible responses based on opponent's movements, require compensation strategies. With these individuals, calculating game strategies improves with activity training and active involvement in the game. The training should be skills involving drawing conclusions and anticipating consequences of the actions in the playing arena (e.g., critical thinking). Here the presentation of case scenarios within small groups would stimulate verbal discussions between teammates on how to attack or block the opposition. A dramatization of the actions in the case scenario could be conducted by group members, followed by talk of opinions and plans of action based on possible occurrence of events within that situation. The practice, discussion, breakdown of tasks, written diagrams, and knowledge of meaning behind plays in physical activities aid in a more elaborate understanding of the activity. To assist developing critical thinking behavior of participants within sports and recreation activities, the instructor can do the following:

1. Determine the goal (desired outcome) of the skill and communicate this clearly to the participants.

2. Structure the environment to encourage goal attainment. This is where the instructor helps the participants to verbally identify those factors in the environment to which the participant must attend. The instructor then asks the participants questions about how they think the environmental conditions would affect their skill attempts (e.g., football throw, weather conditions, position of players, skill level of opponent's defensive line, etc.). Structuring the environment appropriately means simplifying the practice conditions so that participants can determine what has to be done; when, where, and how it has to be done; and why it has to be done a particular way. As the group becomes more proficient, the environment should be structured to match, as closely as possible, the conditions under which the activity or game is to be performed.

3. Provide the learner with instruction and feedback. Instruction can be implemented through a variety of teaching methods. Whatever method employed, the purpose is to direct participants to think critically about what it is they are going to do.

Feedback is necessary to reflect upon correct or incorrect responses to a question or action. It should include statements of relevant information as well as questions to encourage the participant to focus on his practice attempts (Clements, 1995, pp. 35-36).

Compensation strategies are only a small part of performing an activity or sport with equal success to a person who does not having learning disabilities. A person with a disability may need something extra, whether it is more time, individual practice or tutorial sessions, special equipment, different arrangements, or personal assistance. These accommodations can improve one's chance of accomplishment in a given activity or sport.

Specific Accommodations and Modifications of Recreation Activities

People having perceptual-motor based learning disabilities most often find comfort in participating in physical solitary activities such as walking, running, weight lifting, swimming, skateboarding, rollerblading, or cycling. The competition in these activities is with oneself. This enables the individual to improve at her own speed, and she experiences no external pressures from others evaluating her performance. If this person wishes to have a friend accompany her during the activity, she will usually select someone who is similar in activity ability level and/or understands her disability. Thus, a feeling of comfort is conveyed in this arrangement and relationship; no feelings of embarrassment or intimidation enter the situation. What can make the transition from participating in physical solitary activities to physical team activities less frightening? Supplying appropriate modifications or accommodations to the situation.

Selecting modifications could consist of something like allowing extra time in a timed word game, painting a baseball yellow, using bright green tape to create the boundaries of an inside foul line on a volleyball court, or teaching all soccer players the following mnemonic to remember a play sequence: **PIFS - P**ass ball with **I**nside **F**oot to **S**tationary player or **PIF SAMP - P**ass ball with **I**nside **F**oot **S**lightly **A**head of **M**oving **P**layer. Accommodations can be as simple as having the catcher wear red gloves under his mitt for administering signals to the pitcher or audio recording someone reading directions to assembling a model project. Complex accommodations might consist of breaking down steps and rewriting the rules of a game. The revised game rules with additional steps are then given to the person to use as a reference guide to follow during participation in the game. The *Technical Assistance Bulletin* (Shields, 1996), published by the Recreation Resources Service at North Carolina State University, states the following guidelines for adapting activities and lists the primary types of adaptations.

Guidelines for Adapting Activities:
- adapt only if essential for participation, success, and enjoyment or to reduce failure and frustration;
- consider adaptations as temporary or transitional changes, if possible;
- adapt on an individual need and age-appropriate basis;
- adapt for normalization by keeping the activity as close to the standard version as possible;
- adapt considering availability and cost in the community;
- ask the consumer, family, or friends for suggestions.

Primary Types of Adaptations:
- Materials—equipment (the weight and size of objects and implements, target size, ball resiliency, etc.).
- Procedural—rule (expectations can be altered, rules can be modified, and choices can be reduced).
- Space—distance from target or between bases, height of targets, etc.
- Force—force or speed required for activity slowed or substituted.
- Skill sequence—use of task analysis to illustrate steps.
- Lead-up activities—tasks, exercises, or games that are prerequisites to activity.
- Communication—interpreter, taped message, magnification of volume or print, other audio or visual needs (p. 2).

Major categories in this section will be Sports and Physical Activities, Passive Activities, Outdoor Activities, Hobbies, and Social/Community Activities. Each category comprises a number of activities with narratives explaining the objectives of the activities, equipment and rules of the activities, and accommodations and/or modifications to the activities.

Sports and Physical Activities

Badminton

The object of the game is to hit the shuttlecock back and forth across the net with a racket without permitting it to touch the ground. The person's quest is to hit the shuttlecock into the opposing court so that it cannot be returned.

1.   Have a number of rackets available with different weights (3.5 to 4.2 ounces) and various racket grips (3.5 to 3" inches).

2.   Metal rackets are more durable than wood rackets and tend to be heavy. Fiberglass and graphite rackets are light, give a whipping action, and provide a subtle sensitivity to the shuttlecock.

3.   Use nylon shuttlecocks for durability.

Problems that occur in badminton:
➻ Miss: failure of the racket to come in contact with the shuttle.
➻ Wood shot: hitting the shuttle with the wood of the racket rather than the strings.
➻ Fault: any violation of the rules. Specifics to this is if either in service or play, the shuttle falls outside the boundaries of the court or passes through or under the net. Also, if the shuttle in play is hit twice in succession by the same player with two strokes.

Solutions to difficulties:
➻ Individual practice sessions of bouncing the shuttle off the racket head, using an underhand swing (shuttle bouncing up toward the sky), and practicing underhanded one-on-one volleys will help cure the miss and wood shots.
➻ *Modifications*—If the shuttle continues to fall outside the boundaries of the court as a result of misjudging distance or regulating exertion of force on the shuttlecock, then lengthen boundary lines of the court or increase the weight of the shuttlecock by gluing or taping a lightweight, small metal washer underneath the shuttlecock.
➻ *Modification*—Poor ability to aim the shuttlecock over the net or for the shuttlecock to reach the net can be helped by having the person having difficulty use an underhand stroke to bounce

the shuttlecock up, while a second player on that team hits the shuttlecock over the net (similar to a set-up play in volleyball).

➥ *Accommodation*—A person having difficulty hitting the shuttlecock over the net will be allowed to have two or three hits per serve or volley.

Racquetball

A rubber ball is batted alternately by the players against the front wall of the one- or four-wall court, the object being to cause the ball to rebound to such a position and in such a manner that the opponent cannot return it before the second bounce. Suggestion is to begin with one-wall (front wall) court play with a player having learning disabilities; it is easier to return shots and master angle shots from one-wall play vs. four-wall play.

1. Racquets can be made of wood, fiberglass, graphite, or various kinds of metals and plastics of differing shapes. Lightweight metal or plastic is beneficial to the beginner. Racquet heads are tear drop or owl head, 9" wide by 11" long.

2. The ball is usually dark in color, 2.5" in diameter, and weighs 14 ounces.

Problems that occur in racquetball:
● Crotch ball: a ball hitting at the juncture of the front wall and floor or the ceiling, sidewall, or corner.
● Out: serving the ball out-of-bounds or hitting the floor before the wall.
● Miss: inability for racquet to make contact with ball.

Solutions to difficulties:
● Teach students basic sidearm and underarm patterns beginning with tapping the ball easily against the wall rather than using strokes requiring maximum force production. Practice in teams of two, alternating hits off the wall and developing a consistent volley. Next, have teams transition to changing the level of the ball against the wall, changing the angle of the shot, and changing the force level of the ball. This type of practice assists in diminishing a miss and crotch ball.

● *Modifications*—To eliminate or control the number of "outs" a player receives, allow for a two-bounce return from serve or move service box up five feet (use 15 feet instead of 20 feet from the front wall). A tennis ball or larger rubber ball can be employed during game play to secure contact with racquet.

● *Accommodations*—For the player who exhibits poor grasping ability due to inconsistent and incorrect exertion of force that causes the player to frequently lose her racquet, the use of a control (grasp) cuff or Ace bandage can help in proper gripping. The Grasp Cuff can be purchased through Access to Recreation, Inc. (see Chapter Seven, Equipment and Materials section, for a complete address).

Golf

Golf is a sport that offers lifestyle enjoyment. The golfer is either pitted against self or opponents. The object of the game is to score as few strokes as possible for each hole. Play starts at the teebox and continues through stroking the ball through the fairway and onto the green. At the green the ball is putted into the hole marked by a flagstick.

1. Clubs are constructed of wood, steel, or graphite, or are titanium-shafted.

2. The golf ball's selection is dependent upon the individual. Construction varies from a solid one-piece ball to a ball having a small hard core wound with rubber bands and sealed with a durable cover. Plastic balls may be used for indoor or small area (e.g., backyard) practice.

3. A tee is a wooden or plastic peg on which the ball is placed and from which the ball is to be driven.

Problems that occur in golf:

◉ Golf swing: backswing is too fast, eliminating good tempo and throwing the golfer off balance; raising the head from its original position; rushing the downswing; uncocking the wrists too soon, which throws off the proper sequence and usually casts the club outside of the correct plane; and failing to complete the follow-through with the hands held high.

Solutions to difficulties:

☺ Individual practice sessions focusing on the swing without use of a ball.

☺ For adults, practice with a swing trainer club. This is a hinged iron that collapses (or becomes flexible) when the golf swing is incorrect (see Chapter Seven, Equipment and Materials section for companies selling swing trainers).

☺ *Modification*—Instead of playing a game of golf, play or competition can focus on "golf individual skills." The purpose of the individual skills competition is to allow athletes to train and compete in basic golf skills. The six skills are in short putting, long putting, chipping, and the pitch shot, iron shot, and wood shot. More information on this type of contest is contained in the book, *Sports and Recreation for the Disabled.* Chapter Seven has the address where one can purchase this book.

☺ *Accommodation*—Use oversized clubs to assist with club contact with the ball and to increase the distance of the ball. There are numerous golf equipment companies manufacturing oversized woods and irons. Oversized golf equipment can be purchased in single pieces or in a club set.

Aerobics

Aerobic exercise is an activity that uses the oxygen system of the body. This activity works on the heart, lungs, and vascular system to deliver oxygen to working muscles. When a greater amount of oxygen can be supplied, the body is able to sustain high levels of work over longer periods of time. In aerobic and calisthenic exercises, participants should perform at least 10 repetitions per set, from one to three sets, resting between sets.

1. Clothing should be comfortable; loose-fitting clothes or stretch cotton exercise outfits; athletic aerobic shoes or comfortable sneakers.

2. An exercise mat should be either a 1" cross-link/closed-cell polyethylene foam filler, which provides the best shock absorbency, or a 2" 100 ILD polyurethane foam filler (for extra light weight; recommended for elementary school use).

3. Equipment could include the Thera-Band® and Thera-Band® Tubing to permit passive to active assistive stretching to help deliver progressive, resistive exercise. Step® contains a non-slip platform with two supporting blocks.Vinyl covered dumb-bells or soft wrist and ankle weights could also be used to build strength in muscles during aerobic exercise. The mat,Thera-Band®, Step®, dumbbells, and weights are available through Sportime Abilitations (see Chapter Seven for their address).

4. The aerobic studio should have floor-length mirrors covering at least one wall.Watching oneself perform exercises can con-tribute to spatial awareness, synchronization of one's move-ments with peers in the group, and a refined performance of exercise routines.

Problems that occur in aerobics:
♥ Directionality:distinguishing separate movements to the front, back, right, left, up, and down.
♥ Interpreting instructor's commands while continuing to move: participant stops to listen to instructor's directions then pro-ceeds with exercise, losing repetitions within a set.
♥ Keeping pace with instructor:participant is a half-step behind group or slow to make changes.
♥ Coordination difficulty: confusion with switching footing in Step® activities, manipulating and stretching the Thera-Band® around limbs, or holding dumbbells in hands and moving both arms in opposite directions.

Solutions to difficulties:
♥ When directionality and coordination are problems, the par-ticipant might look into taking a slower pace class,such as low-impact aerobics. Before enrolling in an aerobics class, talk with the instructor; ask her how often routines are changed during the 10-week exercise program and what basic steps the instruc-tor will be using. In addition to asking about basic steps, in-quire about observing the class for a few sessions. Become aware of the exercise routines;use of equipment,music, and teacher's mannerism;and the way she interacts with students.One should ask herself, "Are the instructor's directions clear and easy to follow?"

♥ *Accommodations*—Participants receive a handout from the instructor depicting illustrations of basic aerobic step sequences that will be used throughout the program. The participant can study these handouts and practice the steps at home, thereby lessening the chances of mistakes during class. A staff member or peer involved in the aerobic exercise could provide an extra verbal or physical cue to the participant, helping this person with direction changes and maintaining pace with the group. To improve coordination, the participant can arrange for one-on-one sessions with the instructor. In these sessions the participant will have the opportunity to practice alone with the instructor, use equipment at her own pace, mimic movements of the instructor at a slower speed or in smaller movement intervals, and can correct mistakes without audience observance and comments. Besides, immediate reinforcement is provided by the instructor to build the participant's confidence level.

♥ *Modification*—The instructor explains to class participants the advantages behind specific exercise movements (e.g., this exercise builds the quadriceps, biceps, cardiovascular system, etc.). A participant may use the explanation as a way to remember the sequence of steps—an association memory strategy.

Passive Activities

Card Games (Deck of Regular Playing Cards)

Crazy 8
The object of the game is for one player to rid himself of all cards first.

Equipment: • two decks of regular playing cards (or more if needed)

Formation: Two decks of cards are needed for more than five players. Eleven cards are dealt to each player and the remaining cards are put in a pile in the middle of the table.

Action: The dealer leads a card in any suit; everyone in turn around the table must follow suit unless he wants to change suit by either matching the last number with a new suit or by using an "8"—the wild card that can name any suit. For example, if the last card put down was a five of hearts, the next player may either play any heart or the five of any other suit, thereby changing the suit. The player can also play an "8," calling the "8" any suit he desires. Anyone who does not have a play draws from the pile in the middle, one card at a time, until he turns over a card that can be played.

Problems that occur in Crazy 8:

♣ Difficulty remembering directions to the game (e.g., matching last number with new suit; asking, "What is the function of 8?" or forgetting to draw cards from the pile when the player does not have a card to play).

♣ Forgetting sequence of playing turn in game.

Solutions to difficulties:

♣ *Accommodations*—Either the player having difficulty or the activity leader can create a game reference guide card stating game rules, objectives, and directions. This information can be printed on a 3x5 card in simple, easy to follow steps of the game. To remember that the person always follows the player to his left, the player could use the first-letter mnemonic strategy of **PTTL** for "Play to the left." The player could also draw an arrow pointing left on the lower outside portion of the thumb of the left hand (if player holds cards in left hand) or draw the arrow pointing left on the lower outside portion of the right hand (if player is holding cards in right hand). This arrow drawing should be designed to be only visible to the player; it is a discreet way to remind one of correct direction.

♣ *Modification*—Creation of an "8" wild card in any suit. Illustration, if the group is playing clubs and the next player, who did not have any clubs or any number to match the last number (e.g., two of clubs) places an "8" of spades down, but calls the suit "diamond" instead of keeping the "8" of spades, the player would change the card to an "8" of diamond. This assists those players whose auditory memory and fluid reasoning are not on the same level as other players in the group. Here, one does not need to remember the auditory change because the new card (e.g., "8" of diamond) indicates the change.

Seven Up

The object of the game is to get rid of all cards in the hand first. The winner receives all the chips placed in the center of the table, plus chips from other players who have cards left in their hands.

Equipment: • one deck of playing cards
                 • chips or beans

Formation: All cards are dealt for four to six players. Each player is given 20 or more chips or beans.

Action: The person to the left of the dealer starts and must have a "7" to lay down. Play is made on "7s", either up or down (see diagram below). If no play can be made, the player must put in a chip. When one's turn comes again, the player may lay down as many plays (e.g., cards) as he can in order to get rid of cards in hand. He does not have to play more than one card, but a player may not pay a chip if he has a card that will play. The first player to get rid of all his cards takes all the chips that have been put into the center. Other players must pay the winner one chip for each remaining card still held. Numbers must be played from six to ace and eight to king in order on either side of "7" and must match the suit of the "7." Four "7s" can be played at one time.

♠	A 2 3 4 5 6	"7"	8 9 10 J Q K
♥	A 2 3 4 5 6	"7"	8 9 10 J Q K
♦	A 2 3 4 5 6	"7"	8 9 10 J Q K
♣	A 2 3 4 5 6	"7"	8 9 10 J Q K

Problems that occur in Seven Up:
♣ Difficulty remembering to play more than one "7" layout, when cards are available.
♣ Forgetting sequence of playing turn in game.

Solutions to difficulties:
♣ *Accommodation*—The first few times playing this game might require the assistance of another person to remind the player

having difficulty to look at all cards, one suit at a time, to see if a card can be laid down on each available "7" layout. The use of two or three card holders allows for easy manipulation of cards and placement of cards in a correct layout. Other accommodations in playing cards consist of utilizing a variety of large print cards and card holders (e.g., hand held or free standing). These materials can be purchased through S&S Worldwide Games (see Chapter Seven for their address).

♣ *Modifications*—Only allowing two "7" layouts at one time. When one layout is complete, the next "7" suit can be placed to begin a new layout.

(Card game instructions adapted from Jane A. Harris, 1970, *File o' Fun: Card File for Social Recreation*)

Table Games
Word Yahtzee ®
Players try to beat the clock in forming words from the letter dice and by building words of different lengths in a variety of categories to end up with the most points.

Equipment: • seven letter dice with number values
• one dice cup
• one timer
• one Word Yahtzee® score pad

Action: One player is chosen to go first, then others follow in a clockwise manner. A player has a maximum of three chances to roll the word dice. These rolls must be completed in one minute. A player receives points if he rolls all vowels, all consonants, an entire word or chance (number value for the word(s) formed from the roll of dice). To determine a final score, the players add the points in the upper sections of the score sheet and add the points in the lower section. The combined total of the upper and lower sections is the grand total. The person with the highest score wins the game.

Problems that occur in Word Yahtzee®:
✍ The player is unable to spell words within the time span of one minute, which might limit the player to only one or two rolls.

✍ Difficulty adding scores or player takes a longer amount of time to total word scores than other players.

✍ Forgetting rules of the game.

Solutions to problems:

✍ Extend the amount of time per roll for the player having the difficulty (accommodation) or for all players in the game (modification), for example, allowing one minute for *each* of the three rolls.

✍ Pair the player having difficulty with another player or person not playing to assist him by giving clues (e.g., an animal that lives in the forest, first letter begins with "D," and this word contains four letters).

✍ *Accommodations*—Using an electronic spell checker or dictionary to aid in spelling words and a calculator to computer scores. A peer could double check the player's score to verify correctness. Either the player or activity leader can create a reference game sheet with procedures, rules, and scoring instructions that the player can use during play of game.

✍ *Modifications* —To assist the entire group in understanding the rules and procedures of the game, the activity leader would conduct the game by categories. Game one will consist of players adding up "all consonants." Game two, all players would obtain a score from "all vowels." The last game consists of adding up "only words"—chance category. The game can be played without a timing and scoring factor. This is the most comfortable method of introducing someone having trouble with spelling, mathematics, and slow processing of information to play a group word game.

(Word Yahtzee®, E.S. Lowe, A Milton Bradley Co., Springfield, MA 01101)

Dominoes

Five-up, also known as Muggins or All Fives, is played with the standard, European six-spot tile set. The goal of the game is to score points by forming chains whose ends total up to some multiple of five (e.g., 5, 10, 15, 20, etc). The player who forms such a pattern immediately scores that total.

Equipment: •   one double-six domino set that contains a 28 tile set; bones, tiles, or stones are the names used referring to domino playing pieces

• paper and pencil to keep score

Action: Each player draws one bone to decide who goes first. The player that draws the bone with the highest total of spots leads off. Players draw five bones from the boneyard, starting with the lead player and proceeding clockwise in turn. The players must play a bone that matches either ends of the bone lead by the preceding player. Double bones are laid crosswise on the chain; up to four bones may be laid against a double, two continuing the chain and two more sprouting off the double to form a cross pattern. If at any point players cannot add a bone to the end of one of the chains, then they must draw bones from the boneyard until they draw a bone that can be played. All bones that cannot be played immediately are added to their hand. The first player to play all of his bones scores points for the bones remaining in other players' hands. If play is blocked such that no player may lay a bone, then all players should total their remaining bones. The player with the lowest total scores the total of all other players' bones. A game is normally 150 to 200 points. If more than one player or team passes this total in the same hand, then the team or player with the highest point total wins.

Problems that occur in dominoes:

Difficulty matching bones, especially with double-nine or double-twelve sets (e.g., the dots seem to run together).

Problems adding bones at the end of chains and remembering that only a score with multiples of five are valid.

Forgetting to draw from the boneyard when he has no bones in hand to play.

Solutions to difficulties:

Play a game of dominoes without keeping score. The only object of this game is for the player to match his bones and rid himself of all his bones, then that player becomes the winner. For persons who dread counting, this game version might prove more suitable for equal participation.

Jumbo Double-six Dominoes and Color and Dot Dominoes are available to aid in matching. With the Color and Dot Dominoes, a player would look at matching the color and correct dot design of the tile. These domino sets are available through S&S Worldwide Games (see Chapter Seven for the address).

Accommodation—Make a couple of bone covers out of a piece of colored poster board. Place the bone on the colored poster board paper and cut out the shape of the bone. When the person's turn comes, he takes the paper bone covers and places them over half of the bone at the end of each chain. Only the outer half of the bone that needs to be connected would be visible to the player. If there are four chains, four bone outer ends are exposed, waiting to receive a connecting bone. After the proper bone is chosen and placed correctly in the chain, then the player can remove the bone covers.

(Rules of dominoes taken from http://www.gamecabinet.com/rules/ DominoMuggins.html and http://www.gamecabinet.com/rules/DominoTerms.html)

Trivia and Information Knowledge-based Games

These type of games include Jeopardy®, Trivial Pursuit®, Scattergories®, Wheel of Fortune®, and Outburst®. The object of the majority of games previously listed is to respond quickly and correctly to information given to a player. The more correct answers, the higher amount of points the player receives during the game.

Equipment: • contents of the game

Action: Players are given category titles and/or clues to topics. Within a given amount of time the player must verbalize or write his or her response to the question. The response is either directed at the leader of the game or the opposing team. When that person or team states an incorrect response, the opposing team or player gets a chance to answer correctly to the given category or clue. Sometimes both teams will answer the same topic at once (Scattergories®), then state their answers to the leader, who then verifies the correct answer and assigns points to the team or player.

Problems that occur in trivia and information knowledge-based games:

? Incorrect interpretation of information (visual or auditory) that results in a wrong answer.

? Player unable to process information presented in time allotted, resulting in no response or frequent guessing.

? Player knowledgeable of the answer, but states the incorrect word, mispronounces the word, or has difficulty spelling the word correctly.

? Due to team atmosphere and a competitive nature, the player may experience overwhelming anxiety to produce consistently correct answers, thereby dropping out of the game after the first round of play.

Solutions to difficulties:

? *Modifications*—All players can ask for information to be repeated, have the option to read the card, and be presented with an example to clarify confusion or uncertainty about the topic. A player can also ask for another clue or category if she has trouble comprehending what the question is asking.

? *Accommodations*—Extend time to better process incoming information. For example, when giving a category, allow a player time to think about it before setting the timer, thus doubling the amount of game time, or pair a player with a peer to discuss the meaning of information before contributing a response. If spelling is a concern, ask players to spell the word anyway they can; credit will be given to verbally stating the word and giving a definition or example of the word. A player is permitted to use a portable spell checker or computer to make lists of words or to produce the answer. A player could also explain the meaning or definition to his partner and the partner could verbalize or write the answer to the question.

Outdoor Activities

Fishing

An outdoor activity whereby the individual by oneself or in a group enjoys being in the surroundings of nature is fishing. In fishing, participants test their skills against water and sea life while savoring the solitude of the moment.

Equipment:
- fishing pole, either constructed of fiberglass or bamboo
- electric or crank arm reel with adjustable drag,
- weights on the line
- hooks, bobbers, and lures
- tackle box
- fishing net and fish stringer—holds all the fish caught
- waders—rubber boots and leg covers
- optional—boat or canoe rental

Action: Organize materials for a fishing excursion, rent a boat or canoe, and pack fishing supplies, food, and drink. The next step is to travel to a desired destination and assemble the fishing gear. The most important task is casting the fishing pole and waiting for fish to arrive. When the bobber goes underwater, the participant gives a slight tug on the pole in order to set the hook into the fish. He then reels the fish in quietly, but smoothly. Once the fish is out of the water, remove the fish from the hook, put fish on the stringer, and place them into an ice- or water-filled ice chest.

Problems that occur in fishing:

∝ Organizational and time management problems when the person constantly forgets or misplaces fishing equipment.

∝ Participant using too much force in extracting pole from the water (losing fish) or in continuously moving pole in water (expelling fish from hook with bait).

∝ Damaging fishing pole, hook, and other equipment due to over angling (e.g., hook gets caught in the trees, bushes, rocks, wood on pier, people's clothing, etc.). The participant can also hurt fellow nature and fishing enthusiasts in the area from lack of awareness about his surroundings.

Solutions to difficulties:

∝ First make a list of "things to do" to prepare self for the fishing trip, for example, check bobbers for cracks, buy more hooks, reserve a canoe at the lake two weeks before the trip, purchase fishing licenses, etc.

∝ Make a second list of equipment and supplies required for fishing excursions. If fishing by oneself, have a friend or spouse double check the person's list before he ventures out to the lake or stream. The list should not only name equipment and supplies, but the location where the supplies will be kept (e.g., bait in 4oz. clear plastic box in tackle box). This compensation strategy aids in organizing self and limits misplacement of supplies before, during, and after the fishing trip. This list should always be kept in the same place all the time (e.g., list of equipment and supplies kept in a plastic bag taped to the top of the tackle box).

∝ Enroll in a safety precaution class that is taught by an experienced recreation leader who offers a multisensory approach. Showing videos of fishing mishaps, role playing the courteous and cautious fishing person, demonstrating correct casting or angling methods in crowded areas (e.g., plant or human inhabitants) and proper handling of hooks, and offering first aid procedures helps to deter major fishing catastrophes.

∝ *Accommodation*—To adjust for appropriate use of strength to expel fish from the water, have an experienced fisherman guide the person using hands-on directions. The fisherman would stand behind the person, place his hands on the hands of the person holding the fishing pole, and guide the person's arm up and out of the water, demonstrating the correct way to retain the fish on the hook. Additional one-on-one practice sessions on casting and reeling is beneficial for improving technique.

Hiking

A means of getting closer to nature by using one's God-given mechanisms for transportation is hiking. Hiking is not only good for one's cardiovascular system but also offers the splendor of magnificent scenery and sounds of natural habitat to provide a boost for one's psyche. A stroll through a country's untouched areas offers lessons in understanding and respecting the fruits of Earth.

Equipment: • comfortable-fitting hiking boots and socks
            • backpack—lightweight frame (tubular aluminum) with an attached nylon pack containing several compartments
            • clothing—wool clothing; long underwear is essential for night and cool days. It is usually best

to "layer" clothing and adjust the number of layers to suit the temperature and degree of physical activity
- sleeping bags, sleeping pads, or air mattresses
- tents or shelters (e.g., lightweight tarp)
- cooking and eating equipment
- pocket equipment (e.g., wooden matches, pocket knife, whistle, and compass)
- food and water
- maps and guidebooks
- first-aid kit

Problems that occur in hiking:

∧   Directionality difficulties and interpreting maps; misreading maps often results in getting lost.

∧   Poor judgment regarding needs of body and or weather condition, resulting in hypothermia or heat stress.

∧   Poor planning, miscalculated water and food supply for hike, or brought wrong type of shoes and clothing for hike.

Solutions to difficulties:

∧   Begin with small day hikes with other experienced hikers. Interested persons should attend a number of hikes sponsored by nature-oriented groups or organized recreation agencies (e.g., Sierra Club, 4-H Club, Boy or Girl Scouts, sporting and outdoor stores, community recreation agencies, or college leisure groups). Attend classes or workshops on hiking preparation and safety. The previous problems listed can happen with experienced hikers; what brings a person out of a potentially hazardous situation is knowing what to do to prevent the situation from getting worse.

There are a number of programs that specialize in providing wilderness experiences for people with disabilities. These programs are as follows:

- ***Colorado Outdoor Education Center for the Handicapped (COECH)*** offers year-round wilderness programs for people of all ages, with a variety of developmental, physical, emotional, medical, and learning disabilities.

- ***Shared Outdoor Adventure Recreation (SOAR)*** facilitates access to outdoor adventure through the following activities: skiing, river rafting, sailing, hiking, camping, rock climbing, and ropes challenge courses.
- ***Wilderness Inquiry*** is designed to integrate disabled and nondisabled individuals in cooperative adventures that facilitate learning, communication, and development of self-esteem (see Chapter Seven for addresses to these wilderness organizations and camping facilities).

Wilderness staff members knowledgeable about the needs and characteristics of people having disabilities are more prepared to deal with unexpected circumstances occurring with this population than a staff person not having any training or knowledge about disabilities. These programs are not being endorsed by this author or publisher. The book is making readers aware that wilderness programs for people having disabilities do exist and information is available for readers to further explore these programs.

Gardening

Recently being recognized as having therapeutic properties, gardening throughout the years has been a favorite outdoor pastime for people of all ages. Gardening relieves the stresses of daily life, builds muscles, stimulates creativity, and promotes the flourishing of beautiful floral life all can enjoy for years to come.

Equipment:
- seedlings, seeds, bulbs, or roots
- soil or clear plot of land
- containers - flat or deep (depending upon plant)
- water and watering can
- cultivator, transplanter, digger/weeder, and trowel

Action: Before one begins planting, prior knowledge about gardening is essential for proper growth and maintenance of plant life. The gardener should be aware of hardiness criteria (zone) in one's geographic area (e.g., rainfall, temperature, and variation between seasons); nutrients for soil; perennial versus annual plants; amount of shade or sun within planting area; insect, animal, or disease damage to plants; and correct time to plant seeds, bulbs, and seedlings during the year. If the gardener is aware of all the previous information, the next action is to purchase the seeds or plants, soil, and nutrients. Plant flowers, seeds, vegetables, fruits, or trees following the directions provided; water plant, prune, or pinch back as directed; and watch it grow.

Problems that occur in gardening:

❀ Time management difficulties and infrequent watering and feeding arise because a schedule was not created or maintained. Harvesting vegetables and fruits too early or too late because the growth time was not noted is also a problem.

❀ Memory problems, such as overwatering plants (e.g., watered plants twice in one day or watered plants immediately after rainfall later in the day, not using proper judgment), forgetting to cover plants (e.g., plants in high altitude and direct sunlight areas), or not winterizing plants for next year.

❀ Organizational problems, such as overextending self by creating a garden that is too large to manage, choosing high maintenance plants requiring a lot of time and money, and having many different varieties of plants that each call for different care and maintenance.

❀ Poor judgment, such as not contacting an expert gardener or nursery personnel for information about helping a sickly or dying plant before it is in its last days of life.

Solutions to difficulties:

❀ Create a checklist or schedule of watering and feeding times for the week.

❀ Note changes in weather, with frequent rainfall or high temperatures one needs to adjust the watering and feeding schedule.

❀ Install a drip or sprinkler system for easier maintenance of the watering schedule.

❀ Attend gardening workshops at local nurseries, 4-H centers, flower clubs (e.g., Iris Club, Rose Club, or Orchid Club) or classes held at community centers or continuing education centers at local colleges or universities to enhance knowledge about gardening.

Hobbies

Photography

Photography is the art of capturing life's wonders on film. Whether taking pictures of the family, one's favorite vacation spot, or nature's spectacular scenery, the joy of reproducing that special moment can last forever.

Equipment:
- camera: 35mm or any other variety
- film: either color or black and white
- optional: supplies and equipment for developing film

Action: Prior knowledge about operating a camera is necessary. With a manual 35mm camera one must become familiar with F-Stop/aperture, distance/focus ring, shutter speed, and film speed. The F-stop determines the amount of light exposed to film. The smaller the hole in the view finder the larger the number setting on the F-stop. The environment (e.g., low light vs. bright light or shooting a moving subject vs. a stationary subject) will be the deciding factor in what kind of film the photographer will purchase and what type of camera settings will capture the best picture. Film comes in graduated speeds from 100 to 1000. For example, when 400 film speed is used the shutter speed number must be low and the F-stop number larger, this depends upon light and movement of the object. To obtain quality photos, the photographer needs to keep the sun behind her for sunny outdoor photo sessions; to hold the camera steady; to adjust the F-stop, shutter speed, and focus ring appropriately (for a manual 35 mm camera); to adjust the zoom lens for close-up shots or move closer to the subject and fill the viewfinder with the subject; to create a frame within the picture, drawing the viewer's attention to the subject; and to try to take pictures of people in unposed, relaxed, natural settings. After photos are developed, they are then stored in photo albums or scrap books ready for public viewing.

Problems that occur with photography:

📷 Difficulty lining up correct placement of F-stop/aperture, shutter speed, and zoom lens.

📷 Forgetting the appropriate method for adjusting F-stop, shutter speed with film speed (e.g., with 600 speed film, the shutter speed is set at a lower number and the F-stop is set at a higher number).

📷 Blurred or out-of-focus pictures.

📷 Pictures that only contain portions of subjects.

Solutions to difficulties:

📷 Using different paint colors to mark correct placement on the F-stop ring and film speed setting. The use of color creates an association with a number range on the F-stop/aperture ring. Creating a reference guide to camera adjustment assists in decreasing the number of mistakes one makes in adjusting camera features.

📷 Blurred or out-of-focus pictures occur when the person makes a quick movement or accidentally sets the focus for the wrong part of the photo (e.g., sets up to take a picture of a house, but decides to focus on a flower in the driveway). Purchasing a camera with an automatic light and zoom setting or a tripod helps reduce the occurrence of blurred or fuzzy photos.

📷 To decrease impulsive actions that result in missing the subject in the photo, the self-talk method can be used to assure the subject is in the correct position before the picture is snapped. "What kind of subject do I want in my picture?" (a flower.) "How do I go about getting this subject in my picture?" (I locate the flower, move closer to the flower, and adjust the focus on the camera.) "Is all of the subject in my picture?" This means, "Is the subject within the circle guideline of the view lens?" (No, I want to capture its leaves, so I need to move back and readjust the focus before I shoot. Or, yes, I have all of the flower that I wish to have in this picture, so I can shoot the subject now.)

Cooking

The art of creating delicious dishes from a variety of nature's ingredients is a hobby that can be as elaborate as serving 50 people at a seven-course dinner party or specialized as perfecting a cream puff pastry for an after-dinner setting of two. The master of creation is delighted in admiring the beauty of his design and having guest's gastronomic desires satisfied.

Equipment: •   recipe with complete directions
             •   ingredients
             •   measuring and cooking utensils
             •   a cooking apparatus (e.g., stove, oven, grill, or microwave)

Action: Depending upon interest in the subject of cooking (e.g., main dishes, appetizers, sandwiches, soups, breads, vegetables, or desserts), the person will select the recipe and go to the grocery store to purchase the ingredients. Upon purchasing the ingredients, the individual will store them in the kitchen for later use or begin using ingredients to create the recipe. The person is to follow the directions written on the recipe.

Problems that can occur in cooking:
— Misreading directions on the recipe.
— Misjudging time to cook the item.
— Poor calculation of ingredients.
— Poor judgment of finished product.

Solutions to difficulties:
— Difficulty interpreting the difference between a tablespoon (T., Tbsp., or Tbs.) vs. a teaspoon (tsp.) or combining ingredients out of sequence may be compensated for by having the person enlarge recipes, especially those attached to or written on 3"x 5" cards, so he can clearly see the difference between the abbreviations. The person can also rewrite the recipe to say "tablespoon" and "teaspoon." In addition to writing out the previous words, the recipe can be rewritten to emphasize order, for example:

>   Step 1: Add eggs to mixing bowl.
>   Step 2: Add sugar to eggs in mixing bowl.
>   Step 3: Mix sugar and eggs together until creamy, etc.

—Misjudgment of cooking time occurs when one has to calculate the weight of the item to cooking time, altitude level with cooking time, or the inclusion of additional ingredients with cooking time. The meat or main dish section of many cookbooks provide a chart on how long certain types of meat should cook; use this as a guide. Some prepared cake recipes on the side of the box state guidelines for baking at a high altitude level. One piece of advice to remember is to allow cakes and sweet breads to cook at five-minute intervals over given cooking time on the recipe when adding ingredients with consistency of dense liquid (e.g., mashed bananas, applesauce, or puree' fruits).

—Misreading one's measuring cup or measuring spoon can produce a miscalculation of ingredients. To decrease the incident of miscalculation, the person might want to use strips of colored tape to mark off common degrees of measurement, for example, if using a two-cup size glass measuring cup, use red tape at the quarter cup mark, blue tape at the 1/3-cup mark, green tape at the half-cup mark, yellow tape at the 2/3-cup mark, and a piece of all four colors at the one-cup mark. A cook can also purchase separate measuring cups (e.g., 1/8, 1/4, 1/3, 1/2, 2/3, 3/4, and 1 cup). This makes measuring easier when a recipe calls for 1 2/3 cups of flour. One would measure one cup of the ingredient first, then select the 2/3 measuring cup and add the remaining 2/3 cups of the ingredient to the recipe.

—Misjudgment of finished product means poor ability to judge when a cake bounces back from a touch by one's finger or pushing one's finger too hard into a cake, thereby leaving an indentation. What is meant by being "creamy," "crumbly," or "finished when cooled to a solid consistency" is also confusing. Again, guides in well-named cookbooks describe in detail what the previous cooking terms mean. Some prepared items, such as cake mixes and brownie mixes, state exactly how many beats by hand or minutes run on an electric mixer the person should use when blending ingredients. Determining a solid consistency is translated to directions of "leave in refrigerator for at least four hours." It is best to find recipes that describe specifics to instructions and are not vague interpretations of results. Attending cooking classes would also help a person to correctly interpret cuisine terminology.

Crafts

Using one's creative ability to produce a purposeful decorative object for the pleasure of the artist and others to enjoy is crafts. The act of creating any craft object promotes personal leisure enjoyment, builds self-esteem, and allows for expression of creative ability.

Equipment:
- exposure to some form of media (T.V., radio, newspapers, magazines, books, computer) whereby the person receives information about the craft activity
- general supplies: glue, glue gun, scissors or exacto knife, pencil, paper, ruler, tape, straight pins, fabric and study table to work on
- craft instructions from print materials or video

Action:
Person selects the craft that appeals to her through exposure to craft activity via some form of media or friend. The person collects information (name and details) about the craft program, then goes to the fabric or craft store to purchase craft supplies (this may include pattern and directions to assemble the craft). The person returns home with the supplies, reads the craft directions, and begins to assemble the craft item. An alternative action is for the interested person to sign-up for a craft course. The first day of class the instructor informs the class on what materials to buy; these materials are then brought to the next class session.

Problems that occur in crafts:
- ✄ Difficulty comprehending and following craft instructions (see Chapter Three, "Mary assembling model airplanes").
- ✄ Incorrect measurement of materials (e.g., cutting materials the wrong length or skipping stitches during knitting or crocheting projects), thus the production of a lop-sided or an increasingly narrow craft project.
- ✄ Difficulty manipulating materials or objects.
- ✄ Incompletion of numerous craft projects.

Solutions to difficulties:
- ✄ Ask someone for assistance or take small group or individual instruction at a local craft store to better understand craft in-

structions. During the individual instructions, the student can mimic the teacher's actions in creating the project. The teacher may need to break down the instructions of the craft project (adding more steps to completing the project). If person is reading instructions or viewing a videotape, the person might need to breakdown the craft steps independently.

- *Accommodation*—For visual processing difficulty, the instructions can be read by a friend or teacher out loud while the student is audio recording the session.
- Always purchase enough material or extra material to cover for mistakes made when working on projects. When cutting, cut over the amount given in directions; it is easier to cut off excess than to add and adjust material. The person can also write down a count of stitches and/or say count to self to prevent skipping a stitch.
- If suffering from a poor ability to judge touch and force exerted by self, begin with larger scale crafts and work down to a smaller scale. The person should allow herself breaks before becoming frustrated, preventing damage to the object. The person can create or purchase holders for working with delicate objects (e.g., decorating eggs, miniatures, or ceramics), thus reducing the handling of the object.
- Set short-term goals for self (e.g., in one month I will complete this flower wreath) and designate what the steps will be in each week or meeting of the craft project. The first week, step one: purchase all materials to make a flower wreath. The second week, step two: create a design out of flowers purchased. When each step is finished, the person checks off the step on a craft progress sheet. These steps continue until the project is completed. After the entire project is complete, the person writes a summary about the craft experience. This summary includes comments on how to approach a certain portion of the craft project differently, how to adjust directions and add different materials to further enhance the project, and how to delete or combine steps to improve efficiency of completing the craft project. The individual should store this summary with craft instructions to be available when constructing the craft project a second time.

Social/Community Activities

Attending Concerts and Sporting Events

Becoming part of the crowd, escaping from the daily routine of life, rooting for a winning team, or applauding the accolades of others' performances are motivations for participating in spectator activities.

Equipment: • exposure to some form of media (T.V., radio, newspapers, magazines, or computer) whereby a person receives information about the spectator activity.

Action: Through media advertisement or promotion, a potential participant learns about an artist or sporting event. Usually before a person attends a spectator event, he knows something about the event (e.g., knowledgeable about sport, follows a sport team, admires an actor's or artist's work, read the book, or spoke with a friend about the theater production or movie). The person determines if he can attend the event based on the date, time, location, and price of the event. The next step is to purchase the tickets to attend the event and store the tickets in a safe, easy to locate place until the date. Before the event, a person must prepare himself to attend; this means determining finances, transportation arrangements, and directions to the event. Once all of this has been accomplished, the person is on his way to enjoy a day or evening of fun.

Problems that occur in spectator events:

- ☒ Forgetting the date of the event or scheduling other obligations during the same time as the event.
- ☒ Misplacing tickets to the event.
- ☒ Arriving late to the event due to problems with mapping directions to location.
- ☒ Incorrect seating placement at the event.
- ☒ Misjudging finances; not taking into account the amount of money needed for an enjoyable spectator event.
- ☒ Difficulty interpreting the meaning of the event (e.g., movie, play, or musical).

☒ Difficulty following the event, game plays, and scoring due to extraneous factors such as crowd noise, music and video pictures, movement of people in the audience, and the fast pace of the sporting event (no viewing of instant replays).

Solutions to difficulties:

☒ When tickets are purchased weeks in advance, the person should make a note of the event's date on a monthly calendar. This calendar should be in visible view to the person on a daily basis. Review the calendar often to prevent over-scheduling self.

☒ In order to avert misplacement of tickets, the individual can do the following things: 1) create a designated place where documents such as tickets, checkbook, passport, and travel documents are kept all the time; 2) when recording the event's date on a monthly calendar, include the location of the tickets; 3) have companion accompanying the individual to the event hold the tickets. The first two suggestions are preferred over the third because it encourages independence and self-responsibility.

☒ A person experiencing difficulties following directional maps or diagrams may need to take a drive to the event area before the event date to familiarize self with the travel route. During this pre-travel time, the person becomes aware of highway exit signs, landmarks, and street signs. The companion can assist the person with navigating to the event either during the pre-travel drive or the day of the event.

☒ If the individual is using mass transportation and is not familiar with bus, subway, or train routes, the individual can pre-travel via mass transportation to the event area; call the transportation company and ask questions regarding the correct stop for the event area; or, together with another person or companion, review the transportation schedule and highlight departure and arrival routes to and from the event area.

☒ Incorrect seating placement occurs when the person misinterprets numbers and letters on the ticket. The individual having this problem might want to underline or highlight seating placement code on the ticket. The person can also ask the event usher to check the ticket and direct the person to the correct seating area (that is the usher's job).

☒ To assure that the individual attending the event has adequate monies, he can make a list about what will be purchased before, during, and after the event, if applicable. For example, food and drink for self, companion or children; sovereigns; parking; gas; train or bus tickets, etc.

- ✉ To alleviate difficulty in interpreting the meaning of events, the person can read the art critic's reviews about the play/musical or movie before attending. The person can talk with peers or theater enthusiasts about the storyline of a play/musical or movie or obtain a copy of the book based on the play or musical on audiotape (e.g., especially for dyslexics). This background knowledge enables one to follow along with less difficulty than not knowing anything about the topic of event.

- ✉ To avoid environmental distractions, the person should plan to sit as close to the front of the event as possible. This might call for the person buying tickets very early or wanting to take advantage of handicapped seating arrangements. There is minimal or no audience interference with box seats at sporting and concert events. At some concerts and most sporting events, the person might choose to watch the large video screen monitors placed on the stage or above the field to keep him abreast of the singer's movements, game plays, scoring, and following the action during a game.

Travel

Travel is using a particular mode of transportation to get one to a destination of enjoyment. Travel encompasses learning, exploring, escaping, relaxing, socializing, admiring, discovering, and self-fulfillment. Whether one travels to the nearest main town, next state, adjacent country, or a far away continent, the experience gained from that adventure lives forever.

Equipment:
- travel documents: passport (if applicable); transportation ticket (e.g., train, plane, bus, or ship); hotel name, address and confirmation number; and travel itinerary
- luggage that contains clothing and other personal items
- finances: cash, personal check, or credit card
- map of destination: points of interest, restaurant and shopping locations, plus information about other means of transportation once arrived at the hotel

Action: It is helpful if the person having interest in visiting a location knows something about the place before visiting. The person usually talks with a travel agent, family member, or friend to obtain information about the geographic location.The world wide web has city sites whereby the potential traveler can download information about lodging, food, entertainment, transportation, etc. Once a person has decided this is the place for her to visit, the next step is making the arrangements. The person determines the date, time, and length of travel based on available leave from work, other obligations, finances, and possibly weather conditions. The traveler then will purchase a vacation package (this includes transportation, lodging, tours, food, and other travel perks) or just a transportation ticket. If the person is only purchasing a ticket, then she must arrange for a place of lodging, so the next step is to make lodging arrangements (e.g., hotel, motel, bed and breakfast, inn, or friend's house) and confirm length of stay. The ensuing phase is to set aside or budget monies to pay for the trip. One needs to calculate the cost of food, souvenir, tours, tips, and taxes. The most important phase in travel is to organize arrangements at home to assure an enjoyable travel experience. These arrangements can include hiring a house sitter, boarding animals, hiring a sitter for children, reassigning job duties in one's absence from the job, purchasing clothing and personal items for travel, storing automobiles, locking up home and setting the alarm, and notifying the post office to halt mail delivery temporarily (for extended length of travel, e.g., over a month). If children are traveling, their clothing and personal items must be organized. If traveling by car, select what type of food to bring. After all the home and preliminary travel details are attended to, the person or group is ready to go and have fun.

Problems that occur in travel:
✈ Forgets to pack vital clothing and personal items or packs wrong type of clothing.

✈ Misreads travel itinerary, misses plane, or arrives late to tour.

✈ Forgets to complete all home arrangements before leaving.

✈ Misplaces tickets or other travel documents.

✈ Not cognizant to travel agent's advice on traveling (e.g., safety measures).

✈ Gets lost during tour, misses return transportation to hotel, or has the tour agency wait for the person or party.

✈ Misjudges finances, overspends on the trip, or runs low on money the last day.

✈ When packing luggage in hotel, forgets personal items and clothing.

Solutions to difficulties:

✈ The key to having a successful travel experience is being organized and aware of time. For the person who has trouble with organization, sales personnel at a local luggage store or travel agent can provide the person with guide booklets. These booklets instruct the traveler as to the type of clothing to wear and the correct way to pack clothing for travel.

✈ *Accommodation*—Use a checklist obtained from a book as a reminder to what type of items must be packed (see Chapter Seven for name of travel book).

✈ A solution to the misplacement of tickets or other travel documents is similar to the suggestion given in "Spectator Events"; create a designated place where travel documents are placed all the time (e.g., the outside front zipped pouch of the beige carry-on bag).

✈ Highlight arrival and departure times in different colors to decrease misreading travel itineraries.

✈ *Accommodation*—Use a dictation recorder or personal palm-size computer to record travel itinerary. The person may wish to ask a friend or travel companion to record the itinerary or have a friend check the itinerary inputted by the person for correctness of times, names, and addresses.

✈ Just as one may use a checklist to guarantee that all items were packed in the suitcases before leaving home, one can also use a checklist to assure that all home arrangement are taken care of before leaving home. This list should be created at least a month before departure; ask a travel companion or friend to aid in the creation of this list. Once the list is complete, make copies to be used in preparing for future excursions. If one has a house sitter, allow enough time for both persons to review home arrangements together.

✦ The traveler needs to pay attention to subtle remarks made by a travel agent. If she makes remarks like, "I noticed at about three o'clock people were not in that area," "I would not walk past main street," or "It is difficult to get a taxi in this part of town after five o'clock in the evening," the traveler should make a note of these types of comments. Being aware of one's environment can deter a potentially hazardous situation. Unfortunately today, it is important for travelers to ask their travel agent or friends who traveled to the same location about the safety of a particular area.

✦ If one is aware that she has a tendency to get lost, the best suggestion is not to be separated from the crowd. Many tours offer a couple to hours of "free time" for travelers to sightsee or shop independently. If this is the case, make a written note of where the tour bus is parked, the name and color of the tour bus, and landmarks walking from the bus to the shopping area. One could also make an oral recording of the tour guide's instructions for the group using a dictation recorder. Also, using a cueing watch enables the traveler to set a time to return back to the bus for departure from the tour (allow 15 minutes to return to the bus).

✦ With misjudging finances it might prove beneficial to separate money by days or weeks, depending upon the length of the trip. In general, people usually estimate how much money they intend to spend each day (e.g., $50 per day). If one is going on a five-day trip, she would bring $250 for spending money. A person can separate the $250 into five (5) $50 money packets attached with paper clips. If the person did not spend the entire $50 for that day, the remaining monies can be carried over to the next day. Another suggestion is to purchase large money items the day before departure, assuring the funds would be available after taking care of all the travel essentials (e.g., eating, tips, taxes, gifts for others, etc.).

✦ The same checklist one used to pack her suitcases at home can be used when packing to leave the hotel. What travelers usually forget are pajamas or bath robe hanging behind the bathroom door and slippers under the bed. Before leaving the hotel room, open every drawer and scan tops of bedside table, desks, or sitting tables, and the dresser. Also, look under the bed and pillows, in the bottom and top shelf of the closet, and in the bathroom—tub/shower stall, bathroom floor, and behind the door.

Volunteering

Donating one's time and talent to build a better community is commendable. Volunteering produces meaningful interactions; is a process in social issues, new ideas, and completion of short- and long-term goals; and is an outlet for growth.

Equipment:
- exposure to community organizations through some form of media (T.V., radio, newspaper, magazine, or computer)
- transportation to agency where person will be volunteering
- uniform and materials (if applicable)

Action: First, the individual must be aware of what kind of skills and talent he can offer the agency. The question one needs to ask oneself is, "What skills and talents do I have and how can I use these attributes to assist others?" Volunteering is very similar to working in some agencies. Agency employees depend upon the volunteer being present, arriving at the site on time, carrying out tasks efficiently, displaying appropriate social behavior, being knowledgeable about the agency's purpose and operations, and representing the agency in a positive manner. Once an individual has decided what he would like to do, the next step is to locate an agency that could utilize the individual's talents and at the same time satisfy that individual's leisure needs in volunteering (e.g., helping people, teaching other skills, creating a product for display, raising funds, gaining knowledge from others or situation, etc.). An agency can be found through types of media advertising for volunteers or the person can search the yellow pages of the telephone book under the heading of "associations" or "society" to obtain the telephone number and address to contact the agency of one's choice. Any organization that recruits or uses volunteers has an application form the potential volunteer must complete, then the person is interviewed by a supervisor within the agency. After acceptance into the program, volunteers participate in an orientation session. This orientation covers the agency's philosophy, goals, and methods of operation (e.g., policies and procedures). The orientation will also extend to informing the volunteer about his job duties and expectations the supervisor and agency have of their volunteers. In completing the previous steps, one is on his way to being a full-fledge volunteer.

Problems that occur in volunteering:
- Forgetting to schedule volunteer time into one's weekly routine.
- Overcommitting self and neglecting volunteer work.
- Difficulty understanding oral and/or written instruction.
- Misplacing material and supplies.

Solutions to difficulties:
- Place the volunteer work schedule on a monthly calendar. This schedule should be highlighted in color to separate it from work or other activities scheduled within that same week. The calendar is placed in full view for easy daily access.
- When the volunteer work schedule is placed on a monthly calendar this deters overcommitment or a conflict in scheduling from occurring. Depending upon the amount of work, length of time in work, and frequency of volunteer work, one needs to use judgment regarding scheduling other activities. For example, a person volunteers for Habitat for Humanity, assisting with the building of homes for low-income persons every weekend for the next 10 weeks. After the second or third day on the project, the person might realize that this is physically exhausting work. In using correct judgment, it would be in the person's favor to postpone any weekend date for dancing, doing heavy yard work, or running numerous errands, thereby saving energy to work effectively on the building project.
- Difficulty in comprehending oral and written directions requires one to inform his supervisor of this problem. If the person did not disclose the nature of the learning disability during the application or interview process, then here is when the disability should be discussed. The area of concern is teaching

the person who is supplying the oral and written directions what different techniques can be used to deliver the information, not what deficiencies one has due to the learning disability. The person with the learning disability must be knowledgeable of his own learning style, multisensory techniques, accommodations, and job modifications to complete his job more efficiently.

If materials and supplies are a main feature of one's volunteer duties, it is the person's responsibility to have these available in his possession when at the volunteer agency. The person should first compile a list of what materials or supplies are needed all the time or only on certain days. For example, wearing a name tag and uniform (e.g., apron) are required all the time for a kitchen help versus casual clothing for attending the community center's picnic outing. If one is volunteering at a senior center teaching a craft project three days a week (e.g., Monday, Wednesday, and Friday) this person must make a note on a weekly calendar or monthly calendar stating what type of craft activity will be taught on Monday, Wednesday, and Friday. The volunteer should have already created a list of supplies needed to produce a particular craft project; this list is developed before putting the craft schedule on a calendar. Now, having the list of supplies for the craft project and the date to conduct the craft project, the volunteer can pack supplies in a totebag the night before, eliminating the act of guessing about supplies and being prepare to teach the next day's activity.

References

Clements, R.I. (Ed.). (1995). *Games & great ideas: A guide for elementary school physical educators and classroom teachers*. Westport, CT: Greenwood Press.

GED Items. (1992, September/October). Practitioner page: Teaching tips, *GED Items, (9)*4/5, pp.15-16.

Harris, J.A. (1970). *File o' Fun: Card file for social recreation*. Minneapolis, MN: Burgess Publishing Company.

Job Accommodation Network. (1995). *The new facts about disability*. The President's Committee on Employment of People with Disabilities. Morgantown, WV: West Virginia University.

Konstant, S.B. (1992, May-June). Multi-sensory tutoring for multi-sensory learners. *Writing Lab Newsletter,* 5, pp. 6-8.

McCarthy, J.P., Jr. (1995). *The parent's guide to coaching football (2nd ed.).* Cincinnati, OH: Betterway Books.

Next Generation gamers' guide. (1997, February). Next Generation, pp. 137-138.

Reade, B. (1994). *Coaching football successfully.* Champaign, IL: Human Kinetics.

Schuck, J. (1992, Winter). Teaching with (com)passion: A lifeline for students with learning disabilities. *Faculty Development, 5*(2), pp. 1-3.

Shields, J. (1996) Disability awareness—adapting activities. Recreation Resources Service Technical Assistance Bulletin. [On-line]. Available: http://ww2.ncsu.edu/ncsu/forestresources/resource/disaware.html.

Swanson, H.L. (1989, Winter). Strategy instruction: Overview of principles and procedures for effective use. *Learning Disabilities Quarterly, 12*, pp. 3-14.

United States General Accounting Office. (1990). *Persons with disabilities: Reports on costs of accommodations* (Human Resources Division Report GAO/HRD 90-44BR). Gaithersburg, MD: Author.

Wooten, M. (1992). *Coaching basketball successfully.* Champaign, IL: Leisure Press.

Yellen, A.G., & Yellen, H.L. (1987). *Understanding the learning disabled athlete: A guide for parents, coaches, and professionals.* Boston, MA: C.C. Thomas Publishing.

Chapter Seven

RESOURCES
▬────────────────────────────────▬

This chapter explores the vast variety of resources available to professionals, parents, and people having learning disabilities. This information contributes to fostering the betterment of people having learning disabilities living in society.

Organizations and Associations

The following are names and addresses of national long-standing organizations and associations that provide resources in the way of support, training, professional development, expertise, and research to the field of disabilities, especially learning disabilities.

American Alliance for Health, Physical Education, Recreation and Dance is a membership organization of professionals in the fields of physical education, recreation, health and safety, and dance. Their Adapted Physical Activity Council has a nationwide network to provide information about adapting curricula and activities to the needs of people with disabilities. The organization also publishes the journal, *ABLE BODIES*.
American Alliance for Health, Physical Education, Recreation and Dance, 1900 Association Dr., Reston, VA 22091, (703) 476-3400.

American Occupational Therapy Association (AOTA) is a nationwide organization of professionals concerned with all aspects of the occupational therapy field. This association is knowledgeable about the use of sensorimotor training and integration techniques to alleviate sensorimotor processing difficulties evident in some individuals having learning disabilities.

American Occupational Therapy Association (AOTA), 4720 Montgomery Lane, Box 31200, Bethesda, MD 20824-1220, (301) 652-2682, Fax: (301) 652-7711.

American Speech-Language-Hearing Association (ASHA) is the professional, scientific, and credentialing association for speech-language pathologists and audiologists that provide services to people with speech, language, and hearing disorders. It also provides public education materials about communication disorders and professional treatment.

American Speech-Language-Hearing Association (ASHA), 1081 Rockville Pike, Rockville, MD 20852, (301) 897-5700 or 1-(800) 638-8255.

ASCLA/American Library Association operates a program called "Roads to Learning, The Public Libraries' Learning Disabilities Initiative." This program disseminates information about learning disabilities through text and internet resources. It also promotes teaching persons with learning disabilities about library research skills.

ASCLA/American Library Association, 50 East Huron St., Chicago, IL 60611, 1-(800) 545-2433 ext. 4027 or 4399.

Association on Higher Education and Disability (AHEAD) is an international, multicultural organization of professionals committed to full participation in higher education for persons with disabilities. The association sponsors numerous training programs, workshops, publications, and conferences.

Association on Higher Education and Disability (AHEAD), P.O. Box 21192, Columbus, OH 43221-0192, (614) 488-4972, Fax: (614) 488-1174.

Children and Adults with Attention Deficit Disorder (CHADD) is an nonprofit, parent-based organization that disseminates information on ADD and has over 460 parent support groups. It publishes a semiannual magazine, *CHADDER,* and a newsletter, *Chadderbox.* Website address: http://www.chadd.org

Children and Adults with Attention Deficit Disorder (CHADD), 499 Northwest 70th Ave., Suite 308, Plantation, FL 33317, (954) 587-3700, Fax: (954) 587-4599.

Colorado Outdoor Education Center for the Handicapped (COECH) offers year-round wilderness programs for people of all ages with a variety of developmental, physical, emotional, medical, and learning disabilities.

Colorado Outdoor Education Center for the Handicapped (COECH), P.O. Box 697, Breckenridge, CO 80424, (303) 453-6422.

CSUN Center on Disabilities serves students with disabilities on the California State University, Northridge campus. The center also conducts major conferences on Technology and Persons with Disabilities and Virtual Reality and Persons with Disabilities; both conference contain sessions on technology and learning disabilities. Its research area developed a screen reading device and universal access system to benefit learning disabled users.

CSUN Center on Disabilities, California State University, Northridge, 1811 Nordhoff St., Northridge, CA 91330-8340, (818) 885-2578, Fax: (818) 885-4929, e-mail: LTM@csun.edu

Council for Exceptional Children (CEC) contains a membership of educators who are concerned about children with disabilities and those who are gifted, parents, and students.

*Note: It is not uncommon for persons to be dual-diagnosed or twice exceptional, this occurs when a person is diagnosed "gifted/LD."

Council for Exceptional Children (CEC), 1920 Association Dr., Reston, VA 22091-1589, (703) 620-3660, Fax: (703) 264-9494, Website address: http://www.cec.sped.org

Council for Learning Disabilities (CLD) serves professionals who work with individuals having learning disabilities. It sponsors conferences, publishes the *Learning Disability Quarterly* and the *L.D. Forum*, and also endorses grants and awards for research on learning disability issues.

Council for Learning Disabilities (CLD), P.O. Box 40303, Overland Park, KS 66204, (913) 492-8755, Fax: (913) 492-2546.

DIRECT LINK for the Disabled is a public benefit organization that provides information and resources for any disability-related questions. This organization contains a database of over 11,000 organizations and social service agencies and locates the closest local organization that meets the individual's specific needs.

DIRECT LINK for the Disabled, Inc., P.O. Box 1036, Solvang, CA 93464, (805) 688-1603.

Disability Rights Education and Defense Fund (DREDF) is a national disability rights laws and policy center dedicated to equal opportunities for persons with disabilities. The center offers education and training programs on disability civil rights issues, legal support, and advocacy. To receive a publication write the following organizations:

Disability Rights Education and Defense Fund (DREDF), 2212 6th St., Berkeley, CA 94702, (415) 644-2555 or 1-(800) 466-4232, Fax: (510) 841-8645

Governmental Affairs, 1616 P St., N.W., Suite 100, Washington, DC 20036, (202) 328-5185.

DO-IT's (Disabilities, Opportunities, Internetworking, and Technology) purpose is to increase the participation of individuals with disabilities in science, engineering, and mathematics academic programs and careers. The DO-IT program contains education programs in high schools, mentoring, summer study, projects, and workshops. It also has a database of electronic resources and DO-IT publications, and sponsors science-oriented events.

Sheryl Burgstahler, DO-IT Director, College of Engineering/Computing & Communications, University of Washington, Seattle, WA 98195, (206) 685-DO-IT, Fax: (206) 685-4045, e-mail: doit@u.washington.edu

EASI: Equal Access to Software Information's mission is keeping professionals informed about developments and advancements within the adaptive computer technology field. This information is beneficial to professionals in the area of education, employment, leisure, and social services.

EASI: Equal Access to Software Information, One Dupont Circle, Suite 360, Washington, DC 20036-1110, (714) 830-0301, Fax: (714) 830-2159, e-mail: EASI@EDUCOM (Bitnet) or EASI@EDUCOM.EDU (Internet).

Exceptional Child Education Resources (ECER) maintains a database of published literature covering the education and development of individuals with disabilities and those who are gifted.

Exceptional Child Education Resources (ECER), 1920 Association Dr., Reston, VA 22091-1589, (703) 620-3660 or 1-(800) CEC-READ, Fax: (703) 264-9494.

HEATH Resource Center is a federal clearing house mandated to collect and disseminate information naturally about disability issues and resources.

HEATH Resource Center, One Dupont Circle, Suite 300, Washington, DC 20036, 1-(800) 544-3284 or (202) 939-9320.

IBM Independence Series Information Center responds to requests for information on how IBM products can help people with a wide range of disabilities use personal computers.

IBM Independence Series Information Center, P.O. Box 1328, Internal Zip 5432, Boca Raton, FL 33430, 1-(800) 426-4832, Fax: (407) 982-6059.

International Dyslexia Association is an international non-profit organization concerned with the complex issues of dyslexia. The society promotes effective teaching approaches, clinical educational intervention strategies, and research. It conducts an annual conference and publishes a newsletter—*PERSPECTIVES*—and a professional journal—*Annals of Dyslexia*.

International Dyslexia Association, The Chester Building, Suite 382, 8600 LaSalle Rd., Baltimore, MD 21286-2044, (410) 296-0232 or 1-(800) 331-0688, Website address: http://www.interdys.org

General information on the **Americans with Disabilities Act (ADA)**

Office of the Americans with Disabilities Act, Civil Rights Division, U.S. Department of Justice, P.O. Box 66118, Washington, DC 20035-6118, (202) 514-0301.

Learning Disabilities Association of America is a non-profit association containing 60,000+ member information and referral service. It provides some free information on learning disabilities, publishes a newsletter and a biannual journal, *Learning Disabilities Multidisciplinary Journal,* and sponsors an international conference. For more information about the association's information and referral service, contact the following organizations:

Learning Disabilities Association of American, 4156 Library Rd., Pittsburgh, PA 15234, (412) 341-1515 or (412) 341-8077, Fax: (412) 344-0224, Website address: http://www.ldanati.org

Learning Disabilities Association of Canada, 323 Chapel St., Ottawa, Ontario K1N 7Z2, Canada, (613) 238-5721, Fax: (613) 235-5391, e-mail: ldactaac@fox.nstn.ca

Learning Disabilities Association of Puerto Rico, GPO Box 361905, San Juan, PR 00936, (809) 777-2253.

Learning Disabilities Network provides educational and referral services for individuals with learning disabilities, their families, and professionals, primarily in the northeast portion of the United States. The network offers conferences, seminars, workshops, and a semiannual newsletter, *The Exchange.*

Learning Disabilities Network, 72 Sharp St., Suite A-2, Hingham, MA 02043, (617) 340-5605, Fax: (617) 340-5603.

National Center for Learning Disabilities (NCLD) is committed to improving the lives of individuals with learning disabilities. Its services include raising public awareness and understanding, national information and referral, educational programs, and legislative advocacy. The center produces a newsletter, *THEIR WORLD* and a five-part video series entitled, "We Can Learn." For more information about the NCLD's referral base of professionals to assist the public, contact the organization below:

National Center for Learning Disabilities (NCLD), 381 Park Ave. South, Suite 1420, New York, NY 10016, (212) 545-7510, Fax: (212) 545-9665, Website address: http://www.ncld.org

National Center for Youth with Disabilities (NCYD) is an information and resource center that seeks to raise awareness of the needs of adolescents and young adults with chronic illnesses and disabilities. NCYD maintains the National Resource Library, a computerized database containing current information about youth with disabilities.

National Center for Youth with Disabilities (NCYD), University of Minnesota, Box 721, 420 Delaware St., SE, Minneapolis, MN 55455, (612) 626-2825 or 1-(800) 333-6293, Fax: (612) 626-2134.

National Consortium for Physical Education and Recreation for Individuals with Disabilities (NCPERID), along with other organizations, assisted in the development of national standards for the field of adapted physical education; these standards will serve as the foundation for creating a national certification examination in adapted physical education. For more information, contact the organization below:

National Consortium for Physical Education and Recreation for Individuals with Disabilities (NCPERID), Dr. Hester Henderson, Treasurer, Dept. of Exercise & Sport Science, HPER N-255, University of Utah, Salt Lake City, UT 84112; or Dr. Manny Felix, Membership Chair, Dept. of Exercise & Sport Science, University of Wisconsin-La Crosse, 115 Wittich Hall, La Crosse, WI 54601.

National Council on Disability is an independent federal agency comprised of 15 members appointed by the U.S. Senate. The council addresses, analyzes, and makes recommendations on issues of public policy that affects people with disabilities. The National Council originated and developed the first draft of the Americans with Disabilities Act. The council also distributes a free newsletter - *FOCUS*.

National Council on Disability, 800 Independence Ave., S.W., Suite 814, Washington, DC 20591, (202) 267-3846.

National Information Center for Children and Youth with Disabilities (NICHCY) provides parents, professionals, and others with information and referral on issues of concern to children and youth with disabilities and their families. This includes information on specific disabilities, early intervention, special education, related services, transition planning, and many other issues.

National Information Center for Children and Youth with Disabilities (NICHCY), P.O. Box 1492, Washington, DC 20013-1492, 1-(800) 999-5599.

National Institute of Art and Disabilities (NIAD) conducts an innovative, interdisciplinary visual art studio program, encourages exhibition of NIAD artists' work, and allows opportunities for NIAD artists to earn income and recognition through the marketing and reproduction of their work.

National Institute of Art and Disabilities (NIAD), 551 23rd St., Richmond, CA 94804, (510) 620-0290, Fax: (510) 620-0326.

National Institute of Child Health and Human Development (NICHD) funds a research center and projects on learning disabilities. For detailed information contact the person below:

Dr. G. Reid Lyon, HLB/CRMC/NICHD/NIH, 6100 Building, Room 4B05, 9000 Rockville Pike, Bethesda, MD 20892, (301) 496-6591, Fax: (301) 402-2085.

National Network of Learning Disabled Adults (NNLDA) is an organization run by and for people who have learning disabilities. It publishes a free newsletter and has a listing of self-help groups.

National Network of Learning Disabled Adults (NNLDA), 800 N. 82nd St., Scottsdate, AZ 85257, (602) 941-5112.

National Organization on Disability (NOD) promotes the fuller participation of Americans with disabilities in all aspects of community life. Its Community Partnership Program implements activities to improve attitudes toward people with disabilities; to expand educational and employment opportunities; and to eliminate physical barriers and expand participation in religious, cultural, and recreational activities. The organization also publishes a quarterly newsletter–*REPORT*.

National Organization on Disability (NOD), 910 16th St., NW, Suite 600, Washington, DC 20006, (202) 293-5960.

National Parent Network on Disabilities (NPND) is a nonprofit organization dedicated to improving the lives of children, youth, and adults with disabilities and their families. Among some of the services that NPND currently provides are legislative representation, reference and referral, a national conference, outreach to parents, available materials, and a database to link parents to local, state, regional, national, or international services.

National Parent Network on Disabilities (NPND), 1600 Prince St., #115, Alexandria, VA 22314-2836, (703) 684-6763.

National Recreation and Park Association (NRPA) is the nation's largest nonprofit service, research, and education organization dedicated to improving the quality of life through effective utilization of natural and human resources.

National Recreation and Park Association (NRPA), 22377 Belmont Ridge Rd., Ashburn, VA 20148, (703) 858-0784, website address: http://www.nrpa.org

National Rehabilitation Information Center (NARIC) is a library and information center on disability and rehabilitation. NARIC collects and disseminates results of federally-funded research projects, contains a REHABDATA database in which it performs searches, and publishes a free newsletter—*NARIC Quarterly*—along with other brochures and resource guides.

National Rehabilitation Information Center (NARIC), 8455 Colesville Rd., Suite 935, Silver Spring, MD 20910-3319, (301) 588-9284 or 1-(800) 346-2742.

National Therapeutic Recreation Society (NTRS) is a branch of the National Recreation and Park Association that promotes all aspects of therapeutic recreation. This membership society encourages networking and research, plus sponsors regional and national institutes. It also publishes a quarterly journal—*The Therapeutic Recreation Journal*—devoted to publishing scholarly and substantive manuscripts in the field of therapeutic recreation.

National Therapeutic Recreation Society, 22377 Belmont Ridge Road, Ashburn, Virginia 20148, (703)858-0784. email: ntrsnrpa@aol.com

Parents Educational Advocacy Training Center (PEATC) assists parents and professionals to translate the legal rights of children with disabilities into genuine opportunities for full participation in school and community life. PEATC sponsors the training of parent-professional teams to work directly with parents of children with disabilities. It also publishes a quarterly newsletter, *The PEATC Press*.

Parents Educational Advocacy Training Center, 228 S. Pitt St., Alexandria, VA 22314, (703) 836-2953, Fax: (703) 836-5869.

Parents Helping Parents (PHP) is a nonprofit, parent-directed family resource center providing information, support, and training for families of children with any kind of special needs (mental, physical, emotional, or learning disability).

Parents Helping Parents (PHP), 535 Race St., Suite 140, San Jose, CA 95126, (408) 288-5010, Fax: (408) 288-7943, Website address: http://www.portal.com/~cbntmkr/php.html

The Rebus Institute is a 501 (c) (3) nonprofit organization committed to the management of problems related to specific learning disabilities and/or attention deficit disorder (ADD) in adults. It serves parents, youth, adults, professionals, employers, organizations, and agencies in their effort to meet the needs of this growing population. For more information contact the following institute:

The Rebus Institute, 1499 Bayshore Blvd., Suite 146, Burlingame, CA 94010, (415) 697-7424, Fax: (415) 697-3734, Website address: http://www.cenatica.com/rebus/

Shared Outdoor Adventure Recreation (SOAR) facilitates access to outdoor adventure through the following activities: skiing, river rafting, sailing, hiking, camping, rock climbing, and ropes challenge courses.

Shared Outdoor Adventure Recreation (SOAR), P.O. Box 14583, Portland, OR 97214, (503) 238-1613.

Sibling Information Network was established to assist individuals interested in the needs of families of persons with disabilities. It offers a state-by-state listing of sibling support groups and also publishes a quarterly newsletter–*Sibling Information Network News*.

Sibling Information Network, 1776 Ellington Rd., South Windsor, CT 06074, (203) 648-1205.

Trace Research & Development Center is an interdisciplinary research, development, and resource center on technology and disability. Its mission is to advance the ability of people with disabilities to achieve their life objectives through use of communication, computer, and information technologies. For more specific information use the following address:

Trace Research & Development Center, University of Wisconsin-Madison, 1500 Highland Ave., Rm. J-151, Madison, WI 53705, (608) 262-6966, Fax: (608) 232-8848, website address: http://trace.wisc.edu

Wilderness Inquiry is designed to integrate disabled and nondisabled individuals in cooperative adventures that facilitate learning, communication, and development of self-esteem. Activities include canoe, kayak, and white water trips; bike trips; and winter wilderness adventures.

Wilderness Inquiry, 1313 Fifth St. S.E., Suite 327, Minneapolis, MN 55414, (612) 379-3858 or 1-(800) 728-0719.

Worldwide Disability Solutions Group (WDSG) at Apple works with key education, rehabilitation, and advocacy organizations nationwide to identify the computer-related needs of individuals with disabilities, then relates that need to third party vendors who develop products for people with disabilities. It also provides information about Macintosh Disability Resources.

Worldwide Disability Solution Group (WDSG), Apple Computer Inc., 20525 Mariani Ave., MS: 2-SE, Cupertino, CA 95014, (408) 974-7910, Fax: (408) 062-5260.

Equipment And Supplies

The following are names and addresses of well-known national companies serving professionals with equipment and supplies to enhance the living experience of those having disabilities.

Access to Recreation, Inc., is a publication that offers a variety of equipment and supplies for persons having disabilities, enabling them to participate more fully in the recreational activity of their choice.

Access to Recreation, Inc., 2509 E. Thousand Oaks Blvd., Suite 430, Thousand Oaks, CA 91362, 1-(800) 634-4351.

Don Johnston, Inc., is a 15-year-old company dedicated to providing quality products for people with special needs. The company designed software such as K.C. & Clyde in Fly Ball, Co:Writer, Write: Outloud, Ukandu, and Blocks in Motion for young people with learning disabilities.

Don Johnston, Inc., 1000 N Rand Rd., Bldg 115, P.O. Box 639, Wauconda, IL 60084-0639, 1-(800) 999-4660 or (708) 526-2682, Fax: (708) 526-4177.

Easy Listener by Phonic Ear is a listening device that is known to improve a student's attention level and concentration. It projects the teacher's voice at a consistent level above background noise to capture and retain student's attention. The Easy Listener personal FM and freefield sound system are recommended by special education professionals to improve communication abilities for students with auditory attention deficit, mild hearing impairment, autism, and central auditory processing disorders.

Phonic Ear, 3800 Cypress Dr., Petaluma, CA 94954, 1-(800) 227-0735.

Franklin Learning Resources has supplied teachers and students with learning tools helpful in improving language and communication skills for over a decade. Tools useful to persons with learning disabilities are the Speaking Language Master Special Edition, Franklin Bookman with Merriam-Webster's Collegiate Dictionary, Franklin Bookman with Dictionary & Thesaurus, and Franklin Spelling Ace.

Franklin Learning Resources, One Franklin Plaza, Burlington, NJ 08016-4907, 1-(800) 266-5626, Fax: (609) 239-5943.

Independent Living Aids, Inc., publishes a catalog named "Can-Do™ Products." The products featured in this catalog range from electronic magnifying viewers and games to household items like cooking equipment.

Independent Living Aids, Inc., 27 East Mall, Plainview, NY 11803, 1-(800) 537-2118, Fax: (516) 752-3135.

Kurzweil Applied Intelligence, Inc. produces optical character recognition systems; these systems scan printed or typed documents automatically and display the text in either digital speech or Braille. Kurzweil VOICE for Windows 2.0 supports voice input for navigation, which drives the Windows operating system and Windows-based applications on a command and control basis, and dictation, which enables the user to create text and enter data simply by speaking.

Kurzweil Applied Intelligence, Inc., 411 Waverly Oaks Rd., Waltham, MA 02154, 1-(800) 380-1234, Fax: (617) 893-6525, e-mail: info@kurzweil.com, Website address: http://www.kurzweil.com.

Matzie Golf Co., Inc., sells three types of golf swing trainers. One is the ASSIST, which has a special training grip, a heavy head to buildup golf muscles, and a patented bent shaft that creates a rotational force to teach the proper release action. The second trainer is CAST-AWAY, a hinged practice club that teaches the power angle, delaying the release of the wrist cock to eliminate casting. It puts an end to thin, fat, and topped shots. The third trainer is E-Z Tempo, it has a highly flexible shaft to help the golfer swing slow and smooth.

Matzie Golf Co., Inc., 112-gfw Penn St., El Segundo, CA 90245, 1-(800) 722-7125.

Recording for the Blind and Dyslexic (RFB&D) is a national nonprofit organization that provides taped educational books free on loan, books on diskette, and a variety of other services through its registration program. RFB&D borrowers require documentation of a disability and submit a yearly registration fee in order to receive equipment and services. The organization also has a number of 2- & 4-track portable tape recorders with variable speed control useful for taping class lectures or instruction sessions. Write to the address below for an application form:

Recording for the Blind & Dyslexic (RFB&D), 20 Roszel Road, Princeton, NJ 08540, (609) 452-0606 or (609) 520-8014, Fax: (609) 520-7990, e-mail: jkelly@rfbd.org

Refiner Golf has a hinged five iron engineered to hit golf balls and teach a smooth, instinctive, model swing. The Refiner comes with an instructional video.

Refiner Golf, 15307 Amberly Dr., Suite 5, Tampa, FL 33647, 1-(800) 756-3665.

Sportime Abilitations, a division of Sportime International, sells equipment for development and restoration of physical and mental ability through movement. The company has equipment and supplies in the area of movement, positioning, furniture, sensorimotor, recreation, exercise, and aquatics.

Sportime Abilitations, One Sportime Way, Atlanta, GA 30340, 1-(800) 850-8602 or 1-(800) 845-1535.

S&S Worldwide Games has served the needs of professionals in education and recreation for 40 years with quality products. These products range from sporting equipment to music and instruments. All products are carefully selected to give you the best possible price, quality, and performance.

S&S Worldwide Games, P.O. Box 517, Colchester, CT 06415-0517, 1-(800) 243-9232 or 1-(800) 937-3482.

The Trace Center at the University of Wisconsin-Madison has a CD called Cooperative Electronic Library on Disability. This CD contains information on the following:

ABLEDATA - description and ordering information for over 20,000 assistive technology products.

Cooperative Service Directories - these list thousands of disability related services by name, type of service, geographical location, and other criteria.

DATABASE - which contains books, pamphlets, videos, and other information resources on disability, including the 44,000 entry REHABDATA database.

Text Document Library - this library's inventory has complete texts of key disability-related documents providing information on legislation, regulations, guidelines, and funding.

For more information contact the following:

The Trace Center, at the University *of Wisconsin-Madison*, 1500 Highland Ave., Rm. S-151, Madison, WI 53705, (608) 262-6966, Fax: (608) 263-8848, e-mail: info@trace.wisc.edu, website address: http://www.trace.wisc.edu

Books, Newsletters, and Electronic Publications

The resources in this section will equip professionals, family members, or a person with learning disabilities with strategies, equipment, support services, and personal insight in to the management of learning disabilities. Some of the books in this section might be available at local or college libraries.

Books

A Travel Guide and Trip Diary (1991) by **Louis & Clark Travel Suppliers** informs the traveler about the essentials to organizing self for a prosperous travel experience. This book can be obtained from local luggage stores or writing to the address below:

Louis & Clark Travel Accessory Supplier, 1680 West Irving Park Rd., Chicago, IL 60613.

The Americans With Disabilities Act: Questions and Answers and ADA Self-evaluation Guide can be obtained from any of the ten **Regional Disability and Business Assistance Centers**. Toll-free number for reaching any of the following centers is 1-(800) 949-4232.

Region I: Maine, New Hamsphire, Vermont, Massachusetts, Rhode Island, Connecticut, (207) 874-6535.

Region II: New York, New Jersey, Puerto Rico, (609) 392-4004.

Region III: Pennsylvania, Delaware, Maryland, District of Columbia, Virginia, West Virginia, (703) 525-3268.

Region IV: Kentucky, Tennessee, North Carolina, South Carolina, Georgia, Alabama, Mississippi, Florida, (404) 888-0022.

Region V: Ohio, Indiana, Illinois, Michigan, Wisconsin, Minnesota, (312) 413-7756.

Region VI: Arkansas, Louisiana, Oklahoma, Texas, New Mexico, (713) 520-0232.

Region VII: Iowa, Missouri, Nebraska, Kansas, (314) 882-3600.

Region VIII: North Dakota, South Dakota, Montana, Wyoming, Colorado, Utah, (719) 444-0252.

Region IX: Arizona, Nevada, California, Hawaii, Pacific Basin, (510) 465-7884.

Region X: Idaho, Oregon, Washington, Alaska, (206) 438-3168.

Community Recreation and People with Disabilities: Strategies for Inclusion (2nd ed.) (1997) by Stuart J. Schleien, Tipton M. Ray, & Fredrick P. Green. This book continues with providing information on developing and implementing inclusive recreation environments. This book can be purchased by contacting the company below:

Paul H. Brookes Publishing, P.O. Box 10624, Baltimore, MD 21285-0624 , 1-(800) 638-3775.

Equal Access: Information Technology for Students with Disabilities. For more information contact the following address:

McGraw-Hill, Inc. Primus, Princeton Rd., S1, Highstown, NJ 08520, (609) 426-5867 or 1-(800) 962-9342, Fax:(609) 426-5900.

Guidelines for Directors of Non-Specialized Camps on Integrating Children with Learning Disabilities into their Camps by Doreen Kronick. This Canadian–based publication provides an overview to understanding learning disabilities, the preparation of child and staff member to the camping experience, and the implementation of a camping program for children with learning disabilities. This book can be obtained by writing the following address:

Learning Disabilities Association of America, 4156 Library Rd., Pittsburgh, PA 15234-1349.

Learning Strategies for Adults: Compensations for Learning Disabilities by Sandra C. Crux (1991). A useful resource for educators working with adults in a variety of settings. The publishing company to contact is below:

Wall & Emerson, Inc., Six O Connor Dr., Toronto, Ontario, Canada M4K 2K1, (416) 467-8685.

No One to Play With: The Social Side of Learning Disabilities by Betty Osman (1982). An account of learning disabilities affecting social and emotional behavior. The book can be purchased from the following publisher:

Random House, 201 East 50th St., New York, NY 10022.

On Being LD: Perspectives and Strategies of Young Adults by Stephen T. Murphy. The book was published by Teachers College, Columbia University in New York (1992). The author of this book explains firsthand accounts of the academic, social, and personal experiences of students with learning disabilities. This book imparts knowledge gained through practical experience that can be used as a reference to improve and understand the real environment of people living with learning disabilities.

Peterson's Colleges with Programs for Students with Learning Disabilities, Third edition. Charles T. Mangrum II, Ed.D., and Stephen S. Strichart, Ph.D., are the editors. The most complete guide to nearly 1,000 4-year and 2-year colleges. This book is available at most public libraries and in college libraries.

Peterson's Guides, P.O. Box 2123, Princeton, NJ 08543-2123, 1-(800) 338-3282.

Sports and Recreation for the Disabled, Second edition by Michael J. Paciorek and Jeffery A. Jones. This book features modifications and accommodations for 53 physical activities. The primary emphasis of the book is assuring equal opportunities for persons having physical and developmental disabilities. Some of the information in the book could be used on a temporary basis with persons having learning disabilities. This book is published by the group below:

Cooper Publishing Group, 701 Congressional Blvd., #340, Carmel, IN 46032.

Succeeding Against the Odds: Strategies Insights from the Learning Disabled by Sally L. Smith (1991). This book provides information and insights on adults with learning disabilities. Contact the publishing company below:
Jeremy P. Tarcher, Inc., 5858 Wilshire Blvd., Los Angeles, CA 90036, (213) 935-9980 or 1-(800) 631-8571.

Newsletters

Closing The Gap, Inc., is a publication dedicated to resources and technology updated for persons with special needs.
Closing The Gap, Inc., P.O. Box 68, Henderson, MN 56044, (612) 248-3294, Fax: (612) 248-3810.

The Postsecondary L.D. Network News is published three times per year by the Postsecondary L.D. Unit of the A.J. Pappanikou Center on Special Education and Rehabilitation at the University of Connecticut. The newsletter covers various issues concerning students with learning disabilities in college.
Postsecondary L.D. Network News, A.J. Pappanikou Center on Special Education and Rehabilitation, University of Connecticut, U-64, 249 Glenbrook Rd., Storrs, CT 06269-2064.

Electronic Publications

DO-IT News is a newsletter distributed periodically by the staff of the NSF-funded project DO-IT (Disabilities, Opportunities, Internetworking, and Technology) at the University of Washington. To subscribe, send a request to: doit@u.washington.edu.

Information, Technology, and Disability is a quarterly journal devoted to computer use by people with disabilities. To obtain complete issues, send a message with a blank subject line to listserv@sjuvm.stjohns.edu. In the body of the message type SUB itd-jnl Firstname Lastname (example: SUB itd-jnl John Doe).

The Journal of Virtual Reality in Education periodically has information pertinent to learning disabilities. To receive issues, e-mail jvre-all@sjuvm.stjohns.edu; to receive each issue's table of contents, e-mail jvre-toc@sjuvm.stjohns.edu

Recreation Resources Service Technical Assistance Bulletin periodically publishes articles pertaining to recreation and disabilities. "The Disability Awareness - Adapting Activities" by Joyce Shields, MS, CLP is an especially beneficial issue in providing accommodations and modifications to recreation activities for those having disabilities. To download or print this issue write to http://www2.ncsu.edu/ncsu/forest resources/recresource/disaware.html (short version is http://www2.ncsu.edu)

Under the category of **Newsgroups** on the Internet, many articles are written pertaining to learning disabilities. To explore the contents of these articles a person could either locate the newsgroup with the search engine then type in the words learning disability or learning disorder or type in this address: *news:alt.support.learning-disab*. For the newsgroup in education, its address is *news:alt.education.disabled*, which may also contain information about learning disabilities.

Videos

How Difficult Can This Be? Understanding Learning Disabilities through the F.A.T. City Workshop (70 mins). This film features a unique workshop wherein adults have the opportunity to experience learning disabilities first hand. Contact PBS Video 1-(800) 328-7271 for video and teacher's guide:
I'm Not Stupid (51 mins). This video gives an enlightening and compassionate introduction to and overview of the nature of learning disabilities. Contact the following:
LDA, 4156 Library Rd., Pittsburgh, PA 15234, (412) 341-1515.

We Can Learn. A five-part video outlines procedures in determining if a child has learning disabilities and what to do it he does. It profiles the success of strategy intervention of children and young adults with disabilities.
NCLD, 381 Park Ave. South, Suite 1400, New York, NY 10016, (212) 545-7510.

Degrees of Success: Conversations with College Students with Learning Disabilities (1992) focuses on the experiences of college students with learning disabilities as described by students themselves.

GeorgeAnn du Chossois, Access to Learning Program,
New York University, 566 La Guardia Place, #701, New York, NY
10012, (212) 998-4980.

Internet

Information about learning disabilities is available via the
World Wide Web (WWW). Connections to obtain information about
learning disabilities are accessible by inputting the web address to
open file or by topic name through a search engine. Discussion
about issues, topics, trends, experiences, or just networking occurs
in electronic discussion lists. These lists accumulate large amounts
of very beneficial information that is continuously exchanged
through users (people) by e-mail. The following is an inventory of
www addresses and discussion lists to assist those with disabilities,
their families, friends, and professionals in acquiring resources to
enhance the daily living environment of persons having disabilities.

Gophers

**The Americans with Disabilities Act - Title II Technical
Assistance Manual** covering state and local governments programs
and services. Address: http://gopher.usdoj.gov/crt/ada/taman2.html

Cornucopia of Disability Information, SUNY at Buffalo,
has an exhaustive collection of resources that includes search en-
gines, independent living, employment, etc. Address: gopher://val-
dor.cc.buffalo.edu/1

DO-IT from the University of Washington site has information on general disabilities, adaptive technology companies, legal
resources, and other disability links. Address: gopher://
hawking.u.washington.edu:70/11/disability-related

HEATH Resource Center contains materials on
postsecondary education for people with disabilities, college, vo-
tech, adult education, and other training. Address: gopher://
bobcat-ace.nche.edu

The World Wide Web (WWW)

Access First provides the best in sales, training, and support for the sight impaired, print handicapped, and learning disabled community. It has more than 40 years experience in the areas of high technology sales and technical support, application design, community networking, and funding resources. Address: http://www.nforamp.net/~access/af1.html

The Americans with Disabilities Document Center contains the ADA statute, regulations, ADAAG (Americans with Disabilities Act Accessibility Guidelines), federally reviewed tech sheets and other assistance documents. Address: http://janweb.icdi.wvu.edu/kinder/

Camp Nuhop, nicknamed The Warm Fuzzy Camp, is a summer residential program for any youngster from 6 to 16 with a learning disability, behavior disorder, or attention deficit disorder. About 50-55 campers and two staff members live on site in groups of 6-7 campers to every two counselors (see Appendix S for more details). Address: http://www.bright.net/~cnuhop/#INDEX

Conferences and general information dealing with learning, learning disabilities, and/or learning disabilities and technology contacting LD Resource. Snail mail address: LD Resource, 202 Lake Rd., New Preston, CT 06777, (860) 868-3214, e-mail: ldr@ldresources.com, Website address: http://www.ldresources.com

Disability, commercial sites contains newsletters, disability tips, and a disability mail address: http://disability.com/links/cool.html, http://disability.com (then search its home page), http://www.eskimo.com/~jlubin/disabled.html

Dyslexia 2000 Network, launched on January 11, 1995 and run by the Adult Dyslexia Organization in the United Kingdom, contains the latest information for dyslexic adults: details on events and publications and promotions for higher education, and collects the input from professionals in the field of dyslexia and its Buddy service. Address: http://www.futurenet.co.uk:80/charity/adoldescript.html

Family Village Sports & Recreation provides links to recreation resources for individuals with disabilities. Address: http://www.familyvillage.wisc.edu/recreat.htm#camps

The Instant Access Treasure Chest has comprehensive collections of resources and articles on ADD, dyslexia, auditory deficits, and other learning disability-related topics. Address: http://www.fln.vcu.edu/ld/ld.html and http://www.fln.vcu.edu (then search its home page).

Language–based Learning Disability: Remediation Research is collaborative research at the University of California at San Francisco (UCSF), Keck Center and Rutgers University, CMBN - sponsored by the Charles A. Dana Foundation and Hearing Research Inc. Address: http: //www-ld.ucsf.edu/, or address for publications about remediation research: http://www-ld.ucsf.edu/pubs.html

LD Online exclusively covers all aspects of learning disabilities. Address: http://www.Idonline.org

Learning Disabilities Organizations: An International Web Home was developed by LDA Alaska for organizations involved with learning disabilities. Address: http://www.lda.org

Learning Disabilities Research & Training Center conducted by the University of Georgia and Roosevelt Warm Springs Institute for Rehabilitation focuses on four research stands that primarily correspond to the conceptual, regulatory, and consumer framework surrounding the needs of adults with specific learning disabilities. Address: http://www.coe.uga.edu/LD/

Marin Puzzle People have an outstanding site that brings insight and warmth into its presentation of learning disabilities. Marin Puzzle People provide information on various learning disorders and links to other resources on the Net. Address: http://www.hooked.net/users/dyslexia

National Adult Literacy and Learning Disabilities Center (NALLDC) produces publications, discusses hot topics, and maintains links to LD and adult literacy websites. Address: http://novel.nifl.gov/nalldtop.html

Other Disability Resources on the Internet include the following address: http://primes6.rehab.uiuc.edu/pursuit/dis-resources/inet-dis/inet-dis.html. The shorter version: http://primes6.rehab.uiuc.edu (then search its home page).

The Rebus Institute is devoted to the dissemination of information related to adults with learning differences. Address: http://www.cenatica.com/rebus

The Summit Camp, Inc., offers therapeutic camping for boys and girls with learning disabilities and/or attention deficit disorders. This camp is prepared to meet the social, emotional, psychological, and educational needs of its campers via exciting and rewarding activities. The camp provides an extraordinary staff ratio (three adults to each four campers), and the staff is renowned for its talent, enthusiasm, warmth, and caring. Additional information about Summit Camp and its travel program is described in Appendix T. The camp's e-mail address: summitcamp@aol.com; Website address: http://www.castlepoint.com/summit/

Therapeutic Recreation Directory is the home page for therapeutic recreation and recreation therapy. Address: http://www.pacificnet.net/computrnet/

University of Kansas Department of Special Education has a disability-related web site for disabled K-12 and postsecondary students. Address: http://www.sped.ukans.edu/speddisabilitiesstuff/ld.html, a shorter version is: http://www.sped.ukans.edu (then search its home page).

YAHOO: DISABILITIES is a disability-specific search engine. Address: http://www.yahoo.com/Society_and_Culture.Disabilities/ (the _ denotes a space)

Discussion Lists

Addults is for discussion among adults with attention deficit disorder. To subscribe, send a message with a blank subject line to listserv@sjuvm.stjohns.edu. In the body write "subscribe ADDULTS Firstname Lastname" (i.e., subscribe ADDULTS Jane Doe).

Altlearn discusses different learning styles. To subscribe, send a message with a blank subject line to listserv@sjuvm.stjohns.edu. In the body write "subscribe altlearn Firstname Lastname" (i.e., subscribe altlearn Jane Doe).

CanAdapt-L is access technology with particular emphasis to Canadian individuals, groups, and suppliers that discusses issues, problems, and solutions of technology for persons with disabilities and information about Canadian legal context. To subscribe, write to mailserv@odie.ccs.yorku.ca or zcameron@orion.yorku.ca, and in the message write "subscribe CanAdapt-l."

Dsshe-l is a list about services for students with disabilities in higher education; address: dsshe-l@ubvm.bitnet

Information on families and support systems for persons with disabilities also advocates issues discussed and promoted by persons having disabilities. Address: listserv@sjuvm.stjohns.edu

LD-list is the learning disability information exchange list. To join, send a request to majordomo@curry.edu, subscribe to ld-list (Firstname Lastname i.e., subscribe ld-list Jane Doe).

PLLD-L has information on libraries and learning disabilities. To become a part of this list send a message to listproc@ala.org, to subscribe write PLLD-L (Firstname Lastname, i.e., subscribe PLLD-L Jane Doe).

APPENDICES

APPENDIX A
Evidence Checklist: Referral for Learning Disabilities

Directions: Place a letter before observed characteristics:
N = not shown, S = sometimes, 0 = often.

Attention Deficits

_____ 1. cannot sit still
_____ 2. cannot stand without some body movement
_____ 3. impulsive; acts without thinking
_____ 4. low frustration tolerance; angers quickly
_____ 5. cannot finish assignments in allotted time
_____ 6. environmental distractions; looks up and around, focusing on what is being seen or heard
_____ 7. fidgety
_____ 8. has short attention span
_____ 9. produces very little work due to daydreaming
_____10. disorganized; constantly losing books, papers, keys, supplies, etc.

Social Behaviors

_____ 1. constantly exhibits a "negative disposition"
_____ 2. always attends to the affairs of others (e.g., cannot seem to mind own business)
_____ 3. often exhibits cruel behavior; is mean to or makes fun of others
_____ 4. does not take criticism well
_____ 5. withdrawn; avoids groups, and has little communication with others
_____ 6. displays immature behavior; babyish; constantly depends on others
_____ 7. does not understand body language
_____ 8. exhibits lack of enthusiasm for everything
_____ 9. never assumes responsibility for actions
_____10. anxious; insecure; tense

Perceptual Problems

Visual

_____ 1. complains of tiredness while reading
_____ 2. complains print blurs while reading for short periods of time (Scoptic Sensitivity Syndrome)
_____ 3. has slow reading speed
_____ 4. experiences reversals: b for d, p for q, E for 3

_____ 5. experiences inversions: u for n, w for m, 6 for 9
_____ 6. identifies number sequences incorrectly (e.g., 23 as 32)
_____ 7. loses place frequently during reading
_____ 8. rereads lines or skips lines
_____ 9. if does not recognize word, substitutes similar sounding or looking word in to the reading
_____10. identifies words backwards (e.g., was/saw, on/no, top/pot)
_____11. shows poor ability to determine likenesses-differences in words
_____12. sees uneven spacing between letters (e.g., "goes" as "go es");
_____13. combines certain words in sentence sequence (e.g., "Bob went in the house" as "Bob wentin thehouse")
_____14. shows a poor ability to discover change in environment

Auditory

_____ 1. has poor auditory processing; cannot understand conversation or learning delivered at the normal rate of speech
_____ 2. avoids working in small groups
_____ 3. shows problems in auditory discrimination; has difficulty hearing differences in letter sounds
_____ 4. shows difficulty in determining what direction a particular sound is coming from
_____ 5. cannot filter out extraneous noise (e.g., dishes rattling in restaurant while listening to someone talk)
_____ 6. does not follow oral directions correctly

Spatial/Motor

_____ 1. becomes lost in familiar surroundings (e.g., school, neighborhood, or grocery store)
_____ 2. has directionality problems; shows difficulty distinguishing between right, left, forward, back, up, and down
_____ 3. has poor ability to keep columns straight in math
_____ 4. shows poor ability to maneuver around things; clumsy; accident prone
_____ 5. does not place letters on line
_____ 6. does not form letters correctly
_____ 7. does not copy letters or words correctly from the board
_____ 8. mirror writes (i.e., hold paper up to mirror and you see it as it should look)
_____ 9. shows major problems coloring within the lines on paper
_____10. has illegible handwriting

_____11. exhibits poor eye-hand coordination (e.g., has difficulty hitting a ball with a bat)

Cognitive/Conceptual Deficits

_____ 1. cannot see relationship between similar concepts
_____ 2. perseveration; gives same response again and again
_____ 3. does not understand abstract relationships such as in time: *yesterday, today, tomorrow, after/before*
_____ 4. does not understand abstract concepts such as *life/love, more/less*
_____ 5. has difficulty associating an act with its logical consequence
_____ 6. requires assistance cues or examples to evoke imagination
_____ 7. has a delayed reaction to recognizing a joke or pun
_____ 8. slow to respond, needs more time to think about information
_____ 9. understands information on a literal level
_____10. does not use inferential thinking–the "wh" questions to derive an answer: "who, what, where, when, why, and how"
_____11. numerous rereading of sentences or paragraphs to comprehend meaning
_____ 12. has difficulty organizing thoughts in a sequential manner for writing
_____13. can express ideas about a story or paragraph, but experiences major difficulty in writing it
_____14. discovers correct answers derived in nontraditional thinking methods
_____15. has difficulty thinking in an orderly, logical way (circular thinking)
_____16. mispronounces common words

Memory Deficits

_____ 1. cannot remember information that was just shown (visual)
_____ 2. cannot remember information that was just heard (auditory)
_____ 3. cannot remember sequence of steps in a complex math problem
_____ 4. cannot remember spelling for commonly used words
_____ 5. has poor sight vocabulary; knows few words on the automatic level
_____ 6. knows something one day but doesn't know it the next
_____ 7. word finding problems

_____ 8. has difficulty remembering newly learned vocabulary

_____ 9. exhibits poor use of using problem–solving strategies

_____10. exhibits poor memory for English grammar rules

When the "O" marks (for often) are predominant within this evidence checklist, these continuous behaviors are indicators to learning disabilities. The next step for the professional is to refer the student for diagnostic testing.

APPENDIX B
Learning Styles Sensory Modality Inventory

Directors: There are eleven incomplete sentences and three choices for each. Some of those choices contain more than one option. If any one of those options seems typical of you, score that answer. Score the three choices by rating: 3 = most typical of you; 2 = somewhat typical of you; 1 = not typical of you.

1. When I want to learn something new, I usually

    _____ A. want someone to explain it to me.
    _____ B. want to read about it in a book or magazine.
    _____ C. want to try it out, take notes, or make a model of it.

2. While traveling, I decided to visit a friend whose address I do not know. In calling this friend, I would want him to

    _____ A. tell me the directions by phone.
    _____ B. fax me a map or e-mail me directions.
    _____ C. meet me in front of the hotel and follow the friend to his house.

3. At a party, most of the time I like to

    _____ A. listen and talk to two or three people at once.
    _____ B. see how everyone looks and watch people.
    _____ C. dance, play games, or take part in some activities.

4. If I were helping with a musical show, I would most likely

    _____ A. compose the songs while playing or sing the songs.
    _____ B. design the costumes or select paint color or lighting for the scenery.
    _____ C. make the costume, build the sets, or take an acting role.

5. When I am angry, my first reaction is to

    _____ A. tell people off, laugh, joke, or talk it over with someone
    _____ B. visualize a picture of what happened in the event or think by myself.
    _____ C. walk away from the person, exercise to release anger, or throw something.

6. A happy event I would like to have is

_____ A. hearing thunderous applause for my accomplishments.
_____ B. seeing my picture in a newspaper or magazine recognizing my achievements
_____ C. being chosen to demonstrate my knowledge and ability to important people.

7. I prefer a teacher to

_____ A. lecture using informative explanations, stories, and discussion.
_____ B. write on the chalkboard, use visual aids, and read assigned resources.
_____ C. assign projects, experiments, or homework and conduct in–class activities.

8. I know that I talk with

_____ A. different tones of voice.
_____ B. my eyes and facial expressions.
_____ C. my hands and gestures.

9. If I had to remember an event so that I could recall it later, I would choose to

_____ A. hear an audio recording of the event or tell it aloud to someone.
_____ B. see pictures of it or read a description.
_____ C. replay it using practicable rehearsal like dance, a role-play technique, or by drawing the actual event.

10. When I cook something new, I like to

_____ A. have someone tell me the directions.
_____ B. read the recipe and judge the dish by how it looks.
_____ C. experiment, using combinations of known ingredients, feeling their texture, and taste.

11. In my free time, I like to

_____ A. listen to the radio, talk on the telephone, or attend a musical event.
_____ B. go to the movies, watch TV, or read a magazine or book.
_____ C. get some exercise, go for a walk, play games, or make things.

12. If I am using equipment such as a VCR, camcorder, or computer for the first time

_____ A. I want someone to tell me how to use it.
_____ B. I want to read the directions or watch someone else do it.
_____ C. I want to jump right in and do it; I'll figure it out sooner or later.

To interpret your sense modality, add up your score for each letter.

Total number: A. _____   **Auditory**

B. _____   **Visual**

C. _____   **Kinesthetic or Tactile**

If your hightest score was

A. – **you learn best through listening**
B. – **you learn best by seeing it in print or other visual modes.**
C. – **you learn best by getting physically involved.**

A score can indicate a near equal or dual sensory modality preference. It is not uncommon to have an auditory/visual or visual/kinesthetic sensory modality preference.

Reports in educational research suggest that most individuals have a preferred way to gain information. Results of the three common styles are:

• Visual learners rely primarily on vision for input, whether it is text, pictures, graphs, or symbols. This group represents about 65% of the population.
• Auditory learners gain most from what they hear. The process of talking about and hearing one's own and other's ideas about a topic assist in understanding the subject. This group represents about 15% of the population.
• Tactile and Kinesthetic learners understand information through doing, feeling, tasting, and touching. This group represents about 10% of the population. (Harwell, 1989, p. 42)

(Adapted with permission from *Learning Style Preference* by Adele Ducharme and Luck Watford)

APPENDIX C
Sample Educational Diagnostic Evaluation Report

Name:_J. Smith_   Evaluation Completed:_October 15, 1996_
Student #:_999-99-9999_   Tested by: C. Green, Certified Ed. Diagnostican
DOB:_July 15,1972_
Age: 23
Sex: Male
Education level: Freshman
Referral source: J. Bea, Special Services Counselor
Reason for referral: poor test grades, difficulties completing English 101

Test Administered
Weschler Adult Intelligence Scale-Revised (WAIS-R)
Woodcock-Johnson Psychoeducational Battery–Revised (WJ-R: Achievement)
Nelson-Denny Reading Test
Diagnostic Spelling Potential Test (DSPT)
Woodcock-Johnson Psychoeducational Battery–Revised (WJ-R: Cognitive Processing)
Bender Visual-Motor Gestalt Test
Written Language Sample (Non-standardized)

Background Information
   J. Smith is a 23-year-old male who was seen for a complete educational evaluation through the University Psychological Testing Center. He was referred by J. Bea, a counselor at Special Services, because of his difficulties taking tests and completing in-class essays in English 101. Information provided by Mr. Smith from his case history indicated that he attended parochial schools throughout his school career. Following graduation, he went to Jardin Community College. He related that he first began having difficulties in the ninth grade. He also has received speech and language therapy from the first through third grades. This therapy was in response to Mr. Smith's poor ability to pronounce "s," "sl," and "w" in certain words. He is currently a junior and a biochemistry major. He also works at Presbyterian Hospital on the weekends as an aide.
   J. Smith is the youngest of six children, having one older brother and four older sisters. Both parents were in the home during his childhood and appear to have been supportive. His health history is unremarkable for serious illness; however, when he was a child he sustained a broken leg. Mr. Smith also wears glasses and lists his last vision exam in 1995. His last hearing exam was in 1989. He reports possible hearing loss due to playing in a rock music band and working summers on a construction site.

Learning Characteristics (Self-rated by student)

When asked to complete a "behavioral checklist," Mr. Smith marked the following factors as being significant in interfering with his ability to learn or function:

- *written language* - Unclear written expression (trouble getting ideas across)
- *work and study habits* - Poor organization and budgeting of time

Test Results and Analysis

All scores, unless otherwise noted, are reported with a mean (average) score of 100 and a standard deviation of 15.

Wechsler Adult Intelligence Scale-Revised (WAIS-R)

	*Scaled Score		*Scaled Score
Information	9	Picture completion	10
Digit Span	12	Picture arrangement	8
Vocabulary	7	Block design	14
Arithmetic	9	Object assembly	13
Comprehension	6	Digit symbol	10
Similarities	7		

Verbal IQ = 90   Performance IQ = 106   Full scale IQ = 96

*   *Scaled scores relate to a mean score of 10 when compared to the individual's own age group.*

These state standards for special education in the public schools define "expectancy" as a standard score obtained in an intelligence test. When testing for a specific learning disability, all other scores (in the areas of academic achievement and processing) will be compared to this level of expectancy or educational potential. On the WAIS-R, Mr. Smith achieved a Performance IQ score of 106 that classifies his non-verbal cognitive skills within the "average" range. This ranks him at the 65th percentile when compared to other individuals his age. In contrast to this was his Verbal IQ score of 90 that falls at the 25th percentile. The discrepancy between the Verbal (90) and the Performance (106) IQ scores is considered to be statistically signficant at the .01 level. This discrepancy of 16 points, as well as the overall pattern of scores, suggest Mr. Smith's Verbal IQ score does not reflect his true intellectual functioning or potential, consequently, the Full Scale IQ score is also somewhat low. The Performance IQ of 106 will be considered as the most representative of his present level of functioning. *(Whether a Full scale or Subscale measure is used depends upon the discretion of the diagnostic evaluator.)*

When looking at individual subtest scores on the WAIS-R, Mr. Smith demonstrated no significant strengths or weaknesses (when compared within his own total performance) as all subtest scaled scores fell within a range considered to be average for him.

When looking at general areas of performance (as derived from various subtest combinations), Mr. Smith's strengths were in the areas of perceptual-motor development and spatial ability. General areas of performance found to be low for Mr. Smith included verbal comprehension and conceptualizing ability. It should be noted that while these areas were low when compared to his overall performance, all areas ranked no lower than within the "average" range of performance for a population of 23 year olds.

Woodcock-Johnson Psychoeducational Battery-Revised (WJ-R): Achievement

	Approximate Age Level	Grade Level	Percentile	Standard Score	Discrepency from Expectancy
Broad reading	17 - 5	11.7	26th	90	-16
Basic reading	24	14.8	46th	99	-7
Reading comprehension	17 - 0	11.5	20th	87	-19
Broad mathematics	29	15.3	52nd	101	-5
Basic math Skills	26	16.9	80th	113	+7
Math reasoning	19 - 4	13.1	35th	94	-12
Broad written language	14 - 7	9.4	12th	82	-24
Basic writing skills	14 - 3	9.1	11th	82	-24
Written expression	15 - 6	10.0	8th	79	-27
Broad knowledge	16 - 6	10.9	19th	87	-19

Significant discrepancy is defined in the literature concerning adults as a negative difference of 15 to 20 standard score points between expectancy and achievement scores. Standard scores (and percentiles) on the Woodcock-Johnson compare the individual's performance to others in the same age group. This discrepancy of 20 points approximates a span of 1.5 standard deviations. In that Mr. Smith's expectancy score is 106, the significant discrepancy level for him would be at or below a score of 86.

This will also be used when analyzing his performance on various processing skills as measured by the Woodcock-Johnson Psychoeducational Battery-Revised: Cognitive Processing.

Achievement (basic academic) testing indicates Mr. Smith is demonstrating a significant discrepancy in standard scores when compared to his own level of expectancy (on the WAIS-R) in the areas of reading and written language. Somewhat surprisingly, Mr. Smith has excellent word attack skills, indicating that he has done a great deal of works with a good speech and language therapist. Within the written language cluster, punctuation, capitalization, usage/grammar, and sustained attention to a writing task were the areas that were most difficult for Mr. Smith. His errors on the writing task stemmed from writing words that did not constitute a sentence. It should be noted, however, that when the elements of punctuation, capitalization, and grammar were not of paramount importance, Mr. Smith could communicate his thoughts in a manner commensurate with his expectancy. It should also be noted that math appears to be an area of relative strength for him. Within this area, however, he seemed to have some difficulty with stated math problems, basic math errors, and not remembering formulae needed to set up the problem.

Nelson-Denny Reading Test

	Grade Level	Percentile	Standard Score	Discrepency from Expectancy
Vocabulary	10.6	7th	78	-28
Comprehension	8.6	5th	75	-31
Total	9.9	5th	75	-31
Reading Rate	—	10th	81	-25

The Nelson-Denny Reading Test was administered in order to obtain additional information concerning Mr. Smith's current reading abilities. The vocabulary section of this test consists of 100 items, each with five answer choices, and has a time limit of 15 minutes. Mr. Smith obtained a significant discrepancy in standard scores of this section in comparison to his own level of expectancy. The comprehension section contains eight reading passages and a total of 36 questions, each with five answer choices. The time limit for this section is 20 minutes, the first minute being used to determine reading rate. Mr. Smith's performance on the Nelson-Denny indicates significant difficulties in vocabulary, comprehension, and reading rate.

Diagnostic Spelling Potential Test (DSPT)

The Diagnostic Spelling Potential Test (DSPT) was administered in addition to the Woodcock-Johnson Written Language Cluster in order to obtain more information concerning Mr. Smith's approach to spelling. Three subtests were administered, each containing 90 items. The subtests are as follows:

- *Spelling:* yields a score for accurately spelled words (from dictation).
- *Visual recognition*: yields a score for the individual's ability to recognize the correctly spelled form of a word without the aid of an auditory stimulus.
- *Auditory-Visual recognition:* yields a score reflecting the individual's ability to recognize the correctly spelled form of a word when it is pronounced aloud.

Mr. Smith's performance on the DSPT is as follows:

	Percentile	Standard Score	Discrepency from Expectancy
Spelling	90th	119	+13
Visual recognition	86th	116	+10
Audio-Visual recognition	77th	111	+6

Mr. Smith's standard scores on the DSPT indicate spelling skills are well within his own level of expectancy. Scores from all areas fell within the "high average" range of performance and appear to be a relative strength.

Woodcock-Johnson Psychoeducational Battery-Revised:
Cognitive Processing

	Approximate Age Level	Grade Level	Percentile	Standard Score	Discrepency from Expectancy
Long-term retrieval	24	15.9	57th	103	-3
Short-term memory	17-1	10.1	36th	95	-11
Processing speed	29	14.5	46th	98	-8
Auditory processing	5- 6	K.5	.1	44	-62
Visual processing	13-5	7.8	24th	89	-17
Comprehensive-knowledge	16-9	11.0	15th	84	-22
Fluid reasoning	30	16.1	57th	103	-3

Mr. Smith's performance on the WJ-R: Cognitive Processing indicates a significant discrepancy in scores in the areas of auditory processing, visual processing, and comprehension-knowledge. A suspicion of a hearing impairment might be the reason behind the low auditory processing score.

On the **Bender Visual-Motor Gestalt Test**, Mr. Smith's performance was within his own range of expectancy. This test is designed to measure visual-motor integration abilities and requires the individual to copy geometric forms.

Eligibility Statement

Mr. Smith demonstrates a specific "learning disability" in the areas of reading and written language. This evaluation indicates that his academic performance is related to processing difficulties in the areas of auditory processing, visual processing, and comprehension-knowledge.

Recommendations

1. Due to documented difficulties in the area of processing, extended time accommodations on exams may be necessary based on Mr. Smith's own judgment of the material and arrangements made with the individual professor. Special arrangements for exams can be made through Special Servieces in Broker Hall.

2. Mr. Smith's visual processing difficulties make it impossible for him to move quickly through information presented visually. J. Smith should inform his professors of his visual procesing difficulties so that they understand the need for extended reading time.

3. Due to Mr. Smith's processing deficits, a class schedule of no more than 12 hours per semester is recommended. He should work closely with an academic advisor on a regular basis in order to design his program carefully.

4. Mr. Smith should obtain tutoring and study skills strategies from the Tutorial Center and one-on-one instruction from Special Services. Teaching him the use of employing mnemonic devices or simple drawings could improve his retention of information.

5. Mr. Smith should arrange study sessions with frequent breaks and time allowed for extensive review of materials. He should also arrange to begin studying for an exam at least five days before an exam date, allowing enough rehearsal to get the information into long-term memory.

6. Auditory processing may make note-taking difficult for this student. Note-taking materials (available through Special Services) and/or a tape recorder could relieve him of having to take notes while attempting to process the lecture material simultaneously.

7. Referral to the Speech/Language Clinic to determine hearing loss and how this affects his learning is recommended.

8. Mr. Smith should attempt to obtain reading assignments and a course syllabus from classes he is planning to take prior to the beginning of each new semester so that he can get a "head start" on classwork.

258   *Developing Recreation Skills in Persons with Learning Disabilities*

APPENDIX D
NCAA Academic Requirements Committee
Criteria for Learning Disabled Student Athletes
per NCAA Bylaws 14.3.1.3.4 - 14.3.1.6

Division I - Eligibility

14.3.1.3.1.1 Students with Learning Disabilities
A student diagnosed with a learning disability is permitted to have all core courses completed prior to initial full-time enrollment at a collegiate institution. The determination as to whether courses taken at a high school are core courses shall be made on the basis of the 48 H confirmation statement issued to the high school where the student completed the classes. Courses taken at a collegiate institution must be approved by the Academics/ Eligibility/Compliance Cabinet. (adopted 1/14/97; effective 8/1/97)

14.3.1.3.4 Courses for Students with Disabilities
The Academics/Eligibility/Compliance Cabinet may approve the use of high school courses for students with disabilities to fulfill the core-curriculum requirements if the high school principal submits a written statement to the NCAA indicating that students in such classes are expected to acquire the same knowledge, both quantitatively and qualitatively, as students in other core courses. Students with disabilities still must complete the required core courses and achieve the minimum required grade-point average in this core curriculum. (revised 1/14/97; effective 8/1/97) (Excerpt adapted from *1997-98 NCAA Division I Manual*, pp. 139-140)

Division I: Academic Eligibility Requirements
If you're first entering a Division I college on or after August 1, 1996, or thereafter, in order to be considered a "qualifier," you're required to:

* graduate from high school;
* successfully complete a core curriculum of at least 13 academic courses [this core curriculum includes at least four years in English; two in math; one year of algebra and one year of geometry (or one year of a higher-level math course for which geometry is a prerequisite); two in social science; two in natural or physical science (including at least one laboratory class, if offered by your high school); one additional course in English, math, or natural or physical science; and two additional academic courses (which may be taken from the already mentioned categories, e.g., foreign language, computer science, philosophy)];

- have a grade-point average (based on a maximum of 4.000) and a combined score on the SAT verbal and math sections or a sum score on the ACT based on the following qualifier index scale.

Qualifier Index

Core GPA	ACT[1] (new: sum of scores)	SAT (old scoring system)	SAT (new scoring System)
		before April 1, 1995	on or after April 1, 1995
2.500 & above	68	700	820
2.475	69	710	830
2.450	70	720	840-850
2.425	70	730	860
2.400	71	740	860
2.375	72	750	870
2.350	73	760	880
2.325	74	770	890
2.300	75	780	900
2.275	76	790	910
2.250	77	800	920
2.225	78	810	930
2.200	79	820	940
2.175	80	830	950
2.150	80	840	960
2.125	81	850	960
2.100	82	860	970
2.075	83	870	980
2.050	84	880	990
2.025	85	890	1000
2.000	86	900	1010

[1] *Previously, ACT score was calculated by averaging four scores. New standards are based on sum of scores.*

A "partial qualifier" is eligible to practice with a team at its home facility and receive an athletic's scholarship during his first year at a Division I school and then has three seasons of competition remaining. A partial qualifier may earn a fourth year of competition, provided that at the beginning of the fifth academic year following the student-athlete's initial, full-time collegiate enrollment, the student-athlete has received a baccalaureate degree.

In order to be considered a "partial qualifier," you have not met the requirements for a qualifier, but you're required to:

- graduate from high school;
- present a grade-point average (based on a maximum of 4.000) and combined score on the SAT verbal and math sections or a sum score on the ACT based on the following partial qualifier index scale.

Qualifier Index

Core GPA	ACT* (new: sum of scores	SAT (old scoring system)	SAT (new scoring System)
2.750 & above	59	600	720
2.725	59	610	730
2.700	60	620	730
2.675	61	630	740-750
2.650	62	640	760
2.625	63	650	770
2.600	64	660	780
2.575	65	670	790
2.550	66	680	800
2.525	67	690	810

* *Previously, ACT score was calculated by averaging four scores. New standards are based on sum of scores.*

(Excerpts taken from *1997-98 NCAA Guide for the College-Bound Student-Athlete,* p. 2)

Division II - Eligibility

14.3.1.3.4 Courses for Students with Disabilities

The Academic Committee may approve the use of high school courses for students with disabilities to fulfill the core curriculum requirements if the high school principal submits a written state-ment to the NCAA indicating that students in such classes are expected to acquire the same knowledge, both quantitatively and qualitatively, as students in other core courses. Students with disabilities still must complete the required core courses and achieve the minimum required grade-point average in this core curriculum. (revised 1/14/97; effective 8/1/97) (excerpt adapted from *1997-98 NCAA Division II Manual,* p. 125)

Division II: Academic Eligibility Requirements

If you're first entering a Division II college on or after August 1, 1996, or thereafter, in order to be considered a "qualifier," you're required to:

- graduate from high school;
- have a GPA of 2.000 (based on a maximum of 4.000) in a successfully completed core curriculum of at least 13 academic courses [this core curriculum includes three years in English; two in math; two in social sciences; two in natural or physical science (including at least one laboratory class, if offered by your high school); and two additional courses in English, math or natural or physical science; and two additional academic courses (which may be taken from the already mentioned categories, e.g., foreign language, computer science, philosophy)];
- have a combined score on the SAT verbal and math sections of 700 if taken before April 1, 1995, or 850 if taken on or after April 1, 1995, or a 68 sum score on the ACT.

A "partial qualifier" is eligible to practice with a team at its home facility and receive an athletic's scholarship during his first year at a Division II school. In order to be considered a "partial qualifier," you have not met the requirements for a qualifer, but you're required to graduate from high school and meet one of the following requirements:

- specified minimum SAT or ACT score; or
- successful completion of a required core curriculum consisting of a minimum number of courses and a specified minimum grade-point average in the core curriculum.

(Excerpts adapted from *1997-98 NCAA Guide for the College-Bound Student-*

Athlete, 1997-98 NCAA Division I Manual, and *1997-98 NCAA Division II Manual*)

For more information about the *1997-98 NCAA Guide for the College-Bound Student-Athlete* write to the NCAA:

The National Collegiate Athletic Association
6201 College Boulevard
Overland Park, Kansas 66211-2422   http://www.ncaa.org
Phone: 913-339-1906   NCAA hotline: 800-638-3731

APPENDIX E
Visual Guiding

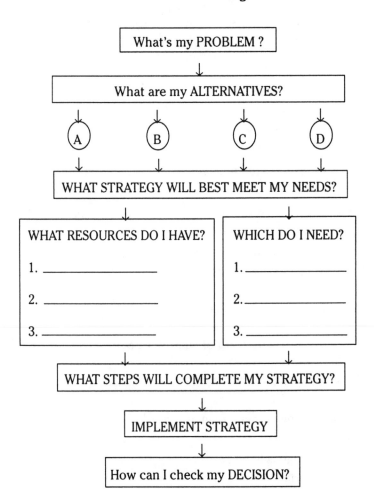

APPENDIX F
Family Air Sangs (Familiar Sayings)

These are actual "mis-heard" sayings from an individual who has an auditory discrimination learning disability. **Directions:** Read these words aloud. Write to the side what these words really mean.

1. Rocker buy bay bee inner tree hops.
2. Ah waits beep a light.
3. Roland's tone gadders nome hoss.
4. Butter laid den ever.
5. Law tent britches full in town.
6. Ink odd weed rust.
7. But tune toot a gather.
8. Up any shave sup any urn.
9. High pled jelly gents two thief lag.
10. A fit furs chewed own suck seed dry egg hen.
11. Want a drain sit bores.
12. Win rum dues a romance stew.

Translation of Family Air Sangs

1. Rock-a-bye baby in the tree tops.
2. Always be polite.
3. A rolling stone gathers no moss.
4. Better late than never.
5. London bridge is falling down.
6. In God we trust.
7. Put two and two together.
8. A penny saved is a penny earned.
9. I pledge allegiance to the flag.
10. If at first you don't succeed, try again.
11. When it rains it pours.
12. When in Rome, do as the Romans do.

(Excerpt adapted from Learning Disabilities Training Project, Western Carolina University. 1989. *The Postsecondary Learning Disabilities Primer.* Cullowhee, NC: Author)

APPENDIX G
What Did the Queen Ask the Magic Mirror?

Directions: Cross out all the letters in the diagram that appear 4 times. The letters that are left will spell the answer. Please complete this task in five to seven minutes.

D	G	K	L	W	M	B
H	O	M	I	D	L	J
G	C	S	J	T	B	H
E	K	D	F	C	G	A
J	I	L	B	R	G	J
E	D	M	S	T	L	C
B	K	C	■	K	M	■

Answer: Who is the fairest?

Taken from *Snow White Fun Pad™: Packed With Things To Do!* No Author, No Publisher. Obtained from a Walmart Store.

Directions to "What Did the Queen Ask the Magic Mirror?" This is an example of how a young sibling having learning disabilities, especially directionality and memory difficulties, would solve this exercise.

Letter D
1. Reads the first and second lines from left to right, crossing out both Ds.
2. Reads the third line from right to left.
3. Reads the fourth line, but skips the "D," forgetting what letter to cross out.
4. Reads the fifth line from left to right.
5. Rereads the fifth line, but from right to left.

6. Reads the sixth line from left to right, crossing out the "D."
7. Reads the seventh line from right to left.

Letter G
1. Reads the first line from left to right, crossing out "G."
2. Skips the second line.
3. Reads the third line from left to right, missing the "G."
4. Reads the fourth line from right to left, crossing out "C" instead of "G."
5. Reads the fifth line from left to right, crossing out the "G."
6. Reads the sixth line from right to left.
7. Reads the seventh line from left to right, crossing out the "C."

Letter K
1. Reads the first line from left to right, crossing out the "K."
2. Reads the second line from right to left.
3. Reads the third, fourth, and fifth lines from left to right, crossing out the "K" in the fourth line.
4. Reads the sixth line twice.
5. Reads the seventh line from left to right, crossing out both "Ks."

Letter L
1. Reads the first line from left to right, crossing out the "L."
2. Reads the second line from right to left, missing the "L."
3. Skips the third line.
4. Reads the fourth line twice from left to right.
5. Reads the fifth line from left to right, crossing out the "L."
6. Reads the sixth line twice from left to right, crossing out the "L" twice, then realizes this line was just read.
7. Reads the seventh line from left to right.

Letter W
1. Reads the first line from left to right, crossing out the "W."
2. Reads part of the second line, then goes to the third line.
3. Reads the fourth line from right to left.
4. Reads the fifth and sixth line from right to left.
5. Rereads the sixth line
6. Reads the seventh line from right to left, crossing out the "M."

Because this person forgot the directions, he did not go back to erase the crossed out "W" because there was only one "W" and not four. Now, finish this puzzle using the correct directions. As you can see, with all the rereading, forgetting directions, and letters being confused, it will take this person longer than 10 minutes to complete this task. It is possible if the sibling managed to obtain the correct answer it might be difficult for him to read it. See example answer (1), produced by someone who solved this puzzle using the directions on this page. Example answer (2) was produced by someone who developed a systematic method of isolating the letters to obtain the correct answer.

Example Answer (1)

Answer produced: Mho ilgs thd fgirmst?

Example Answer (2)

Correct answer: Who is the fairest?

APPENDIX H

Scrambled Pies

Directions: A simple activity like "Scrambled Pies" could cause severe frustration for the child who has trouble distinguishing an object within other objects (whether the objects are similar or different). This child may find less than 10 pies or more than 10 pies, recounting the overlapping pies in the middle of the picture.

Scrambled Pies

How many pies did
Snow White bake?

Answer: 10 pies

Taken from *Snow White Fun Pad™: Packed With Things To Do!*
No Author, No Publisher. Obtained from a Walmart Store.

APPENDIX I

Drawn Fabric Embroidery

  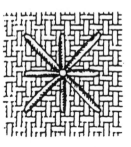

Diagram 1   **Diagram 2**   **Diagram 3**

Star eyelet

A Star Eyelet consists of eight stitches worked over a square of fabric, eight threads each way, all stitches being worked into the same central hole. (Diagram 1)

An individual with problems in directionality may not know the starting point of this design. One must begin in the middle, on the underside of the fabric. Work the thread up from the underside of the fabric, counting approximately three fabric lines on the topside of the fabric. Insert needle in that third line, bring thread underneath fabric, and insert needle up through the beginning point of the design.

If the person begins at the end point of the star design, she would need to circle around twice in order to end up in the middle to continue with the next star point. The person might have cross understitching to take the thread from one star endpoint to the next star endpoint, or bring thread up through the fabric near the central hole showing fabric lines between stitches. One can create a Star eyelet design by doing the previously mentioned steps, but the final product would not look as nice and the person having learning disabilities would know she made mistakes. (Diagram 2)

An individual with figure-ground problems will probably encounter difficulty with interpreting the picture, because it is in black and white. The fabric color is grey and the thread color is a darker gray. The person may not be able to distinguish between warp fabric threads and cross fabric threads, making the star endpoints uneven. (Diagram 3)

(Excerpt adapted from *100 Embroidery Stitches, Coats & Clark's Book No. 1 50-A*, 1975)

APPENDIX J
Case Scenario #1

Henry is a college senior and is required to take a math class before graduating. He knew he had to take a math class, but decided to put it off in the hopes that he would do it later. Henry has always had a fear of math and never performed well on math tests or homework assignments. Now that Henry is in his last year of college he must enroll in the required math course.

During this required math class, the instructor asks students to work in pairs and quiz each other before the exam. Although Henry has kept up with the work, he is fearful of not knowing the answer and being ridiculed by his partner. When it is Henry's turn to answer a question, he has difficulty following the steps in the word problem. Rather than asking his partner for clarification, Henry says he doesn't know the answer.

The student states, "That was in our homework."

Henry explodes, "Get off my back! Answer it yourself."

He leaves the room.

- Is Henry acting passively, aggressively, or assertively?
- Identify the problem(s) in this situation.
- How do you think Henry's partner felt after Henry left the room?
- What could Henry do to handle this situation assertively?
- Have you ever been in a similar situation?
- What did you do?
- How did it turn out?
- Role play a student admitting that he is having difficulty and asking for assistance or clarification.

(Adapted from *Assertiveness Scenarios. Facilitating an Academic Support Group for Students with Learing Disabilities: A Manual for Professionals* by Janis Johnson. Columbus: AHSSPPE)

APPENDIX K
Case Scenario #2

Jill is in her second year at college and is currently enrolled in a history course. One requirement for this course is to complete a 10-page research paper. Jill began to work on her paper three weeks before it was due. She carefully chose her topic, outlined her paper, conducted her library research, and wrote several drafts before she was satisfied with the final paper. Jill completed the paper on time and submitted it to the professor feeling very proud about the results.

The following week Jill received the research paper back from her professor. She was shocked to discover that she had been given a grade of "D." This was the lowest grade she had ever received on a paper while in college.

Jill was extremely angry and confused with this grade. However, she feels intimidated by her professor and is too afraid to approach him with her questions and concerns about this research paper. To deal with her anger, Jill phones her best friend and tells her friend how her professor is being unfair in grading reports. Jill complains at length to her friend. The friend encourages Jill to forget about it, accept the grade, and study really hard for the final exam to improve her overall course grade. Jill decides to do what her friend suggests.

- Is Jill acting in a passive, aggressive, or an assertive manner?
- What are the problems in this situation?
- What could Jill do to handle this situation assertively?
- Write out a sample dialogue of what Jill could say to her professor.
- What would you do if you were in Jill's situation?
- Have you ever had this happen to you? What did you do? How did it turn out?
- Role play Jill assertively approaching her history instructor for clarification on his grading procedures.
- What additional suggestions do you have for students contacting professors?

(Adapted from *Assertiveness Scenarios. Facilitating an Academic Support Group for Students with Learing Disabilities: A Manual for Professionals* by Janis Johnson. Columbus: AHSSPPE)

APPENDIX L
Case Scenario #3

Michael recently graduated from college and accepted a job working at a large insurance company. Throughout college Michael utilized a reader or books on tape to assist him in understanding written text. A large portion of Michael's job consists of revising many medical and home insurance policies, along with handling complaints about claims. After finishing his first two weeks on the job, he noticed that he will need some kind of accommodation (i.e., audio recording of the policies or having a person read the policies out loud to him) because with all the reading, it is difficult to meet job task deadlines.

Michael did not disclose to his employer that he has a learning disability that affects his reading comprehension. He is afraid his supervisor might report this to other management personnel and he might be fired. Michael is pondering, "What should I do?"

Michael, concerned about his position at work, contacted a counselor at the career center at his former college. He told the counselor about his problem, who in turn directed him to the director of special services. The counselor also informed him about his protection under the Americans with Disabilities Act. In meeting with the director of special services, Michael formulated a list on how he would approach his supervisor to disclose his disabilities and difficulties with reading.

1. Make an appointment with supervisor.

2. Calmly describe his learning problems with the supervisor and emphasize success in reading tasks when accompanied by verbal input.

3. Discuss the options of accommodations (i.e., have a secretary audio record each policy Michael would be handling in his job; obtain a computer program with voice features; or the company could purchase a Kurweil machine so any text could be verbally read).

4. Talk about the ranking of priorities with job duties.

Michael carried out his plan as stated above—he discussed accommodation options with his supervisor. He listened attentively when his supervisor was concerned about the cost involved with purchasing a new computer or Kurweil machine. The supervisor's decision to select the accommodation of the secretary audio recording each policy required for Michael's job was accepted by Michael as a reasonable choice. Michael and his supervisor both compromised on what were important priorities for his job.

- Is Michael acting passively, assertively, or aggressively?
- Identify the problem(s) in this situation.
- What could Michael do to improve his situation at work?
- Have you ever had this happen to you? What did you do? How did it turn out?
- What additional suggestions do you have for individuals discussing their disabilities with a supervisor?

(Adapted from *Assertiveness Scenarios. Facilitating an Academic Support Group for Students with Learing Disabilities: A Manual for Professionals* by Janis Johnson. Columbus: AHSSPPE)

APPENDIX M
Recreation Interest Survey

Directions: Please mark in the box which activities you have participated in and what activities you would like to participate in.

Have Done	Would Do	Activities	Have Done	Would Do	Activities
		PHYSICAL			GAMES
___	___	Team sports	___	___	Crossword puzzle
___	___	Swimming	___	___	Table games
___	___	Table tennis	___	___	Lawn games
___	___	Individual sports	___	___	Jigsaw puzzles
___	___	Exercise	___	___	Cards
___	___	Cycling	___	___	Other _____
___	___	Bowling			
___	___	Golf			OUTDOOR
___	___	Jogging/Running	___	___	Fishing
___	___	Walking	___	___	Camping
___	___	Other _____	___	___	Rollerblading
			___	___	Hiking
		ART	___	___	Picnics
___	___	Photography	___	___	Gardening
___	___	Painting	___	___	Other _____
___	___	Drawing			
___	___	Crafts/Sewing			COMMUNITY
___	___	Ceramics	___	___	Church
___	___	Carpentry	___	___	Community cntr.
___	___	Other _____	___	___	Club _____
			___	___	Shopping
		MISCELLANEOUS	___	___	Dining out
___	___	Reading	___	___	Movies
___	___	Television	___	___	Theater
___	___	Video movie	___	___	Concerts
___	___	Travel	___	___	Sporting events
___	___	Volunteering			
___	___	Socializing			HOBBIES
___	___	Pets	___	___	Collectibles ___
___	___	Dancing	___	___	Writing
___	___	Music	___	___	Cooking
___	___	Entertaining	___	___	Investing
___	___	Other _____	___	___	Fixing Things
			___	___	Other _____

APPENDIX N
Assessments of Functional Abilities in Recreation Activities

Functional Assessment of Characteristics for Therapeutic Recreation (FACTR)
(Peterson, Dunn, & Carruther, 1983)

This instrument examines functional skills and behaviors considered to be prerequisite to leisure involvement. Eleven behaviors are in each of three categories: physical, cognitive, and social/emotional. Subcategories are to be rated on 3- or 4-point scales after observation by a therapist. Some reliability studies reported. It is usable with any special population.
Published: Idyll Arbor, Inc. (# 13), 25119 SE 262 St., Ravensdate, WA 98051, (206) 432-3231.

Ohio Leisure Skills Scales on Normal Functioning (OLSSON)
(Olsson, 1988)

OLSSON measures 20 functional abilities in three major areas: functional skills, behavioral skills, and social/communication skills. Its use is intended for clients with cognitive impairments. A therapist implements five activities in which the client is observed and assessed, then summarizes observations in two sections of the instrument. Validity and reliability information are available on this instrument.
Published: Roy Olsson, Dept. of PEHP, Health Education Bldg., University of Toledo, 2801 W. Bancroft, Toledo, OH 43606.

General Recreation Screening Tool (GRST)
(Burlingame, 1988)

GRST measures functional abilities in three areas (physical, cognitive, and affective) according to developmental age groups up to 10 years. This instrument is intended for individuals with developmental disabilities and is designed for scoring after therapist observation. No validity and reliability information are reported.
Published: Idyll Arbor, Inc. (# 111), 25119 SE 262 St., Ravensdate, WA 98051, (206) 432-3231.

Recreation Behavior Inventory (RBI)
(Berryman & Lefebvre, 1981)

This observational tool is used to assess cognitive, sensory and perceptual motor skills as prerequisities to leisure participation. Eighty-seven behaviors are to be observed during 20 recreation activities, then rated on a 3-point scale. Intended for children, but use reported in behavioral and long-term care facilities. Validity and reliability information published on instrument.
Published: Doris Berryman, Dept. of RLPES, 239 Greene St., Room 635, New York University, New York, NY 10003.

APPENDIX O
Cognitive Leisure Indicator Instrument

Components

The Cognitive Leisure Indicator is used to assess the perceived cognitive ability and leisure participating ability of an individual having a disability. This instrument was developed to determine if an individual's cognitive ability has an effect on his ability to participate in leisure activities. This three-page, forced item-Likert questionnaire contains a total of 78 questions. The questions are divided into seven subsections. The subsections consist of the following topics:

1. Attention/Distractibility
2. Organization/Planning
3. Social/Emotional
4. Cognitive Processes
5. Reading/Spelling/Writing/Mathematics
6. Perceptual/Motor
7. Leisure Ability

Instructional Audience

The populations this instrument can be use with are learning disabilities, mild brain injury, stroke, communicative disorder, and attention deficit disorder. Individuals should have or have had (in the case of a head injury) a sixth grade reading level and be 14 years of age or older. This instrument can be use in clinical environments (hospital, outpatient clinic, therapist office) or educational environments (mid-school, secondary, and postsecondary settings). The instrument should be administered to persons in a quiet, non-threatening environment.

Functioning capability required of a person participating in the Cognitive Leisure Indicator assessment is as follows:

- ability to comprehend language of the instrument,
- ability to follow directions of instrument,
- ability to remember one's daily behaviors,
- oriented to reality,
- absence of psychotic features,
- ability to attend and maintain vigilance,
- demonstration of maturity (recognizing importance of testing),
- motivation or vested interest in assessing one's skills.

General Directions

The self-report instrument is administered to person(s) either individually or in a small group setting (having no more than six people). This assessment instrument is not timed, but the average length of time for completion is between 15 to 25 minutes. The test administrator has the option of asking the person the statements on the form and filling out the form, or having the person read the form and complete its contents. For the latter option, the test administrator will inform the person(s) to fill in the demographic information on the top of the first page (name, date, age, sex, education level, disability, and physical limitations of disability, if any). Inform the person to read each statement on the instrument and circle the number under the column that best describes the person. The answer categories are "Not like me," "Sometimes like me," "Most like me," and "Always like me." The person is to only circle one number per statement.

Directions for Scoring

The test administrator is to add all of the numerals circled in the subsection. Place the sum of scores on the "Total" line at the end of the subsection. The total number of each subsection is then transferred to the Cognitive Leisure Indicator Scoring Form. The test administrator uses this scoring scale form to determine the individual's raw score range per subsection.

Directions for Interpreting the Results

Scores of poor or *low average range in any one or more of subsections (1-6) and scores of above average in the leisure ability subsection means that the individual's perceived cognitive abilities do not interfere drastically or prevent one from participating in leisure activities. Above average scores in one or more subsections (1-6) and *low average or poor scores in the leisure ability subsection mean the individual may lack self-confidence and/or could be uncomfortable in competitive or cooperative group situations, thus limiting participation in the leisure activities. In this case, the test administrator would review the scores in the S/E area to determine if a negative social/emotional outlook was reported (obtaining a score in the 12 to 22 range - poor). Poor scores in both the leisure ability subsection and any subsection (1-6) means that the perceived cognitive ability has some effect on perceived leisure ability, hence interfering and/or preventing the individual from participating in leisure activities. In this situation the test administrator would note which particular subsection(s) received the poor score rating, then write recommendations suggesting the recreation leader teach the individual certain compensation strategies and/or deliver accommodations. These recommendations assist in making the leisure activity a more pleasurable and successful experience for the person having a disability.

* Low average refers to a score of 21 in *A/D* and *O/P subsections;* a score of 23 in *CP subsection;* and a score of 23 in *S/E, R/S/W/M, P/M, and LA subsections.*

Management

The Cognitive Leisure Indicator utilized as an initial assessment tool to determine cognitive and leisure abilities provides the following:

- prescription and implementation of a therapeutic recreation treatment plan within the individual's comprehensive treatment plan,
- guidelines for topics of discussion in leisure counseling sessions,
- overall awareness to the person and professional of how the individual's conditions affects leisure participation,
- a reference of information for supplying accommodations or modifications to recreation program,
- results about inept capacities that require improvement through a skill building curriculum,
- information to assist a transitional and educational planning team to determine student's recreation needs (e.g., under "related services") in receiving special education services.

The results from this instrument are beneficial for data collection regarding comparison outcomes of perceived cognitive and leisure inabilities with specific categories of disabilities. It can also be used for pre-post testing of program effects and can supply the baseline scoring to assist documentation of a person's progress (e.g., change in perceived ability after introduction to leisure actvities or implementation of accommodations in a recreation program).

Cognitive Leisure Indicator

Author: Lorraine C. Peniston, Ph.D., CTRS

Name: _____

Date: _____   Age: _____   Sex: _____

Education Level: _____   Disability: _____

Physical Limitation of Disability: _____

Instructions: Please circle the number under the column that best describes you.

Attention/Distractibility	Not like me	Sometimes like me	Most like me	Always like me
1. I often find myself "tuned out"(e.g., staring out the window) when I was really trying to pay attention to something.	4	3	2	1
2. I cannot keep my mind on a project when I hear certain sounds (e.g., people talking, door closing) or something moving.	4	3	2	1
3. I often think about other things and cannot keep my mind on a project long enough to complete it.	4	3	2	1
4. I cannot keep my mind on a project when I work or play with other people.	4	3	2	1
5. I can keep my mind focused when learning something new.	1	2	3	4
6. I am able to complete one project or activity before beginning another.	1	2	3	4
7. I can remain seated for more than 60 minutes when completing a project or activity.	1	2	3	4
8. I can wait until instructions have been given before I begin a project or activity.	1	2	3	4
9. I can do two things at one time very well (e.g., talk on the telephone and write).	1	2	3	4
10. I often have to ask somebody to repeat what he just said.	4	3	2	1

Total A/D _____

	Not like me	Sometimes like me	Most like me	Always like me
Organization/Planning				
1. I often lose track of time.	4	3	2	1
2. I can decide which daily activities are more important than another.	1	2	3	4
3. I can remember an appointment or meeting date.	1	2	3	4
4. I usually show up for an event on time.	1	2	3	4
5. I often forget to bring necessary materials or supplies to activities.	4	3	2	1
6. I use a calendar or daily reminder schedule to keep track of my appointments, assignments, and meeting dates.	1	2	3	4
7. I can adjust easily to a change in plans.	1	2	3	4
8. I can complete most assignments on time.	1	2	3	4
9. When given an assignment to complete in an hour, I can successfully complete the assignment.	1	2	3	4
10. I have difficulty getting started on a project.	4	3	2	1

Total O/P _____

	Not like me	Sometimes like me	Most like me	Always like me
Social /Emotional				
1. I can easily make friends.	1	2	3	4
2. I can talk with people easily.	1	2	3	4
3. I understand what others say to me.	1	2	3	4
4. I can tell if I said or did something that was rude.	1	2	3	4
5. I can work and play quite well with others.	1	2	3	4
6. I can relate to people in charge (e.g., boss, teacher).	1	2	3	4
7. I like myself.	1	2	3	4
8. I am able to ask other for assistance.	1	2	3	4
9. I am open to suggestions by others	1	2	3	4
10. I can meet my responsibilities.	1	2	3	4
11. I often get upset easily.	4	3	2	1
12. When I'm upset, I can tell someone about my problem in a clear, calm manner.	1	2	3	4

Total S/E _____

Cognitive Processes	Not like me	Sometimes like me	Most like me	Always like me
1. I can remember things without writing them down.	1	2	3	4
2. When learning a new game or activity, I can remember it the next day or several days later.	1	2	3	4
3. I often need to refer back to instructions or ask questions when I'm playing a game I like.	4	3	2	1
4. I often forget the next step in a game or activity.	4	3	2	1
5. I often go out of turn during a game or activity.	4	3	2	1
6. When playing a board game (e.g., checkers) I think about what kind of move I'm going to make ahead of time.	1	2	3	4
7. I use ways to stump my opponent in games or activities.	1	2	3	4
8. I know the difference between important and unimportant information.	1	2	3	4
9. I can make decisions with little difficulty.	1	2	3	4
10. I am able to solve problems in my life.	1	2	3	4
11. I often have problems recalling the exact word I want to use.	4	3	2	1

Total CP _____

Reading/Spelling/Writing/Mathematics

	Not like me	Sometimes like me	Most like me	Always like me
1. I can remember what I read.	1	2	3	4
2. I am able to identify the main idea of what I read and explain it in my own words.	1	2	3	4
3. I often need to ask someone to help explain the meaning of words or phrases when I read.	4	3	2	1
4. I often read words and letters backwards or upside down (e.g., "saw" for "was", "b" for "d").	4	3	2	1
5. I often write words and letters backwards or upside down (e.g., "saw" for "was", "b" for "d").	4	3	2	1
6. I often have difficulty spelling words.	4	3	2	1
7. I often have difficulty looking up words in the dictionary due to my spelling.	4	3	2	1

Reading/Spelling/Writing/Mathematics Cont.	Not like me	Sometimes like me	Most like me	Always like me
8. I avoid word games (e.g., crossword puzzles, Scrabble®, etc.).	4	3	2	1
9. I can get my thoughts and ideas on paper with little difficulty.	1	2	3	4
10. I often do not know where to place commas, periods, and capital letters in a sentence.	4	3	2	1
11. I can play games where I have to add a score or follow a certain order of numbers.	1	2	3	4
12. I can work successfully on projects where I am required to measure something, count a pattern, and use math to find a sum.	1	2	3	4

Total R/S/W/M _____

Perceptual/Motor

	Not like me	Sometimes like me	Most like me	Always like me
1. I have difficulty copying written material.	4	3	2	1
2. I have difficulty drawing simple pictures and shapes.	4	3	2	1
3. I have problems following the ball when watching a basketball (or any other sports) game.	4	3	2	1
4. I can usually judge where a ball is going to land and move myself to the area to catch the ball.	1	2	3	4
5. I can locate jigsaw puzzle pieces and place them in their correct position in the puzzle (e.g., puzzle with 500 pieces).	1	2	3	4
6. I can tell where the boundaries and foul areas are located in a game or sport activity I know well.	1	2	3	4
7. I can put together a model or craft project with little difficulty.	1	2	3	4
8. I always know where to stand when playing in a sport activity I like.	1	2	3	4
9. When learning a new exercise or sport activity, I can usually follow the instructions of the teacher quite well.	1	2	3	4
10. I can read a map to locate a place and drive myself to the location without major difficulty.	1	2	3	4
11. I often misjudge when to hit a ball with another object (e.g., bat, racket, hand).	4	3	2	1
12. I often have trouble maintaining my balance.	4	3	2	1

Total P/M _____

Leisure Ability (Leisure Time)

	Not like me	Sometimes like me	Most like me	Always like me
* Definition of leisure time - Free time when a person is not working, in school, or studying. The individual can do what he likes to do, usually participating in a recreational activity.				
1. I am a person who can have fun.	1	2	3	4
2. I know what I want to do in my leisure time.	1	2	3	4
3. I can change the things I don't like about my leisure time.	1	2	3	4
4. I can learn to participate in any game or activity.	1	2	3	4
5. I can find time to participate in weekly recreational activities.	1	2	3	4
6. I can participate in games or activities even when I am having problems understanding the directions and rules.	1	2	3	4
7. My disability does not stop me from participating in the recreational activity of my choice.	1	2	3	4

When I have some problems participating in a recreational activity:

	Not like me	Sometimes like me	Most like me	Always like me
8. I can tell people to slow down.	1	2	3	4
9. I can ask someone to repeat the directions.	1	2	3	4
10. I can ask someone to show me how to do something.	1	2	3	4
11. I can ask someone to write the information down on paper.	1	2	3	4
12. I can ask someone to help me put together a project.	1	2	3	4

Total LA _____

Cognitive Leisure Indicator Scoring Form

Directions for scoring

Add all of the numerals circled in each subsection. Place the sum of scores on the "Total" line at the end of the subsection. The total number of each subsection is then transferred to this form. Read the scoring scale to determine ratings within each subsection. The following abbreviations indicate the following:

A/D - Attention/Distractibility
O/P- Organization/Planning
S/E - Social/Emotional
CP - Cognitive Processes
R/S/W/M - Reading/Spelling/Writing/Mathematics
P/M - Perceptual/Motor
LA - Leisure Ability

Place the total number of each subsection from the Cognitive Leisure Indicator form in the appropriate categories below:

A/D _____   O/P _____   S/E _____   CP _____

R/S/W/M _____   P/M _____   LA _____

Scoring scale for the individual subsections:

A/D and O/P: 40 - 31   above average
                 30 - 21   average
                 20 - 10   poor

CP: 44 - 34   above average
                 33 - 23   average
                 22 - 11   poor

S/E, R/S/W/M,
P/M, and LA :   48 - 36   above average
                 35 - 23   average
                 22- 12   poor

Directions for Interpreting the Results

Scores of poor or *low average range in any one or more of subsections (1-6) and scores of above average in the leisure ability subsection mean that the individual's perceived cognitive abilities do not interfere drastically or prevent one from participating in leisure activities. Above average scores in one or more subsections

(1-6) and *low average or poor scores in the leisure ability subsection mean the individual may lack self-confidence, and/or could be uncomfortable in competitive or cooperative group situations, thus limiting participation in the leisure activities. In this case, the test administrator would review the scores in the S/E area to determine if a negative social/emotional outlook was reported (obtaining a score in the 12 to 22 range - poor). Poor scores in both the leisure ability subsection and any subsection (1-6) means that the perceived cognitive ability has some effect on perceived leisure ability, hence interfering and/or preventing the individual from participating in leisure activities. In this situation the test administrator would note which particular subsection(s) received the poor score rating, then write recommendations suggesting recreation leader teach individual certain compensation strategies and/or delivering accommodations. These recommendations assist in making the leisure activity a more pleasurable and successful experience for the person having a disability.

*   Low average refers to a score of 21 in *A/D* and *O/P subsections;* a score of 23 in *CP subsection;* and a score of 23 in *S/E, R/S/W/M, P/M, and LA subsections.*

Validity and Reliability Report

In the summer of 1994, 27 people who attended the University of New Mexico completed the test-retest reliability experiment for this instrument. The experiment consisted of 10 males and 17 females, ranging in age from 20 to 49 with some displaying disabilities. Disabilities revealed were as follows: two physical, two LD/emotional, one polio, and one chemically dependent. An overall reliability measure of .78 was calculated from the 27 participants using the Pearson Product-moment correlation. Reliability measures of the subsections are as follows: Attention/Distraction $r=.61$, Organization/Planning $r=.83$, Social/Emotional $r=.62$, Cognitive Processes $r=.85$, Reading/Spelling/Writing/Math $r=.86$, Perceptual Motor $r=.77$, and Leisure Ability $r=.74$.

During the year of 1994 (May-October), 15 subjects having disabilities and 15 subjects not having disabilities volunteered to complete the indicator form to determine its validity. Below are the results of each group's rating on the scoring scale:

Mean Scores

Disability Group	No Disability Group
A/D = 25.7 - mid-average	A/D = 30.7 - high average
0/P = 27.9 - average	0/P = 31.5 - above average
S/E = 33.2 - high average	S/E = 38.2 - above average
CP = 27.6 - average	CP = 33.1 - high average
R/S/W/M = 30.5 - mid-avg.	R/S/W/M = 41.5 - above avg.

P/M = 31.6 - mid-average   P/M = 40.0 -above average

LA = 32.1 - high average   LA = 37.0 - above average

The following table lists how subjects per group scored in subsections.

Disability Group	No Disability Group (Mean Scores)
A/D = 2 - poor, 11 - avg., 2 - above avg.	0 - poor, 6 - avg., 9 - above avg.
O/P = 1 - poor, 11 - avg., 3 - above avg.	0 - poor, 4 - avg., 11 - above avg.
S/E = 0 - poor, 8 - avg., 7 -above avg.	0 - poor, 3 - avg., 12 - above avg.
CP = 3 - poor, 10 - avg., 2 - above avg.	0 - poor, 9 - avg., 6 - above avg.
R/S/W/M = 4 - poor, 7 - avg, 4 - above avg.	0 - poor, 0 - avg., 15 - above avg.
P/M = 0 - poor, 11 - avg., 4 - above avg.	1 - poor, 2 - avg., 12 - above avg.
LA = 0 - poor, 11 - avg., 4 - above avg.	2 - poor, 2 - avg., 11 - above avg.

The Mann-Whitney U Test was employed to determine that the scores obtained from the Cognitive Leisure Indicator detected differences in the group (between the disability and no disability subjects). Because subjects were not selected randomly (recruited volunteers to test instrument), the two subject samples were independent (one group having disabilities and the other not having disabilities) and homogeneity of variance was not found in the two populations, the Mann-Whitney U Test would be adequate in analyzing differences between the groups. Seven scores from the disability group and seven scores from the no disability group were randomly selected and assigned ranking. The U statistic was calculated from the selected total test score (total of all test subsections). A calculated U=3 with N=7 and a=.01 was below the critical values range of 6-43. This means that the scores in the two populations were discovered by the Cognitive Leisure Indicator to be different and a change error in sampling did not occur. This instrument is successful in measuring how perceived cognitive ability affects an individual's ability to participate in leisure activities.

The content validity was examined by a psychologist, educational diagnosticians, a psychometrician, special educators, therapists (speech, recreation, and psychology), and individuals having TBI and LD.

APPENDIX P
Cognitive Leisure Checklist©
(Abbreviated form of Cognitive Leisure Indicator Instrument)

Author: Lorraine C. Peniston, Ph.D., CTRS

Name: _____

Date: _____ Disability (if known): _____

Instructions: Please write in the number that best describes you. Response key: 1 - Never occurs, 2 - Sometimes occurs, 3 - Always occurs

___ 1. I can keep my mind on a project long enough to complete it.

___ 2. I can remain seated for more than 60 minutes when completing a project.

___ 3. I always remember what instructions were said, so I don't have to ask for the instructions to be repeated.

___ 4. I usually show up for an event on time.

___ 5. I always remember to bring necessary materials or supplies to activities.

___ 6. I can complete most assignments on time.

___ 7. I can start a project within a short time period without difficulty.

___ 8. I can talk with people easily.

___ 9. I can play quite well with others.

___ 10. I am able to ask others for assistance.

___ 11. I can meet my responsibilities.

___ 12. When learning a new game or activity, I can remember it the next day or several days later.

___ 13. I can always remember the next step in a game or activity.

___ 14. I can always remember taking my turn during a game or activity.

___ 15. I can always make decisions during a game or activity.

___ 16. I am able to identify the main idea of what I read and explain it in my own words.

___ 17. I avoid word games (crossword puzzles, Scrabble®, etc).

___ 18. I can play games where I have to add a score or follow a certain order of numbers.

___ 19. I can work successfully on projects where I am required to measure something, count a pattern, and use math to find a sum.

___ 20. I can draw simple pictures and shapes.

___ 21. I can follow the ball when watching a basketball (or any other sports) game.

___ 22. I can usually judge where a ball is going to land and move myself to the area to catch the ball.

___ 23. I can locate jigsaw puzzle pieces and place them in their correct position in the puzzle (e.g., 500 piece puzzle).

___ 24. I can tell where the boundaries and foul areas are located in a game or sport activity I know well.

___ 25. I can put together a model/craft project with little difficulty.

___ 26. When learning a new exercise or sport activity, I can usually follow the instructions of the teacher quite well.

___ 27. I can judge when to hit a ball with another object (e.g., bat, racket, hand).

___ 28. I can always maintain my balance.

___ 29. I can ask someone to show me how to do something.

___ 30. I can participate in games or activities even when I am having problems understanding the directions and rules.

_____ **Total Numbers**

Scoring: Major difficulties: 30 to 50 points
Some difficulties to average: 51 to 71 points
Good to excellent: 72 to 90 points

Major difficulties require on–going assistance with major accommodations. Some difficulties require periodic assistance with some accommodations; Good to excellent needs little assistance and no accommodations.

APPENDIX Q
Overview of Disabilities

The definition of an individual with a disability, according to the Americans with Disabilities Act, is one who:

1. has a mental or physical impairment that substantially limits one or more of the major life activities of that person; or

2. has a record of physical or mental impairment that substantially limits one or more of the individual's major life activities; and

3. is regarded as having such an impairment, whether he has the impairment or not.

Major life activities are those physical activities an individual carries out in the course of a day, such as dressing, eating, manipulating objects, speaking, seeing or hearing, and cognitive activities such as understanding, problem solving, or remembering (McGovern, 1991).

Physical or Mental Impairments
1. Physiological disorders or conditions;

2. Cosmetic disfigurement; or

3. Anatomical loss affecting one or more of the following body systems: neurological; musculoskeletal; special sense organs (which would include speech organs that are not respiratory such as vocal cords, soft palate, tongue, etc.); respiratory, including speech organs; cardiovascular; reproductive; digestive; genitourinary; hemic and lymphatic; skin; and endocrine.

Disabilities are diagnosed by trained professionals who are knowledgeable about specific disabilities. The professional can be a physician, psychiatrist, educational diagnostician, counselor, and some therapists (speech and language, occupational and physical).

Examples of Common Disabilities
*   Mental retardation—Down's syndrome
*   Developmental disabilities—learning disabilities, attention deficit disorders, cerebral palsy
*   Cognitive impairments—stroke, brain injured (traumatic or acquired)

- Neuromuscular disorders - multiple sclerosis, muscular dystraphy, Parkinson's disease, Alzheimer's disease
- Emotional disorders - anxiety, phobia, severe depression
- Social disorders - anti-social behavior, passive/aggressive, aggressive tendencies
- Psychotic disorders - schizophrenia, delusional tendencies
- Addictive disorders - drugs (legal or illegal), alcohol
- Eating disorders - anorexia nervosa, bulimia nervosa
- Sensory disorders - visually impaired/blind, hearing impaired
- Communication disorders - mute, aphasic, stutter
- Physical - amputee, arthritis, spinal cord injury
- Conditions - epilepsy, cancer, heart disease, diabetes, HIV

There are many other debilitating conditions that can cause someone to become disabled—temporary or permanently.

(Excerpts adapted from *ADA Title II Technical Assistance Manual.* http://gopher.usdoj.gov/crt/ada/taman2.html)

APPENDIX R
Participant Evaluation Form

1. Participant name (Optional): _____

2. Date: _____

3. Name of program: _____

4. Program location: _____

5. Program times and days: _____

6. Program leader: _____

7. Did the program leader explain information in a clear and understandable manner?   Yes___ No___
   If no, please explain _____

8. Was the program leader organized and well prepared?
   Yes___   No___

9. Did the leader appear knowledgeable about the topic she was instructing?   Yes___   No___

10. Did the leader appear knowledgeable about agency operations?   Yes___   No___

11. Were you comfortable asking the program leader questions?
    Yes___   No___
    If no, why? _____

12. Did the program leader listen to your questions and response in an appropriate manner?   Yes___ No___
    If no, please explain _____

13. Was the program leader willing to help you with special problems or needs? Yes___ No___

14. Was the environment ideal for learning and participating in the program? Yes___ No___
    If no, what should be changed? _____

15. Program or class size: ___Too small ___Too large
    ___Adequate

16. Cost of program: ___Adequate   ___Too expensive
    ___Expensive, but worth the price.

17. Was an adequate amount of equipment and/or materials distributed during the program? Yes___ No___
    Not Applicable___

18. Was equipment in good working order?   Yes___ No___
    Not applicable___

19. Were materials easy to read and/or use? Yes___ No___
    Not applicable___

20. Did program meet your needs?   Yes___ No___
    If no, please explain: _____
    _____

21. Overall rating of the program: ___Excellent   ___Good
                                    ___Fair   ___Poor

22. Suggestions for improvement of program: _____
    _____

23. What other questions should we have asked you? Please list:
    _____
    _____

24. Would you encourage family or friends to participate in this program? Yes___ No___
    If no, please explain why: _____
    _____
    _____

Thank you for taking the time to complete this evaluation form.

APPENDIX S
Camp Nuhop

Camp Nuhop, "The Warm Fuzzy Camp," is a summer residential program for any youngster from 6 to 16 with a learning disability, behavior disorder, or attention deficit disorder. It has about 50-55 campers to every two counselors. Camp Nuhop is housed in the facilities of Camp Wesley, a East Ohio Methodist Camp near Perrysville, Ohio. The location is midway between Cleveland and Columbus, and just south of Mansfield. Camp Wesley is surrounded by the 3,000 acre Mohican Forest and Pleasant Hill Lake Park. These areas provide many activities for the program: boating, primitive camping, canoeing, and tubing on the Mohican River and hiking to the fire tower and covered bridge.

The program is more than a summer camp; to assist children to succeed during their stay the program asks a great deal of parents. First, the family completes an application questionnaire that explores the camper's abilities, social adjustment, and desired camp goals. Then a teacher evaluation form helps us understand the student's school performance in these areas as well. Second, the staff assigned to each camper then arranges parent conferences at camp for all new campers. This pre-camp conference provides personal observation, informal discussion, and a general get–acquainted session. Each child gets to meet other Nuhop campers and all staff before camp. This outing also lets staff informally assess social interaction and motor development through group games to help the staff assure compatible groupings of campers. Through application questionnaires and the pre-camp conference, the camp can then plan individualized programs to meet the needs of each camper.

Camp Nuhop promotes "a highly qualified and dedicated staff." Many counselors are college graduates with backgrounds in special education, environmental education, speech therapy, social work, pre-medicine, and psychology. Junior counselors-in-training are high school students, 16 years or older, who are familiar with the Nuhop program. Many have brothers or sisters who have been part of the Nuhop staff.

Nuhop provides a variety of camping experiences in its camping programs. The overall camp program contains: the Exploration Camp, the Wilderness Camp, ACC Camp, Canoe Camp, Crusoe

Camp, Sports Skills Camp, Bike Camp, Leadership Camp, Backpack Camp, Sailing Camp, and Adventure Camp. Our whole camp experience is built upon helping a child see himself in a more positive light. To help each child believe in himself, this camp uses favorite self–esteem activities. These activities concentrate on positive thoughts and attempt to avoid negative thoughts, thus helping each child be his own best friend. To obtain a brochure explaining the programs in detail, or to obtain information about costs and camperships, write to: Camp Nuhop Offices, 404 Hillcrest Dr., Ashland, OH 44805

(Excerpts taken from Camp Nuhop Page, http://www.bright.net/~cnuhop/#INDEX)

This book is not endorsing Camp Nuhop or suggesting readers use its services. It is simply making readers aware that camps are available for persons with learning disabilities. Family members or persons with learning disabilities should thoroughly inquire about the nature of an agency's services to see if it suits your needs.

APPENDIX T
The Summit Camp Program, Inc.

Summit Camp serves boys and girls between the ages of 7 and 17 who are classified as having attention deficit disorder, possible learning disabilities, mild neurological impairment, and/or possible emotional overlay requiring specialized programming and support services. Located in Forest Hills, New York, it is proud to be able to implement its programs within one of the finest facilities in the field of camping.

The Summit Camp can properly be described as an "all weather camp" for its abundant indoor facilities assure ongoing programs despite any weather conditions. The camp Recreation Hall houses an indoor gymnasium featuring regulation basketball and volleyball courts, a large professionally lighted stage, and a make-up room. Educational and enrichment facilities include separate and fully–equipped nature and crafts buildings, a home economics center, a ceramics studio, an industrial arts shop, and a ranch–type structure housing its education and computer center (two classrooms and two computer labs). The camp's outdoor recreation facilities include three surfaced tennis courts, two basketball courts, an in–ground trampoline, nature trails, obstacle course/big toy, low-ropes course, two softball fields, one sand volleyball court, one junior basketball court, one outdoor field hockey court, and camping sites.

The Summit Camp Program offers a core of highly experienced, well–trained, special education professionals to provide counseling staff with the programmatic, educational, and emotional support they require in order to work effectively with campers. The camp's staffing plan provides three adult staff members to every four children. Summit also provides "support and intervention specialists" to assist campers as well as staff. Individuals holding this position provide support to staff through in-service training in behavior management and group-counseling techniques. They provide direct support services to campers by helping them acquire improved social skills, learn techniques for improving self–esteem, self-control, and coping with frustration.

The camp's recreation programs focus on land sports; team sports, including Summit Olympics; waterfront activities; creative arts; computer workshops and lab usage; and the Summit Super-Teen Program. Its camping philosophy is, "Every camp must strive to assure the health, safety, and happiness of each and every child while meeting his/her basic need for acceptance, recognition, and respect." These goals are met through a program of *therapeutic recreation* in which recreational, social, and education activities have as a primary goal the establishment or reinforcement of feelings of success, confidence, enthusiasm, and self-worth within the child. The program is structured so that the campers receive regular instruction in the widest possible variety of recreational skills and are able to judge and appreciate their own progress.

The Summit Travel Program

Summit Travel represents the logical extension of the camping program for young adults (ages 17+) who have outgrown the traditional camping experience, but still require opportunities for structured and supervised social experiences, as well as recreational opportunities of a more adult and mainstream nature. Summit Travel offers one-, two-, three- and six-week programs of domestic and/or foreign travel. Its overseas tours have visited all of the British Isles, Israel, Spain, Italy, Holland, and France. The domestic travel programs have concentrated on the scenic West, Canada, and Hawaii. The one- and two-week programs cater mostly to working young adults, while the three- and six-week programs cater to young people with a greater expanse of time available for summer recreation. To learn more about Summit Camp Programs write to: The Summit Camp Program, Inc., 110-45 71st Rd., Suite 1G, Forest Hills, NY 11375, phone: (718) 268-0020 or 1 (800) 323-9908.

(Excerpts adapted from Summit Camp: Therapeutic camping for boys and girls with learning disabilities and/or attention deficit disorder, 1997 brochure booklet)

This book is not endorsing The Summit Camp Program, Inc., or suggesting readers use it services. It is simply making readers aware that camps and travel programs are available for persons with learning disabilities. Family members or persons with learning disabilities should thoroughly inquire about the nature of an agency's services to see if it suits your needs.

AUTHOR'S PAGE

Lorraine C. Peniston

Lorraine C. Peniston, Ph.D., is a learning disabilities specialist at the University of New Mexico in the Center for Academic Program Support (CAPS). She is also a certified therapeutic recreation specialist and certified leisure professional. Possessing B.A. and Ph.D. degrees in recreation (option - therapeutic recreation) and a Master's degree in special education, she has 17 years experience working with special populations in clinical and educational settings. Within this time span she has written numerous articles about leisure and learning disabilities, study skills strategies for persons with disabilities, and accessibility and accommodations for persons with disabilities. Workshops, presentations, and college courses teaching compensation strategies, study skills, leisure skills, and accommodations for persons with disabilities are also added to her credits.

Dr. Peniston has been a board member for the Southwest Branch (International Dyslexia Association), chairperson of the College and Reading Association Special Interest Learning Disabilities Group, and associate editor for the *Therapeutic Recreation Journal.* Her favorite pastime activities are spending time with family and friends, aqua jogging, gardening, crafts, and traveling.

INDEX